Embodied History

D0671348

EARLY AMERICAN STUDIES

Daniel K. Richter and Kathleen M. Brown, Series Editors

Exploring neglected aspects of our colonial, revolutionary, and early national history and culture, Early American Studies reinterprets familiar themes and events in fresh ways. Interdisciplinary in character, and with a special emphasis on the period from about 1600 to 1850, the series is published in partnership with the McNeil Center for Early American Studies.

A complete list of books in the series is available from the publisher.

Embodied History

The Lives of the Poor in Early Philadelphia

SIMON P. NEWMAN

PENN

University of Pennsylvania Press

Philadelphia

Property of Library
Cape Fear Comm College
Wilmington, N. C.

Copyright © 2003 University of Pennsylvania Press
All rights reserved
Printed in the United States of America on acidfree paper

10 9 8 7 6 5 4 3 2 1

Published by
University of Pennsylvania Press
Philadelphia, Pennsylvania 191044011

Library of Congress Cataloguing-in-Publication Data

Newman, Simon P. (Simon Peter), 1960-
    Embodied history : the lives of the poor in early Philadelphia / Simon P. Newman.
        p.   cm. (Early American studies)
    ISBN 0-8122-3731-5 (cloth : alk. paper). —ISBN 0-8122-1848-5 (pbk. : alk paper)
    Includes bibliographical references and index.
    1. Poor—Pennsylvania—Philadelphia—History—18th century. 2. Poor—Pennsylvania—
Philadelphia—History—19th century. 3. Public welfare—Pennsylvania—Philadelphia—
History—18th century. 4. Public welfare—Pennsylvania—Philadelphia—History—19th
century. 5. Philadelphia (Pa.)—Social conditions—18th century. 6. Philadelphia (Pa.)—
Social conditions—19th century. 7. Philadelphia (Pa.)—Economic conditions—18th
century. 8. Philadelphia (Pa.)—Economic conditions—19th century. 9. Philadelphia
(Pa.)—Population—History—18th century. 10. Philadelphia (Pa.)—Population—
History—19th century.

HV4046.P5 N48   2003
305.5′69′097481109033—dc21   2003042615

for my friends

Contents

Illustrations

Let not ambition mock their useful toil,
Their homely joys and destiny obscure,
Nor grandeur hear with a disdainful smile,
The short and simple annals of the poor.

—Thomas Gray, "Elegy Written in a Country Churchyard" (1750)

Introduction

Early national Philadelphia was a "large, populous & beautiful city . . . regular and well built," filled with "wide and straight" streets flanked by trees. To citizens and visitors alike, this "metropolis of the United States" appeared to be the nation's "finest town, and the best built."[1] Such impressions of space and grandeur were portrayed quite beautifully by William Birch in a series of popular engravings that displayed a city of broad and almost empty streets, in which impressive civic and private buildings were set off by a variety of fully leafed trees. Birch's "View in Third Street from Spruce Street," with the Bingham family mansion in the background, is typical in this regard, with buildings and large public spaces dwarfing a small number of respectable inhabitants (Figures 1 and 2).

Conspicuously absent from these engravings and from many contemporary descriptions are Philadelphia's poorer residents. Even Birch's renderings of such buildings as the almshouse or the Pennsylvania Hospital, structures designed for the city's poor, seem positively bucolic, and the very Philadelphians for whom these institutions were intended are nowhere to be seen (Figures 3 and 4). The population of the city grew extremely fast during the decades following the Revolution, making Philadelphia a far more compact and densely populated city than Birch's prints suggest. By 1800 the city proper consisted of little more than two square miles, and with under half of this area actually settled the population density stood at 45,800 persons per square mile[2] (Figure 5). For all its unusually wide streets, early national Philadelphia was teeming with people, and many of them looked very different from the finely dressed young men and ladies who strolled along the streets of Birch's imagined city.

As fast as the colonial town developed into a thriving and populous city of commerce, manufacturing, and trade, so too grew urban poverty. In stark contrast to Birch's prints were the words of those men and women of wealth and power who felt themselves surrounded and increasingly threatened by the "children, dogs and hogs" who swarmed through the streets; the "dissipated men, and idle women" who filled the

Market; the young chimney sweeps "clothed in rags," who were most "unpleasant to the sight" of refined Philadelphians; the newly arrived indentured servants, who presented "a most revolting scene of want and misery"; and the almshouse residents, comprising a picture of "all that misery and disease can assemble."[3] In the eyes of more fortunate Philadelphians, the innumerable poor of their city appeared more akin to those satirized in William Hogarth's representations of the streets of London than to any of the handful of respectable people in William Birch's wistfully bucolic cityscapes (Figure 6). However, Birch's prints were not flawed attempts to portray the reality of early national urban life, but rather idealized images of Philadelphia as the city's elite might have wished it to appear, as a place in which the troublesome poor were neither seen nor heard but rather controlled by and confined within civic institutions.

Impoverished Philadelphians were readily identifiable, for their appearance contrasted sharply with that of their more affluent neighbors. Periods of un- or underemployment and low wages took physical form in undernourished, undersized, and poorly clad bodies, which were far

Figure 1. William Birch, View in Third Street from Spruce Street, Philadelphia, 1800. Courtesy of the Library Company of Philadelphia. The handsome Federal style mansion dominating this view was built in 1789 by William Bingham, a wealthy merchant, banker, and legislator. Set amid extensive formal gardens, William and Anne Bingham's home was the preeminent center of elite social life in early national Philadelphia.

more likely to be scarred by disease and accidents than were the bodies of the well-to-do. Status, class, and poverty were embodied in their appearance, and thus their very bodies reveal a great deal about the ways the lives and bodies of the poor had been molded by their circumstances. The embodiment of poverty had enormous significance, for medieval and early modern concepts of "ranks" or "estates" in society had imbued white early Americans with a strong sense of a relatively complex hierarchy of social status, which served to legitimate power and authority in a world of inequality.[4] Different types of poverty—and thus different kinds of poor people—were accommodated within this hierarchy, and early modern social commentators and civil and ecclesiastical authorities had made much of the difference between, on the one hand, those who were poor "by impotency" or "by casualty" and, on the other hand, the "thriftless" poor.[5] The former constituted the "deserving poor," who, by demonstrating a willingness to work and by exhibiting an

Figure 2. William Birch, Bank of the United States in Third Street, Philadelphia, 1799. Courtesy of the Library Company of Philadelphia. Adjacent to Dock Street and between the waterfront and the Walnut Street Jail, this was the heart of the city. In the alleys behind and around these buildings lived the city's lower sort, yet in presenting this image of the power and promise of the new nation and its government, Birch again neglected to include any but a handful of respectable men and women, and even fewer respectable working men.

acceptance of their lot through respect, civility, and deference in their dealings with their betters, claimed a right to the support of the community. In contrast, the "thriftless" poor appeared dangerously disrespectful and subversive; they were held responsible for their condition and as a result were judged to be undeserving of aid and the objects of just punishment.

Trade, population, and wealth inequality all grew rapidly in the cities of post-revolutionary America, and as the ranks of the poor increased a simplified discourse of "sorts" of people replaced the rhetoric of a complicated hierarchy of "orders" and "estates," blurring distinctions between the deserving and undeserving poor.[6] At its simplest, this new system divided people into the "better sort" and the "meaner," "poorer" or "lower sort," a value-laden set of terms in which wealthy people

Figure 3. William Birch, Alms House in Spruce Street, Philadelphia, 1799. Courtesy of the Library Company of Philadelphia. Several hundred yards from Independence Hall, Pennsylvania Hospital, and Walnut Street Jail lay another of the city's great buildings, the Alms House. Designed as a place for the incarceration, correction, and betterment of the bodies of deserving and undeserving poor alike, the almshouse was for and about poor bodies, yet it appears here without any such bodies in evidence. Instead, it is a scene of bucolic delight in which a farmer heading to market attempts to capture an escaped pig.

appeared good while the poor were low, mean, and vulgar. Between these two extremes was emerging a new category—the "middling sort," whose merchants, lawyers, craftsmen, and professionals sought to emphasize how far they had risen above the lower sort and who eagerly aspired to join the ranks of the better sort. The better and middling sort employed this language of "sorts" to stigmatize and distance themselves from the "lower sort," and the rapid growth of urban poverty led better and middling sort Americans to believe that proper control and regulation of the lower sort was imperative. Members of the impoverished lower sort often looked alike, and over time a growing proportion of the ablebodied poor came to be classified and treated by their betters as wilfully idle vagrants, paupers, idlers, loafers, criminals, and masterless men who required punishment and incarceration rather than the charitable care afforded the deserving poor of the medieval era. Philadelphia's better and middling sorts feared that the masterless lower sort were quite literally out of control and that they constituted a highly visible and very tangible

Figure 4. William Birch, Pennsylvania Hospital in Pine Street, Philadelphia, 1799. Courtesy of the Library Company of Philadelphia. Although the hospital was intended for the sick and injured bodies of the deserving poor, this engraving excludes images of such folk, despite the fact that many lived in the streets around the impressive building.

threat to the persons, property, and republican society of their betters. The bodies of such men and women were to be controlled, thus preserving social stability, and a new language of class replaced older ideas of orders and ranks in society.[7]

Civic authorities and more prosperous citizens characterized and judged their poorer neighbors by their appearance, embodying a whole host of social problems in the flesh and blood of impoverished men, women, and children. The lower sort included the large mass of working men, women, and children who sometimes experienced poverty during their lives. An economic downturn, the prolonged absence of a seafaring husband, or the illness or injury of a primary breadwinner could drag

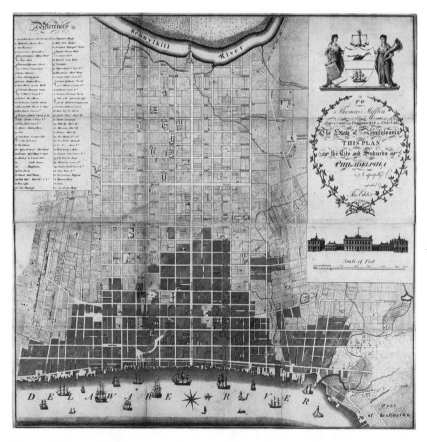

Figure 5. Plan of the City and Suburbs of Philadelphia, 1794. Courtesy of the Library Company of Philadelphia. This contemporary map illustrates the relatively small size of Philadelphia (including Southwark and the Northern Liberties), although by 1800 the population of the area exceeded 60,000.

Figure 6. William Hogarth, Gin Lane (Beer Street and Gin Lane Series), 1751. Courtesy of the Library Company of Philadelphia. In this famous print, the buildings of London appear relatively neutral; the tone of the picture is set by the people in and around them. Hogarth presents the bodies of the poor of mid-eighteenth-century London as drunken, disorderly, depraved, and potentially dangerous.

individuals and families with limited means below the poverty line. Full employment and an income sufficient to meet the expenses of food, fuel, clothing, and shelter could seldom be taken for granted, and members of the lower sort slipped in and out of dire poverty with debilitating regularity. To contemporaries, poverty and lower sort status were proclaimed by bodily appearance, and Philadelphia's ruling authorities and wealthy citizens judged their fellow townsmen and -women accordingly. Although these human bodies were objects with a material reality, they were commonly perceived through a cultural lens that shaped how people saw and interpreted each and every body.[8]

Elite Philadelphians were far better nourished and better dressed than the city's lower sort, and they wore clothing fashioned from fine fabrics and tailored in order to make manual labor demonstrably impractical. Immaculately cleansed and well-groomed bodies further emphasized their distance from such work, while erect posture and dignified bearing signified their elite status.[9] Proper display, self-control, and adornment of the body had long been interpreted as evidence of social status and moral worth.[10] Gender, however, provided some common ground between the bodies of elite, middling, and poorer Philadelphians, for childbirth and medical intervention could injure and deform the bodies of all women, rich and poor alike. But even these experiences were conditioned by class and material circumstances, for while a woman of means would be well nourished, spared from arduous work, and attended by a midwife and doctor in her own home, a hungry and poorer woman in the almshouse or even in her own home could expect to enjoy few of these advantages.

For financially secure Philadelphians, then, the body could become both project and projection, the embodiment of class and status, while the lower sort were dependent on their bodily labor and were thus forced to employ their bodies as tools, as the means of survival.[11] The results were readily apparent, for class and social status were indelibly inscribed on their bodies. During childhood and indeed throughout their lives, poorer Philadelphians were less well nourished and consequently failed to grow as tall and healthy as their richer neighbors, and their less resilient bodies were marked by disease, illness, and the accidents and injuries associated with their lives and work. This book will illustrate the embodiment of class and condition among the lower sort, how these impoverished bodies were judged and controlled by middling and elite Philadelphians, and how the poor struggled to retain some control over their own bodies and lives.

The better sort of Philadelphians often equated the impoverished appearance of lower sort bodies with low social status and moral worth, and drunk, sick, and contaminated bodies appeared to demonstrate flawed character.[12] Deference was required from the lower sort, whose deprived social status required them to shape their bodies to a more slumped and servile posture in their encounters with social betters. The clothing that covered their bodies confirmed their lowly status, for the poor bought and traded cheaper clothing fashioned from coarse fabrics, cut in a loose and generic fashion so as to fit different sized people and allow them freedom of movement at their work.

The rapidly increasing number and concentration of poor bodies disturbed and disgusted their betters, filling them with fearful Hogarthian visions of a world without order. Through their roles as magistrates, overseers of the poor, almshouse and hospital keepers, doctors, jailers, and the masters of servants and slaves, middling and elite Philadelphians set about imposing control over impoverished bodies, thereby defending social order and hierarchy. In such institutions as the prison, almshouse, hospital, and churches, and in servitude and slavery, we can trace the efforts of Philadelphia's rulers to classify and regulate impoverished bodies, often by means of discipline and incarceration.

Classifying, restraining, and medicalizing bodies thus constituted an exercise in social power. Institutions like the almshouse and the prison documented the bodies of those they sought to control, such as servants and slaves who ran away from masters, vagrants and masterless men and women, and even the sick and injured. As a result, the surviving records describe the bodies of the poor in very revealing ways. Sources such as runaway slave and servant advertisements and almshouse and prison records attest to the ways class and the conditions and material circumstances of their lives had shaped and scarred the bodies of the poor. More than that, these records demonstrate the ways these institutions impressed their power upon and strove to recondition impoverished bodies.

Philadelphia's prison, almshouse, and hospital were part of a larger development, in both Europe and America, of a variety of strategies designed to render subordinate bodies passive and then to regulate and even remake these impoverished bodies. For much of medieval and early modern history, the power of the state had been employed to brutalize the bodies of the masterless, homeless, and jobless vagrants who populated town and countryside alike, employing corporal or capital punishment to mark these offenders and other criminals. In early national Philadelphia, however, such medieval practices were replaced by social disciplining, by which means the bodies of impoverished citizens were regulated in an attempt to inculcate order into society. Thus, the records of the almshouse in early national Philadelphia reveal concerted attempts by civic authorities to record, categorize, and then transform the bodies of transgressors from their status as "thriftless" poor into hard-working, productive, and deferential members of society. While almshouse authorities sometimes had sympathy for the wretched souls in their care, their judgments of the bodies of many inmates were more often harsh and unforgiving. The men who ran the almshouse evaluated and judged the bodies of the poor who came before them, holding these—the poorest of all Philadelphians—responsible for their bodily condition and status, and they then attempted to remake their very bodies.[13]

The hospital, too, was an institution organized around such judgments about the bodies of the poor. It was not the impoverished condition or poor health of a person's body that entitled him or her to admission, but rather his or her moral status as evaluated by members of the elite. Within a hospital that had been created not for all of the poor but rather for the deserving poor, the bodies of only a few of Philadelphia's sick poor received expert medical treatment. Previously, their sick and injured bodies would have been cared for by family and friends, but within the hospital they became patients, impoverished but deserving bodies with symptoms and conditions to be analyzed and acted upon. Such treatment was not always a boon, however, for the hospital was a place of sickness and disease that might just as easily kill patients as cure them.

Philadelphia's Walnut Street jail, just like the almshouse and the hospital, was an institution that categorized, controlled, and conditioned the bodies of the poor. During these years it changed from a simple holding place for those awaiting trial or physical punishment into a place and instrument of punishment and reformation in and of itself, wherein the minds and bodies of criminals might be attuned to responsible work. As he toured the prison, J. P. Brissot de Warville neatly encapsulated the prison's larger social purpose, describing it as a "house of correction" in which prisoners were "obliged to work," approvingly noting that this was "the best method of ameliorating men."[14] During an era of rapid and unprecedented urban growth, social instability, and political radicalism, those who failed to control their bodies as all citizens were required to do—in short, those who failed to respect the law and private property—could expect to have their troublesome bodies incarcerated and reformed. Even the contractual obligations between seafarers and the ships' captains and owners for whom they worked, and the indentures and legal codes that regulated servants and slaves, were attempts to control the bodies of men, women, and children, while supposedly providing them with the necessaries of life they might not otherwise be able to provide for themselves, and perhaps even some vocational training into the bargain. In early national Philadelphia an impoverished body without home or work was a vagrant, by definition a villain, who was likely to be punished for his or her crime in the prison, in which the criminally poor were made to work and prepared for a more socially acceptable and productive role in society.

The records employed in this book reveal the ways in which the poor of early national Philadelphia found themselves enmeshed in a series of structural and institutional contexts that marked, contained, and disciplined their bodies. Buried deeper in some records is evidence of the ways the poor endeavored to recast these contexts and reclaim control over their bodies in terms of their own interests, beliefs, and desires. Almost all the records illustrate the ways lowly status and condition physically affected impoverished bodies, from illness and disease, to the scars that resulted from dangerous and poorly paid work, to the poor clothing and rags with which they were covered. Thus such records place the circumstances and experiences of poverty in a new light by recording its embodiment and showing the ways in which it was physically experienced and manifested. At the same time, some records demonstrate the ways their betters sought to control and remake the bodies and lives of the poor, illuminating how the bodies of lower sort men, women, and children were interpreted, regulated, and controlled. On occasion these records reveal the spirit and initiative of poor Philadelphians who sought to resist such control, illustrating the ways they demanded respect, championed individuality, and celebrated life and culture in a host of different ways.[15] Runaway advertisements, for example, tell stories of the bitter battles over bodies: in servitude or slavery, the unfree poor contested their masters' control over their bodies in battles over, for example, work, deference, and appearance. Such battles over the servile body predated but informed the ultimate struggle, wherein runaways sought to steal ownership of their own bodies.

The pride, the passion, and the joie-de-vivre of the early national lower sort can be detected in the pages of almshouse and burial records, runaway advertisements, and prison dockets, providing rare glimpses of how the lower sort imagined and used their own bodies in opposition to the construction of these bodies by their betters. From the undernourished child who played in the streets and on the waterfront; to the slave who did not even own his body yet who took pains with his personal appearance before stealing himself away; to the sailor who marked his body with tattoos that celebrated his work, beliefs, and relationships; to the indentured Irish servant who refused to mold her body into a meek and deferential stance toward her master and mistress; to the young laborer whose drunken frolics on Independence Day cost him his life—these were people who refused to surrender all control of their bodies, either to the impoverished condition that marked their bodies or to institutions such as the almshouse, the prison, or the hospital that regulated them.

The bodies of lower sort Philadelphians thus functioned as texts, and their contemporaries could read and learn much about their experiences of poverty and the struggle between coercive power and personal independence simply by looking at them.[16] Some looked like Dick, a black American slave who was twenty-eight years old when he ran away from his New Jersey master, Abraham Hunt, in 1795, and like many other runaway servants and slaves headed toward Philadelphia. Standing about five feet five inches high, Dick's body was not his own, and he was permanently scarred by the whipping that Hunt (or a previous master) had inflicted on him, vividly marking his status. Quite possibly as a result of such treatment, when white men wielding power over his body "attacked" Dick with questions he was liable to "stammer in his answers," but perhaps when in the company of other black Americans like Ned, who ran away with him, Dick was able to talk and function without fear and with pride and self respect. Dick could be identified by the old, workingmen's clothes given to him by his master, including an old fur hat, blue jacket, and homespun trousers. Yet in some small fashion Dick resisted Hunt's control of his body: he asserted his bodily integrity and his membership in an emerging African American community with its own style and culture by adopting a distinctively black American hairstyle, and had carefully styled his hair by having the "fore-top lately cut off" while leaving the sides and back "bushy."[17]

Other poorer Philadelphians resembled Augustus Reading. Taken together, Reading's small stature, his "brown" tanned complexion, distinctive clothes, and rolling gait, and especially the scars and tattoos that marked his body all proclaimed the fact that this man was one of the city's many seafarers. Thirty-four years old as he walked through the streets of Philadelphia in the spring of 1805, Reading was several inches shorter than was average for native-born white men. His visibly broken left elbow and the vivid scar on his right wrist illustrated the toll that seafaring could take on the bodies of men who worked in this dangerous and poorly paid profession, while the tattoos of the word "Liberty" and the flag of the United States showed Reading marking his own body in a way that advertised his profession, his nationalism, and his engagement with contemporary partisan politics. His body had been marked by his class and profession, and it was regulated and might even be incarcerated by his betters, yet it displayed a vigorous sense of independence.[18]

Like Dick, Augustus Reading had been marked by his status. His broken and scarred limbs bore witness to his work as a seafarer, one of the most dangerous and poorly paid occupations. Yet he, too, took symbolic ownership of his body, marking it with the tattoos that were worn only by sailors in the new republic. His tattoos allowed him to celebrate his American citizenship and his hatred of the British royal navy, whose impressment of sailors threatened him and thousands of other American seafarers. Reading had been three years old when Thomas Jefferson first came to his home town of Philadelphia, and five years old when Jefferson penned the Declaration of Independence, but like many early national sailors, Reading had taken Jefferson's radical affirmations of equality and liberty to heart. By the early nineteenth century, most sailors identified themselves with this ideology, and to a lesser extent with the Republican party led by Jefferson, and Reading's tattooed celebration of "Liberty" marked his body with a striking affirmation of political rights and freedom that transcended his poverty.[19]

In the descriptions of the bodies of Dick and of Augustus Reading can be found evidence of the subculture of those who owned little and struggled to survive, yet who maintained their own culture, values, and beliefs in the face of the control over their bodies exercised by masters, ship captains, and civic officials in such institutions as the almshouse and prison. The bodies of Philadelphia's poor thus emerge as privileged sites for understanding social relations during the late eighteenth and early nineteenth centuries, during which time the city emerged as a major center of commerce and manufacturing. First and foremost, these bodies displayed the scars and badges of class and condition, and as such they were acted upon by people and institutions of power, yet they also reacted and acted on their own behalf. Exploring and analyzing the primary sources documenting the bodies of the poor adds a new dimension to the social and cultural history of the fast growing cities of the new American republic.[20] We have very few firsthand accounts by the poor and the many working men and women who might so easily have experienced poverty, yet historians have rarely examined records of bodily form and performance and the significance of the ways in which people have clothed, inscribed, and decorated their bodies, or the ways in which they employed gesture, style, and performance to take control of themselves and their circumstances.[21] By treating impoverished bodies as our texts we may learn much about the ways lowly social standing and poverty were experienced; how straitened circumstances marked the bodies of the poor; the ways these bodies were coerced and controlled; and the ways they resisted and asserted their independence. Embodied history—the history of bodies—reveals a complex relationship between the body, personal identity, and the power of social elites. By developing our view of the workings of power on the bodies and in the daily lives of the early national poor, this history enhances our understanding of how class, social power, and personal identity were lived and experienced on the streets of Philadelphia.

This is a book about the people whose bodies are missing from or are misrepresented in William Birch's idealized vision of early national Philadelphia. Many of the people described in almshouse, prison, and burial records lived in Philadelphia, while others such as some seafarers and many runaways either passed through the city or spent significant periods of time there. Runaway advertisements reveal that Philadelphia was the single most popular destination for slaves and servants alike both from the surrounding area and from states as far away as Virginia; the city's racial and economic diversity and the existence of a growing free black community with its own church created against the backdrop of the gradual abolition of slavery all served to make the Quaker city particularly attractive to African Americans.[22] As the city grew, middling and elite Philadelphians became increasingly uncomfortable with the rapid increase in newcomers, whose ranks included apparently rootless men, women, and children, unemployed or under-employed laborers, runaways, migrants from the countryside, and immigrants from Europe who either passed through the city or made it home. Whether an individual in the hospital or the almshouse was a long-term city resident or simply passing through, he or she was—in the eyes of many Philadelphians—part of a growing problem.

Resting on contemporary descriptions and accounts of these people's bodies, this book employs these records—and thus the bodies they detail—as texts to be read and interpreted. The sources describing their bodies have been used by historians to shed valuable light on the material circumstances of the poor, yet many of them were kept—quite deliberately—as records of and about bodies.[23] Indeed, the belief that bodies might be read and deciphered would have made sense to the people of late eighteenth- and early nineteenth-century Philadelphia. This book recognizes and indeed employs that perspective, by using their bodies in order to learn more about lower sort Philadelphians during the decades following the American Revolution, for the tension between these bodies as lived and independent, on the one hand, and as constrained and acted upon, on the other hand, illuminates a vital aspect of the lived experience of poverty. Through these records, the bodies of Philadelphia's early national poor reveal much about the nature of their lives and deaths, about their experiences of social and economic power, and sometimes about their experiences, their beliefs, values, and culture. In most cases, the words and voices of these long-dead men, women, and children are long forgotten, but their bodies may yet speak.

The pages that follow are focused on the bodies of the lower sort Philadelphians who furnished the labor that fueled the city's expansion into a major center of commerce and manufacturing. All six chapters illustrate how social class and condition molded the bodies of the lower sort in ways that reveal a great deal about the physical nature of their lives and deaths. The first three chapters examine the bodies of those who were incarcerated in early national Philadelphia's prison and almshouse or were treated in the city's hospital. During the late eighteenth and early nineteenth centuries these institutions exercised an increasing amount of coercive power over the fast growing ranks of the poor, and their records reveal much about both the physical experience of poverty and the ways the power of upper and middling sort Philadelphians was inscribed upon the bodies of the poor. Even in the records of the jail and almshouse, however, there are examples of the agency of impoverished individuals and communities of the poor who sought to retain control of their bodies, a theme developed in the final three chapters, which explore the bodies of runaway servants and slaves, the bodies of professional seafarers, and the dying bodies of impoverished Philadelphians. These, too, illustrate the bodily experience of low social status and poverty, but they also reveal a wide variety of bodily forms of resistance and agency employed by impoverished Philadelphians. Thus, their very bodies become the sources from which we may learn more about life and death, work and play, and belief and culture among the people who are missing from William Birch's engravings of early national Philadelphia.

Chapter 1
Almshouse Bodies

During the 1780s and 1790s Joseph Marsh, Jr., compiled a series of hefty ledgers. Today Marsh's dusty and crumbling Daily Occurrence Dockets of the Philadelphia Almshouse lie in the Philadelphia City Archives, and they constitute a detailed inventory of the bodies of distressed and suffering Philadelphians who—whether by choice or not—found themselves passing through this "asylum of beneficence."[1] The almshouse was a vital part of Philadelphia's limited system of poor relief, a place containing "all that misery and disease can assemble," wherein the bodies of the poor were incarcerated, cared for, and reformed.[2]

On occasion, Marsh's language suggests that he was moved by the condition of those who entered the almshouse. John Smith was admitted "lame naked helpless & Distressed for every Necessary,"[3] and Isabella Wallington came in "almost naked & every way wretched & abandoned."[4] Ambrose Robinson was "a decent looking old Man" whose work with arsenic in dyeing fabrics had occasioned a stroke and rendered him "much Debilitated," while an old black man named Thomas White was so "much emaciated with disease and swarming with Vermin" that staff were forced to strip and clean him and burn "all the Cloaths he had on—which were indeed only Rags & not worth any trouble to clean them if it were even practicable."[5]

For every one of Marsh's humanitarian sentiments, however, there were many more expressions of strikingly caustic and negative judgments, symptomatic of a larger social tendency to regard all the poor, regardless of the cause of their poverty, as morally and physically responsible for their situation and condition. For every kind word Marsh penned many more cruel ones, and some of the poorest and most distressed of Philadelphians were dismissed as "a very worthless old Woman," "a sullen Idle fellow," or even "lame and worthless."[6] Marsh accurately reflected the values of middling and elite Americans who believed that they could differentiate between the deserving and undeserving poor: the former were those who through no fault of their own were unable to keep themselves and their dependants, while the latter were fit, healthy, and able to work, but sought to take advantage of poor relief. In the fast expanding city, Marsh and his ilk were inclined to treat an ever-increasing proportion of the poor who passed into the almshouse as undeserving. The almshouse records—indeed, the institution itself—illustrate how close many lower sort Americans were to dire poverty and dependence of a sort that the elite could hardly imagine, but which they were quick to judge.[7]

The Daily Occurrence Dockets show the bodies of the poor being evaluated and held accountable by the Overseers of the Poor and the city they represented.[8] Better food and kinder treatment were regularly withheld from those judged undeserving. The almshouse authorities required them to work, in part to help defray the expense of their upkeep and in part to prepare them for work outside the almshouse, so that these troublesome indigents might be released back into the city as better and more productive citizens. But although the differentiation between deserving and undeserving poor persisted, almshouse residents were increasingly judged, incarcerated, and conditioned as a single group of dangerously poor and undesirable bodies.[9] As the city and population of Philadelphia mushroomed in the late eighteenth and early nineteenth centuries, with an accompanying rise in urban poverty, the almshouse played a crucial role in controlling and remolding the bodies of the ever-increasing mass of impoverished urban residents. Such treatment and control were, however, contested by many residents, and early national Philadelphia's almshouse was the site of many struggles for self-determination by thousands of poor, ill, homeless, and socially undesirable bodies. To the elite and middling Philadelphians who constructed, organized, and ran the almshouse, the bodies of the poor were improvement projects, to be undertaken and accomplished. To impoverished Philadelphians in the almshouse, however, their bodies were often virtually all that they owned and thus the primary means whereby they might achieve some measure of control over their own lives. Just as seafarers like Augustus Reading celebrated their membership in a working group of low social status with distinctive dress, tattoos, and language, or black slaves and servants like Dick sought some measure of personal integrity through distinctive dress, hair styles, and bodily adornment, many of those in the city's very lowest ranks used their bodies to carve out some small degree of independence.[10] Embattled bodies populated the almshouse, defining a contest between the authorities who saw residents' bodies as objects to be controlled and residents who defended their bodies as the loci of individual agency and power (Figure 7).[11]

The status and indeed the very nature of the impoverished lower sorts who passed through the almshouse were recorded in explicitly moral terms based upon observation of their bodies. Bodily appearance and actions were both crucial here, and such factors as demeanor, stature, clothing, and intemperance all contributed to the ways residents were judged. The Daily Occurrence Dockets are filled with bluntly formulaic assessments, "embodied characterisations"[12] of the deserving poor, like Hugh Stewart, "an orderly useful old man," or the undeserving, like Mary Chubb, "a very worthless body often here."[13]

To Marsh and those who administered the almshouse, it was all too clear that they were dealing with bodies as objects to be controlled and shaped, rather than as subjective entities to be respected, with the result that the Dockets often dismissively refer to people as no more than bodies.

Figure 7. William Birch, Alms House in Spruce Street, Philadelphia, 1799. Based on the original at the Library Company of Philadelphia, with additions by Anthony King. While the almshouse lay on the outer reaches of the settled area of 1790s Philadelphia, it was only four blocks west of the Walnut Street Jail and was hardly the pastoral paradise presented by Birch. Farmers passed by as they brought their produce to market, but this was a building of the urban and transient lower sort, men, women, and children who were incarcerated and made to work within its walls. The fence made escape from the none-too-tender care of the almshouse keepers difficult but far from impossible, and especially during the warmer months many decamped from the "bettering house," only to be incarcerated again, whether by choice or not, during the colder winter months. As the largest residential structure in the city, it was a place defined by the people who lived within, and by those who sought to control and "better" them.

In some cases the tone was one of approval, as in the case of Clara McCord, "an orderly quiet old Body [who] Spins industriously," or Elizabeth White, "a very orderly willing Industrious old Body Knits &c."[14] More often, however, bodies were described and dismissed in more negative terms. The only words used to describe Ann Newgent were "a very so, so, body," while Elizabeth McClinch, "this vile little *drab*," was dismissed as "a very worthless Idle body."[15] Bodies were objects, even property, as in the case of Sarah Summers, "Lately imported from England," or the former servant Sarah Overturf, "who was unsound (blind) when imported."[16] However, while the poor condition of male bodies was often noted in the records, it was only women who were dismissively referred to as "bodies" by Marsh; given that women of this era were far more likely than men to be referred to as "nosybodies," "busybodies," and the like, it may be that it seemed appropriate and even natural to reduce impoverished women to the status of unworthy and unsound bodies in the almshouse records.

The rapidly growing number of impoverished bodies populating Philadelphia appeared problematic and even dangerous, threatening to run out of control, break down social order, attract and spread disease, and generally contaminate the carefully ordered urban society of the new republic.[17] Admitted time and time again was Robert Aitken, "the worthless, drunken Laughing Barber," "as Lousey filthy & dirty as ever." The prostitute Sarah Simpson was recorded as "a woman & one of the Softer, or tender Sex—for she is very *soft* and *tender,* as to be nearly or quite Rotten with the Venereal Disease," while Ann Johnson was brought from her usual spot near the Coffee House, "a drunken deranged old Woman, brot on a dray very drunk almost naked & near Pewking."[18] People such as these were undesirable, ill fitting the model republic desired by the men and women of means and property and imagined by Birch. To keep society and indeed the republic safe, these troublesome bodies had to be incarcerated and then refashioned: once cleansed, reclothed, and trained to work, these bodies could return to the community as members of the respectable and deserving poor, who would employ their bodies in subservient work and present themselves in an appropriately deferential fashion.

The Daily Occurrence Dockets, then, tell us something of the ways social control was exercised over distressed and impoverished bodies. But these were lived bodies as much as they were objective bodies, and how these men, women, and children experienced hunger, nakedness, cold, filth, disease, and drunkenness, and the ways they chose to employ and resist the almshouse and its system of poor relief, can tell us much about life and culture among the very lowest of the lower sort.[19]

For centuries, European and then colonial American civil authorities had attempted to differentiate between the deserving poor, whose distressed situation was no fault of their own and who merited charitable assistance, and the undeserving poor, who were responsible for their condition and required discipline and subordination. According to the sixteenth-century English commentator William Harrison, for example, the former group of poor "by impotency" or "by casualty" included "the fatherlesse child," "the aged, blind, and lame," "the diseased person that is judged to be incurable," "the wounded soldier," "the decaied houseeholder," and "the sicke persone visited with grievous . . . diseases." In contrast, the "thriftless" poor included "the riotour that hath consumed all," "the vagabound that will abide no where," and "the rog[u]e and strumpet."[20] These categories were more than familiar to early national Philadelphia authorities, and they were employed by Joseph Marsh as he made entries in the Daily Occurrence Dockets.

Philadelphia's almshouse was intended to function as both a refuge and a prison.[21] For the deserving poor the almshouse provided shelter and even a rudimentary hospital, a place of last resort where the ill and wounded might recover or die peaceably, where those without support might live and work, and from which some might be bound out to serve others. Alternatively, city officials or night watchmen often interned the bodies of the undeserving poor for whom the almshouse was a place of correction, even a prison, and a growing proportion of those entering had been arrested in this manner. Located on Spruce Street, the almshouse's imposing buildings lay on the outskirts of the densely populated urban core. Apart from the streets and public places, the almshouse and its workhouse were intended to force such people who appeared fit and able into socially acceptable and productive lifestyles. This dichotomy between sanctuary and prison was reflected in the policies of the Guardians of the Poor, the city officials with responsibility for poor relief and the almshouse, who sought to "take great care to make proper distinctions between the different Classes in separating with Regard to their several Characters & Conduct." Such differentiation was all too real for the men and women who passed through this system: while the deserving poor might enjoy tea, for example, undeserving prostitutes suffering from venereal disease faced a diet of bread and water.[22]

J. P. Brissot de Warville fully appreciated the dual purpose of the almshouse, entitling his description "Visit to a Bettering-House, or House of Correction." He described the almshouse as being "constructed of bricks, and composed of two large buildings; one for men, and the other for women." Included among its residents were "the poor, the sick, orphans, women in travail, and persons attacked with venereal diseases . . . vagabonds, disorderly persons, and girls of scandalous lives." The two wings were subdivided into various rooms and wards "appropriated to each class of poor, and to each species of sickness." While impressed by the almshouse, an experienced European like de Warville was nonetheless horrified by the interior scenes of "misery and disease."[23]

The brief yet illuminating descriptions contained in the Daily Occurrence Dockets illustrate that there were residents who met the Overseers' criteria for deserving poor, people whose bodies were too sick, diseased, injured, or aged to enable their owners to support themselves. James Berry, for example, had continued to work hard despite a sore leg, possibly the result of a painful case of gout. He was admitted in the spring of 1791 as "a poor man, who hath long labour'd under the affliction of a very bad sore leg; & which same leg was again unfortunately caught & severely mash'd between two Hogsheads or Casks last Monday." Full of sympathy for an honest working man who could no longer work, the clerk maintained that Berry "is therefore of real Necessity sent in here."[24] Daniel McCalley and his five-year-old son were admitted because he was "an old man & lately much hurt, at his work, at a mast yard."[25] Similarly, Murdock Morris was admitted as "an old Higlander formerly a laborious man now rhumatic," just as James Smith, "a Ship Carpenter, looks as if he hath been a laborious working-man—now ill with rheumatism &c.," while the old soldier William Payne was "mostly full of ulcers and sores, yet he works duly in the Garden & is very orderly & willing."[26] Those men who had worked their bodies hard and striven for self-sufficiency, and who were willing to work as best they might inside the almshouse, were judged by Marsh to be deserving of institutional support.

Some of the bodies of women were judged in similar ways. Catherine Burley, for example, was "an old bl[ac]k woman, who hath been here for several years, & altho she had *at times* a very bad sore leg, she was mostly a very useful honest house servant in the Stew family."[27] Others proved their willingness to work and serve within the almshouse, as indicated by such approving notations as "Spins industriously" or "very orderly willing Industrious old Body Knits &c."[28] The poverty of Hannah McDonald— "a Sturdy young Womn"—and her young child was the result of her husband's imprisonment, while Mary Hensel was "a Poor Woman with very bad disordered Legs," who was recommended as a suitable candidate for support by Elizabeth Drinker, the wife of one of the wealthiest Quaker merchants in Philadelphia.[29] Such recommendations were important: good, useful, respectable bodies such as Cudgo Briant, "a poor lame old black man" were often legitimized by the recommendations of "Reputable Citizens," upon which their admission to the almshouse as the deserving poor, worthy of support, was dependent.[30]

However, as time went on, more and more bodies were judged rather less favorably. George Mullen is an interesting example. Ordinarily "a frequent very worthless customer," on one rare and noteworthy occasion he was admitted as a member of the deserving poor, for "he is now a proper object as his leg is broke."[31] Only the breaking of his body, which rendered him unable to work and support himself, allowed Mullen to move from the ranks of the undeserving to the deserving poor. Many others were incarcerated as undeserving bodies to be punished and reformed, rather than as bodies to be cared for and helped. Jacob Howtchel was dismissed as "a frequent sore leg'd customer [who] does little or nothing," John Vent as "a sullen Idle fellow," and Daniel Boyd as "a worthless skulking fellow" who was readmitted a year later as "a very worthless Idle skulking pocky former Customer."[32]

If anything, Marsh was even more caustic in his dismissal of women who did not meekly accept aid and quietly work for their own support. He described Jane Burns as "a very so, so body," while Ann Smith was both "lame & worthless."[33] Others combined uselessness with negative attitudes: Judith Boyd was "Past all description Impudent," while for all that Mary Lindsey "spins a little" she "scolds & brawls a vast deal more."[34] Similarly, Mary Bursly was recorded as "a grumbling helpless old woman," after which he added the postscript "Died 28 Sept. 87."[35] The fact that this old woman was fast approaching the end of her life when admitted to the almshouse was all but irrelevant: the true and proper objects of public charity were expected to accept their good fortune quietly, obey the rules, and do all they could to contribute to their upkeep.

Resignation and compliance was expected of all the hundreds of men, women, and children who were forced to call the almshouse home. At any time between 25 March 1801 and 25 March 1802, for example, an average of more than 500 men, women, and children inhabited the almshouse, a figure representing close to 1 percent of the population of Philadelphia, Southwark, and the Northern Liberties.[36] Survival was somewhat easier during the warmer midyear months, during which time the monthly population fell below 500, but during the coldest winter months the almshouse housed as many as 600 souls (Table 1).

Throughout the early national period, native-born white residents formed the largest single group of almshouse residents, although in the face of a rising tide of immigration and the aging of a large class of redemptioners and indentured servants, the proportion of native-born white and black residents declined over time (Table 2).

While raw numbers can tell us something about the overall character of the almshouse population, it is only by delving deeper into the records that details of life in and out of the almshouse emerge. The ledgers that record the disbursement of clothing to residents begin to add life to the numbers as one reads of the shoes, shirts, and trousers handed over to George Taverner in 1806 and then again in 1807. Such items constituted the core elements of a complete—albeit basic—wardrobe, meaning that the almshouse authorities had decided how best to clothe Taverner's body. Eleanor Frailey, too, depended on the almshouse for the most basic of clothing, and in consecutive years she received shifts, petticoats, stockings, aprons, and shoes; unlike George, however, Eleanor was given 2 yards of flannel in October 1806, and then 2 yards of tow linen in May 1807, for she was expected to make some of her own clothing. Mary, the young child of Ann Chandler, received only a petticoat and slip in October 1806, which were supplemented by two frocks, two petticoats, and two slips a year later; perhaps her mother had secured shoes for the child that still had some wear in them, or more likely she ran around the almshouse in bare feet.[37]

TABLE 1. Number of Poor Maintained in the Almshouse

Month	Year	Men	Women	Children	Total
April	1801	172	201	111	484
May		170	197	109	476
June		183	198	106	487
July		178	189	99	466
August		177	187	114	478
September		178	194	122	494
October		193	193	119	505
November		223	225	117	565
December		235	242	114	591
January	1802	257	244	110	611
February		248	245	111	604
March		218	237	105	560
Total		2432	2552	1337	6231
Monthly average		203	213	111	527

Source: *The Accounts of the Guardians of the Poor, Managers of the Alms House and House of Employment of Philadelphia, From 25th of March, 1801, to the 25th of March, 1802* (Philadelphia: broadside, 1802), Library Company of Philadelphia.

TABLE 2. Ethnicity of Almshouse Residents

	1806		1810	
Ethnicity	Number	Percent	Number	Percent
Black	54	14.1	55	9.8
Irish	89	23.2	166	29.4
British	18	4.7	46	8.2
German	26	6.8	45	8.1
Other foreign	28	7.3	18	3.2
Native-born white	169	44.0	234	41.5

Source: Gary B. Nash, *Forging Freedom: The Formation of Philadelphia's Black Community, 1720–1840* (Cambridge, Mass.: Harvard University Press, 1988), 156.

The almshouse functioned as a shelter, a basic hospital, and even a hospice, for the poorest of the terminally ill were as likely to end their days in an almshouse ward as in the hospital or in a residence of their own. At the same time, the almshouse and its directors hoped to remake the able-bodied, cleaning, clothing, and feeding them while preparing them for a productive and independent life. The records, then, reveal the stories told by the bodies of the most impoverished of people in early national Philadelphia, people who could not, or people who their betters believed would not, use their bodies in order to provide for themselves and their dependants.

As a place of refuge for the deserving poor, the almshouse was intended only for those born in or with a legal right of residence in Philadelphia and the outlying districts of Southwark and the Northern Liberties. However, residents and non-residents alike who were judged to be members of the undeserving poor might find themselves incarcerated within its walls for a variety of offenses and bodily conditions, from petty crimes to drunkenness to venereal disease. Many almshouse residents were homeless, so no place of residence was recorded by their names in the Daily Occurrence Dockets, although in most cases the area of the city from which they were drawn or referred was recorded. Thus, Randal McDonald and his wife Ann were admitted from Southwark, "he Sick, she Drunk," while Ann Pettit came in from the city of Philadelphia, "an Infirm poor woman but of a Respectable character."[38] Many of the poor and distressed in Philadelphia came from elsewhere, yet only 2 percent of those for whom a place of referral was recorded came from outside the city and its suburbs; whether Philadelphians or not, such bodies were clearly present in the city and alarming elite and middling residents. Almost 65 percent came into the almshouse from the city of Philadelphia itself, with a further 12 percent coming from the Northern Liberties and 21 percent from Southwark.[39] Perhaps it is not surprising that the fast growing suburban ghetto of Southwark, filled with the teeming houses of those who serviced the waterfront, accounted for a higher proportion of almshouse residents than either Philadelphia or the Northern Liberties, at least in relation to population. Southwark accounted for less than 13 percent of the area's population in 1790 and under 16 percent in 1800, yet provided the almshouse with more than a fifth of its residents.[40]

During the years between 1787 and 1797 males and females were admitted into the almshouse in almost equal numbers, 510 men and 490 women. Of these, 47 were identified as male children and 30 as female children, but at least 60 parents who were admitted brought children with them who were not fully recorded in the Daily Occurrence Dockets, so the number and the proportion of children were probably higher.

Race is harder to determine, for throughout the 1780s and 1790s it was not a category in the neatly ruled records, and usually only appeared as an occasional adjective to describe certain inmates, such as "a Rhumatic Black Man with his wife," or "a Vagrant Pockey Negro."[41] In this manner 27 males and 26 females were recorded as black, although the actual number was almost certainly significantly higher.

The dockets usually contain some description of the condition of the men, women, and children of the almshouse.[42] Often, adjectives were strung together to communicate the person's situation, as in the case of William Hill, a sailor described as poor, lame and sick, or Eleanor Fitzgerald, who was recorded as both infirm and ailing.[43] While many of these descriptive terms refer to physical state and condition, others were qualitative, reflecting the attitudes shared by Marsh, the Overseers of the Poor, and indeed many in Philadelphia society toward the undeserving poor. Charles Proud, for example, may have been an invalid in receipt of a Continental Army pension, yet he was nonetheless registered as "a frequent Customer, & a very Worthless one" who contrived to spend his small pension and then rely upon the almshouse for food and clothing. Similarly, when he recorded the entry of Elizabeth Winn in November of 1790, Marsh dismissed her as "a Drunken Dirty Idle frequent Customer."[44]

All these descriptive terms relate to the bodies of impoverished lower sort Philadelphians. Many referred to the physical condition of the body, others to injuries and illnesses inflicted on it, while some dealt with the ways the body was used and presented by its owner. Often the most detailed part of the ledger entry, these descriptions represented a way of categorizing men and women by their bodies, dividing them into the deserving and undeserving poor. As such they express a form of institutional control whereby the Overseers of the Poor would sort the incoming bodies, then house them in an appropriate part of the almshouse and feed, clothe, or care for them accordingly.

The largest single category of descriptive labels refer to the distressed situation of those whose bodies were failing them. During this period, 126 (15 percent) men and women were described as "old," while a further 83 (10 percent) were "distressed"; these and "feeble," "infirm," "helpless," and "ailing" comprised 31 percent of all the labels employed in these records.[45] A second large category of 121 included those rendered helpless by injuries and broken limbs: those described as "lame," "invalid," "crippled," "blind," "deaf," or incapacitated (through such conditions as frostbite, being beaten, a fall, scalding or burning, a rupture, or broken or missing limbs), together accounted for 15 percent of the descriptive terms.[46] A further 14 percent comprised those weakened by disease or other ailment, including rheumatism, consumption, dropsy, fits, pleurisy, fever, and smallpox. By far the largest category within this group is the rather vague appellation of "sore" leg or legs. In many cases this referred to the painful and incapacitating experience of gout, caused by poor circulation and exacerbated by a meager diet and inadequate clothing and housing. Gout was a condition that could be simulated with relative ease, and it was thus regarded with suspicion by almshouse authorities, who interpreted it as the preferred ailment of those who perhaps were not entitled to the food, clothing, and shelter they sought from the almshouse; consequently, the deserving poor could gain admission only by obtaining a certificate from a magistrate or Overseer of the Poor attesting to their good character and genuine need.[47] Finally, a further 59 people (7 percent) were recorded by Marsh as "deranged," and 18 (2 percent) as "insane" or "lunatic."

All told, 70 percent of the descriptive labels employed in these records refer to bodies in a condition that warranted their inclusion in the ranks of the deserving poor, although in many cases this did not result in their being treated as such. Many were neither categorized nor treated as deserving. At least 57 (7 percent) were brought in by city officials in a state of complete drunkenness, while 49 (6 percent) were pregnant women who were unable to care for themselves and the children they were expecting. A further 87 (10 percent) men, women, and occasionally children were suffering from venereal disease, which could be one of a number of ailments, all of them cruel and debilitating, and on occasion deadly. These people were held responsible for their own condition. Their bodies were numbered among the undeserving poor, and they were recorded and treated as such. Often Marsh was explicit in his use of language that dismissed these bodies as "worthless," "useless," or "so-so," and he employed such terms in over 10 percent of the records in this database.[48] Only in a minority of cases do the records indicate the occupation or status of the person in question, and often these serve further to underline deserving or undeserving poverty. Thus 17 women and 30 men were described as "vagrants," "vagabonds" "strollers," and "ramblers," and 32 women as prostitutes; a good many of these were quickly transferred to the Walnut Street jail.

Perhaps not surprisingly, relatively few of the men in the almshouse were referred to by profession: success in an occupation might well have kept them out of the almshouse. More common were references to past occupations, by which means the man was no longer able to keep himself. Some 30 men were referred to as former soldiers, and 31 as sailors, while 40 were described as craftsmen, blacksmiths, and carpenters. Only 13 men were described as laborers, although it is likely that many had worked in this fashion, while 4 men and 12 women were identified as servants and 2 men as former slaves.

Taken together, the destitute, sick, injured and elderly, as well as un-wanted children and pregnant servants appear as discarded bodies, taken into the almshouse because there was no other place for them. In this manner the almshouse might function as a refuge for such people as Sarah Summers and her infant son William, both of whom were "Lately imported from England" and were "in much distress," while John Morison was recorded as "a Distres'd object," having fallen from a brick-layer's scaffold "by which fall he is much Bruised & Injured."[49] Thomas Musgrove, "a painter far gone in consumption," was admitted in Febru-ary 1788 "entirely naked." Two years later he was admitted again, "very weak & feeble" after being caught outside in a snowstorm, and a day later this "poor feeble man" expired.[50] Like Musgrove, many of those entering the almshouse were clothed in rags or even naked, and often they were infested with lice and vermin. John Brown came in as "a sick-man wrap'd in filthy Rags & Swarming with Vermine," while the "old black man" Daniel Stevenson was "wrap'd up in rags, and swarming with vermine."[51]

To the evident consternation of civic authorities, some of the people who were admitted, cleaned and cared for, and then released, would shortly reappear, once again insolvent and distressed. Isabella Walling-ton was admitted in the spring of 1788, with a notation recording that she was "a former Customer" well known as "a Common Beggar about [the] Streets *Naked* &c." Three months later she was back, "almost naked & every way wretched & abandoned."[52] In early national Philadelphia, clothing provided vital markers of status, race, gender, and class, thus helping to establish the wearer's sense of social identity. Thus the ab-sence of clothing, or the wearing of little more than rags, represented a state of privation, dispossession, and even the loss of an identity that had quite literally been stripped off.[53] Whether sitting in the market place or wandering the streets begging, such unfortunates were far from uncom-mon on the streets of the Quaker City.

The almshouse functioned as a refuge in other ways, though not always a kind one. Mary Peel was one of several women who sought an escape from abusive husbands: she entered in the summer of 1794, "an elderly Woman—much beat and Bruised in a drunken fight with her husband, in which, it appears, she was only second best."[54] Similarly, Jane Kean—the "Wife of John Kean a Bottler in Lumber Street"—was admitted after a failed attempt to drown herself because "her Husband has severely beaten her."[55] On occasion children, too, sought an escape from violence, as when nine-year-old William Laird was admitted to escape his master Daniel Kean, a tobacconist "who it seems hath greatly misused the Child."[56]

Some children were admitted with one or both parents, usually their mothers, as in the case of the ailing one-year-old John McLean, who died three weeks after he and his mother entered the almshouse.[57] Other children were admitted alone or taken from their parents into the almshouse. John Yard was "a ragged Deserted Child *Under 8 Years of Age* whose Parents Neglect to provide for him, & who was taken up in the Streets Begging"; Isaac Potter was "a blk. Child of about 3 yrs. Old, whose mother has eloped, & the father is a Lunatic in the Pennsylva. Hospital"; John and Ann Shepherd were admitted as "two children whose Father is in Goal for debt & the Mother not able to support them."[58]

Both children themselves and those who cared for them may well have worked hard to keep youngsters out of the almshouse, in order to evade an institutionalized attempt to mold indigent younger bodies into productive citizens with little reference to the wishes of either the children or their parents. For whatever the motives and actions of parents or guardians, if it appeared that they could not or would not properly care for a child, the child would almost certainly be taken and bound out as a servant or apprentice. Perhaps Frombo Hall, the African American who had cared for the nine-year-old orphan Jane Morton, had been trying to keep her from the servitude that had almost certainly been the lot of her parents.[59] Similarly, Elizabeth Philips entered the almshouse with two young children in order to escape "the abuse of a Worthless Drunken Husband," but her family was soon split up when the older child was bound out as an apprentice.[60]

Other parents appeared less concerned with the fate of their children, or perhaps were less able to protect them. George Yard, who suffered "fitts & his Intalects, are thereby very much impaired," was taken out of the almshouse after two years residence by his mother, "who said she could & would carefully provide for & keep him." Soon, however, George was back, for "She only wanted him out, to send him a beging," but finding him too sick to do this his mother "sends him here again." Several days later the "poor sick deranged boy" died, and the records are venomous in their dismissal of his "worthless mother."[61] Other records are rather more difficult to interpret. Three-year-old Alexander Thomas was found in the street beside the drunk and insensible body of his mother, while the blind John Hutchinson "would go about begging led by a little girl his Daughter."[62] Alcoholism was regarded as a personal weakness and failing of the undeserving poor, unlike a medical condition such as blindness, which would prevent an otherwise willing and able man from supporting himself and his family. But even in circumstances such as these, the almshouse authorities were likely to strip the children from parents who could not provide for them and bind the children out. Hidden in the spare words of these records are the struggles of impoverished parents to keep their children out of the almshouse and away from the authorities who might take the children away.

Such was the likely fate of children born in the almshouse, yet expectant mothers with no home often had little alternative. The almshouse authorities followed the standard practice of trying to establish the identity of the father, for he could be pressed into supporting the child and mother. It is as if the bodies of these children were property, which women alone could not hold; if a likely man was able to take on the child, both child and mother might go free, but failing that the child would eventually be bound out to a master who could properly raise and care for him or her. Thus, Sophia Watson was questioned during "the Extremity of her labor," during which she declared that Cornelius Hyatt was the father of her newborn daughter Sarah, who lived for only three weeks.[63] Similarly, the African American woman Ann Miller admitted that her daughter Mary had been fathered by "one Edwards a Black Man who is now in the service of Mr. Archd. McCall."[64] Both Margaret Summers and Barbara O'Neal were expecting the children of men in jail; Summer was allowed to marry John Hart in the jail, but children of such unions were almost certain to be taken from their mothers, for they and the fathers would have no way of supporting them.[65] It is not too surprising, then, that pregnant women such as Rachel Davis and Sarah Smith sought to escape the almshouse before giving birth.[66]

The masters of servant women who became pregnant faced a choice. They could, as in the case of James Hunter, pay for the pre- and postnatal care enjoyed by his African American servant Sophia and then have the child bound to himself or to another.[67] It is always possible, of course, that the child was Hunter's. Such was the case for Mary Bowgh, who was "pregnant by her *Young Master* Mr. Shaffer." These circumstances did not always work in favor of mother and child, however, and Bowgh was admitted into the almshouse "destitute of Necessaries & somewhat Silley," perhaps shocked by her apparent abandonment.[68] Governor Thomas Mifflin appears to have been outraged by the discovery that his new African American servant was in fact pregnant before she entered his service: in addition to arranging for Ann Williams to be interned in the almshouse, Mifflin arranged a warrant for the arrest of the father, Archibald Galt, the captain of a sloop named the *Willing Lass*, on which vessel he had transported Ann to Philadelphia.[69]

For pregnant women, then, the almshouse was as much a place of incarceration as it was a refuge. Whether married or single, to give birth in the almshouse might well involve surrendering one's child, and a lengthy period of work to finance the period of "lying-in." Thus, while the fathers of such children were—if located and brought to account—held financially responsible for their offspring, it was the mothers who paid the highest cost. In a very real way, the categories of deserving and undeserving poor dissolved, and whatever their backgrounds and circumstances, pregnant women in the almshouse lost control of their own bodies and those of their children.

The almshouse also functioned as a holding facility for the bodies of drunken and prostituted men and women, all of whom were dismissed as among the worst of the undeserving poor. The Daily Occurrence Dockets mention drunkenness in almost 7 percent of admissions, as in the case of John Shepheard, "a very quiet bidable fellow when sober," who worked in the almshouse gardens, or Catherine Johnston, "a most violent Virago when in Liquor," who could "spin or knit."[70] Consumption of large amounts of alcohol was commonplace in early national America, and despite the post-revolutionary dip in drinking occasioned by the decreased West Indian trade in molasses and rum, each American was consuming an annual average of over three gallons of alcohol (contained in all alcoholic beverages).[71] Alcoholic beverages pervaded society, from the rum rubbed on the lips of teething babies, to the hard cider consumed with breakfast, to the ales brewed in many homes, to the distilled spirits drunk in the workplace, in taverns, and at home, and employed as the most readily available painkiller. Most if not all meals, and all social occasions, were incomplete without alcohol, and virtually all men, women, and children in early national Philadelphia consumed significant quantities. The almshouse records of men and women like the "Tallow Chandler & Soap boiler" James Maloy who was "quiet if sober" were far from unusual; to the almshouse authorities, such people were fine unless they overindulged.[72]

More troubling were those incapacitated by a particularly heavy drinking session, or the alcoholics who had lost control of their bodies and were numbered among the undeserving poor. In both cases, such men and women were admitted into the almshouse in order to remove their incapacitated bodies from public spaces and to try to recondition them after a period of excessive drinking. Mary Lane, "a very noted Drunken disorderly woman," was brought in late in the evening "in a Cart & Very Drunk," accompanied by her two children aged about two and six months, while the ragged Ann Johnson was so drunk that she was incapable of walking into the almshouse.[73] The unfortunate barber Alexander Cremsey was brought in "Stark Stareing Mad" by four men, quite possibly his friends and drinking companions, who acknowledged that "his disorder is the effects of hard Drinking." Similarly, "an unknown Woman, found most beastly drunk in the streets & in danger of perishing" was admitted into the almshouse in January of 1796; it was not until she had slept and sobered up that she was able to identify herself as Mary Ann Lawrence. Benjamin Moffat was "a poor young man stupefied with liqr. & afflicted with Fits," but as soon as he had slept off the effects of his hard drinking he eloped. Others were not so fortunate, as in the case of James Lynch, who in November of 1793 was found lying "severely intoxicated" on the streets of Southwark. According to Marsh, Lynch appeared to have suffered several fits, and he astutely noted that Lynch looked "like a man struggling with Death." After a day and night of rest Lynch regained consciousness and reported his name, but the following morning he died.[74] The fits suffered by Cremsey, Moffat, Lynch, and a host of other almshouse residents were most likely the muscle spasms of delerium tremens, which could be occasioned in a heavy drinker by an illness, a decline in consumption of alcohol, or in these cases an alcoholic binge. Following the "fits" the drinkers might become particularly active and even violent, after which they would fall into a deep sleep and then either recover or—like James Lynch—die.[75]

Others came into the almshouse incapacitated by drink in a rather different manner: while they may not have indulged in a dangerously excessive bout of drinking, their dependence on alcohol rendered them unable to work and survive independently. In the case of Mary Carroll, Marsh believed that "if it was not for rum [she] need not be here," while Jacob Houtchel was dismissed as "a very worthless ordinary frequent Customer with Rum-rotten sore legs."[76] On occasion, drunkenness functioned as a label for these bodies, helping to define people in the way that a profession might: Thomas Salvester was "the noted drunken Wood Sawyer," James Boyd the "vile drunken old Hangman," Thomas McCain "the worthless drunken painter," and Robert Aitken "the worthless, drunken Laughing Barber" or "the noted Drunken laughing Barber."[77]

These admissions reveal that public drunkenness was a relatively common occurrence in early national Philadelphia, and one that most residents would have witnessed in the small and densely populated city.[78] While much social drinking among the lower sort may have taken place in cramped alleys and waterfront communities little visited by more affluent Philadelphians, drunkenness knew no such bounds. Public places, especially the market places on High Street and Second Street, provided venues for socialization, drinking, prostitution, and begging. The "drunken derainged old Woman" Ann Johnson was "usually about the Coffee House," and the unfortunate James Lynch was well known "about Market," rather like Patrick Murphy, "a dirty drunken fellow taken up in that condition in the New Market."[79] In fact it was in the section of his travelogue describing the market that Charles William Janson lamented that "spiritous liquors are, unhappily for the lowest orders of society, still easier of attainment."[80]

Market days were originally held on Tuesdays, Fridays, and Sundays, but the latter day was canceled in 1806 after local residents protested, "not from religious reasons only," but because the lower sorts collected in the market place on Saturday evenings with their weekly wages, "and the Market during the whole night is the scene of every species of riot and debauchery."[81] During and after the Revolution, elite and middling Philadelphians had increasingly distanced their own drinking from that of the lower sorts, so that poorer Philadelphians developed their own culture of social drinking, complete with its own venues.[82] In grog shops, taverns, and even out in the market, poorer Philadelphians gathered together to "Laugh Drink and Smoke and leave Nothing to Care," singing, dancing, and forgetting their troubles.[83]

For the lower sorts, the market provided not only a venue for carousing and begging, but even a place to stay. In *Modern Chivalry* Hugh Henry Brackenridge recorded the tale of a young woman who had been thrown out by her family after bearing an illegitimate child; on her arrival in Philadelphia the unfortunate woman could find no shelter, and she joined others with little or nothing and "lay in the market house, upon a bench."[84] Early national Philadelphians would, then, have seen many of the drunken, ragged, diseased, and injured unfortunates who eventually found themselves in the almshouse. Just as the crack houses and drug-infested streets of modern American cities inspire dread among contemporary Americans, so early national travelers and later temperance advocates complained about alcoholic excess and public drunkenness.

Prostitutes were another category of the undeserving poor who came in for harsh criticism. They comprised the largest group of women identified as having any kind of trade or profession, and accounted for at least 6.9 percent of all the female almshouse residents in this database.[85] The frequency with which such women entered and left the almshouse suggests that, just like drunkards and vagrants, prostitutes—many suffering from venereal disease—were common among Philadelphia's lower sorts. More than any other group of men or women in the almshouse, prostitutes were judged by their bodies, their identities defined by biological function and inscribed by sexual disease. An 1800 broadside entitled "Advice to a Magdalen" advised those who sought to escape prostitution to do so by taking control of every aspect of their bodies, and thus rejecting bodily license and abandon: by being "chaste in your Conversation," avoiding "Talkativeness," being "neat and cleanly in your Dress and Person," and avoiding "Finery or Fashion," such women could exercise a control that fallen women had supposedly lost.[86]

In the Daily Occurrence Dockets, prostitutes appear as the most dissolute and lawless of the undeserving poor, as women whose surrender to unlicensed and immoral sexuality threatened the very fabric of society in the new republic. They were judged accordingly. The Daily Occurrence Dockets recorded venereal disease in men as simply one more aspect of their condition, as in the case of Daniel Boyd, "a very worthless

Idle skulking pocky former customer." Infected children might engender some compassion, as in the case of the unfortunate Jane Williams, daughter of a fish-seller, who at the age of five "hath the Venereal disease from *Parents.*"[87] Similarly, married women like Submit Hickman, whose "worthless Husband . . . has communicated that fatal disorder to this poor woman," or Ann Clark, who "says she was diseased by a *bad* husband," might expect a sympathetic reception in the almshouse.[88]

But while there is sympathy in the language of the records for Cato Cox, "an old Black-man, not long here, [who] died last Night in a shocking Condition with the Venrl Disease," there was precious little for prostitutes.[89] As always, women could embody either nurture or corruption, and in the almshouse records prostitutes—especially those suffering from venereal disease—appeared as the embodiment of decay and corruption.[90] Consequently, prostitutes and the unmarried female poor infected with venereal disease were objects of scorn rather than compassion. Catherine Miller was described as "a vile young Hussey severely Pox'd," Ann Wall "a frequent Pockey Customer, of the most worthless kind," and Kitty Jones "our old Pockey Lady from So[uth]Wark as bad as ever."[91] Time and time again, the brief descriptions entered in the almshouse admittance records defined prostitutes by their condition. Thus Sarah Wilson was recorded as "one of the worn-out Venereal Ladies," Susannah Glass as "a Noted Venereal lady & old Customer," and Grace Boon as "one of the Venereal Ladies."[92] There was little pity for these women, who were seen as independent of male authority and as sources of bodily and moral corruption, even though some died horrible deaths within the almshouse. Many prostitutes could expect the same fate as Mary Pothemus, who entered the almshouse for the final time in August of 1793 and died two months later.[93]

While Marsh was caustic in his dismissal of undeserving poor men and women, the language that he used to describe women in general and prostitutes in particular was especially harsh. To a significant extent, early national society defined women of all classes and races by the productivity of their bodies, both the labor they performed and the children they produced. Women who, according to such authorities as Marsh, misused their own bodies were therefore guilty of social crimes above and beyond the lazy worthlessness of undeserving men. Thus Marsh enjoyed punning on the name of Mary Killgallant, a prostitute admitted in February 1796, but his humour was dark: "well surely then Madam, I am really glad that I never was a *gallant* of yours, tho probably many a good fellow has been and that you kill'd them, *all dead, dead, dead over* and *over, again, and again.*" When Margaret White, "a Noted Lady of the Town," was discharged after the symptoms of her venereal disease had abated, Marsh recorded that she left for "the propogation 'NOT OF THE GOSPEL.'" Similarly, Marsh described Sarah Simpson as "a woman & one of the Softer, or tender Sex," but one whose life as a prostitute had rendered her "so very *soft* and *tender*, as to be nearly or quite Rotten with the Venereal Disease."[25] When Simpson was discharged along with Ann Till, "an Idle black Hussey lately severely Pox'd, now, a little prepared, for another Desperate Cruize," Marsh snidely bid them adieu as "a real Fine Ship and a Sukpherous Bomb-Ketch—just turn'd out of Dock (not with clean bottoms) but very fit for Mischief." Such editorial comments are unique in the records, reserved only for the most unworthy of the undeserving poor.[95]

These women were seen as entirely responsible for the diseased condition of their bodies, and even worse as responsible for the suffering of innocent men and their families. Elizabeth Buckman was admitted in November of 1791, "pregnant & Poxed." Her male child died not long after birth, and it was not until August 1792 that the unfortunate Elizabeth was well enough to leave the almshouse, dismissed "on a Cruise to recoup her Loss & renew her Disorder."[96] The death of Elizabeth's son elicited no sympathy and no acknowledgment that prostitution may have provided her only means for survival. Neither did the admission of Catherine Delaney, "our Noted worthless Red-Kate often here venereal, now return'd & Pregnant & so compleats a very expencive Round." Marsh was more concerned about the cost of caring for such worthless women than he was about their health and welfare, and he dismissed Catherine as "an Idle Hussey" when he recorded the birth of her son two days later. The father, "one Cassell," had died several months earlier during the first of the city's great epidemics of yellow fever, yet Marsh expressed no sympathy for the diseased single mother, nor acknowledgment that his death made her escape from prostitution all but impossible.[97]

A year before Elizabeth and Red Kate entered the almshouse, Hugh Henry Brackenridge had included in *Modern Chivalry* an interview with a young Philadelphia prostitute. Brackenridge endeavored to make clear to his readers that the woman and others like her became prostitutes out of cruel necessity rather than choice. She narrates her story of arriving in Philadelphia penniless and being taken in by another young woman with whom she attempted to make a living "in the millinery way." When they could find no work, she sold more and more of her clothes for food, and after her companion died she was reduced to prostitution. While Brackenridge was careful to point out the difference between such as this young woman, whom he clearly thought of as one of the deserving poor, and undeserving "bauds, and strumpets," he nonetheless asserted a degree of sympathy that may not have been replicated in the almshouse.[98]

Not even the shocking symptoms of syphilis elicited sympathy from Marsh. The pox "hath almost blinded" Mary Fitzgerald and left Catherine

Hayes "scarcely able to Crawl with it," and their dire situation prompted many prostitutes to seek relief from the symptoms by ingesting mercury, a cure that was as dangerous as the disease.[100] Eleanor Redman was "deprived of the use of her Limbs . . . by too much freedom with mercury," just as the "frequent Dirty venereal Customer" Hannah Giles "lost the use of her limbs by too much familiarity with mercury."[31] On these and other occasions, the unfortunate women were too ill to make their own way to the almshouse, and it was their fellow prostitutes who brought them in. Eleanor Redman "was introduced by a couple of the Town Sporting Ladies," namely "the Noted Ruth Gilbert & another of her Profession," just as Grace Boon was escorted out of the almshouse "by a Sister of equal fame." Prostitutes were only one group among the poor of Philadelphia who used the almshouse for their own purposes.[101]

Such records suggest something of the community that may have existed among women forced into casual or more permanent prostitution. Much to the annoyance of civic authorities, this community functioned as a support network that helped these women survive, if necessary bringing them into the almshouse for medical treatment or rescuing them from it once recovered. At any one time, the venereal ward was likely to be housing a good number of these women, and they acted together to protect their interests. They objected, for example, to the care provided by Jane Bickerdite, a woman employed as nurse among the women in the venereal ward. When she finally quit her position, "they mob'd her severely & raised a Bawling Clamrous noise & clanger with Beating & Ratling, Frying Pans Shovels Tongs &c. after her, all of which Together, they called '*The Whoars* march."[102] The young Reverend Ezra Stiles Ely, a chaplain in New York City's almshouse, was shocked to find the sick wards filled with "blasted, withered, dying" prostitutes upon their "beds of disease, planted with thorns." But what most shocked Ely were the ways these dying prostitutes mocked him and his religion, preferring each other's company to his as they awaited death.[103]

Even Brackenridge, following his account of the unfortunate young prostitute and her subsequent suicide, had nothing good to say about the sorority of fallen women. Denied a burial in sacred ground by her suicide, the young woman was escorted out to the Potters Field by "old bauds, and strumpets, and cullies, half-drunk, making merry as they went along."[104] Both the rough music accorded the unpopular nurse and this wake attest to the strength of a community derided and imprisoned by civic authorities. Women who survived by using their bodies, and who were consequently defined by others by those bodies, looked to their own for support. All of them, especially those who were more than casual prostitutes, knew that their lives might well end as did Rebecca Tucker's, "a worn down Venerl. Fille de Joie" who died in the almshouse.[105] Yet in their own subculture, complete with its rough music and wakes, they celebrated life far more than they commemorated death.

For all that the almshouse was intended to aid the deserving poor and reform their undeserving brethren, many emulated the prostitutes who strove to retain control of their bodies by living within the almshouse on their own terms. There was a community of the impoverished lower sorts within its walls whose culture and values the Overseers of the Poor were often unable to eradicate. The almshouse authorities had hoped to wrest control of impoverished bodies away from those who could not or would not care for and employ them properly. Cleansed, nourished, and properly clothed bodies would—if they were able—be required to work and, the authorities hoped, be refashioned for a productive role in society. In practice, however, the lower sorts who were institutionalized in this fashion resisted such control as best they could, attempting to retain control over their own and the bodies of loved ones. Reading between the lines of the almshouse records, one soon discovers a world wherein the poor sought to use the almshouse for their own purposes, and the anger and frustration recorded by so many officials testify to their success.

The most simple way in which residents sought to use the almshouse was as a winter refuge. Having lived and survived as best they could during the warmer months, many sought entry as the days became shorter and colder. For those without food, fuel, shelter, and clothing, the Philadelphia winter was harsh and dangerous, and it was not unusual for men and women to be admitted with "frosted" feet and hands. Within the almshouse they could expect new clothing, food, and some warmth in exchange for their work, and in the spring they returned to their former haunts and occupations. The almshouse was not intended for such purposes, and Marsh condemned those like "the Noted Soldier Jem, who comes & goes when he pleases." He described such seasonal occupants as "Autumnal," as in the case of John Smith and his wife, "a very worthless Couple & Constant Autumnal Customers as they then Duly return, covered or Wrap'd up in rags swarming with filth & Vermine." James Connolly defined the type, being "a very worthless Autumnal Customer . . . [who] returns *annually*, ragged Dirty and Diseased, Loiters here all Winter, & in Spring being Cleaned, Clothed, & Cured, commences his opperations, of Idleness & Drunkenness & during the whole summer is one among many others, whose wretched filthy appearance Disgrace our streets."[106]

This use of the almshouse by the undeserving poor reached its apogee with people like Hugh O'Hara, "a very worthless young fellow" who was admitted in December 1788 "in a very wretched condition, with disease & rags." He subsequently "Winter'd here got cured & cloathed," and then left the almshouse in March 1789 "& immediately sold most of his Cloathing and soon drank the whole they produced." A few months later

O'Hara returned to the almshouse, "naked & badly diseased," but having been "cured & cloathed & now very hearty" he "according to Custom ran off."[107] Rather than reforming the undeserving poor, the almshouse appeared to be presenting them with opportunities to continue living largely independent and masterless lives. Daniel Boyd, a "frequent autumnal worthless Customer," entered the almshouse every winter "as idle and impudent as possible," insisting upon "every accommodation of Cloathing &c. (with insolence) *as a matter of right.*" But Boyd suffered from "an old ulcerous sore leg," "Venereal contamination," and drunkenness, which meant that no amount of reform in the almshouse was likely to prepare him for work in Philadelphia that would support him. In a republican age in which independence was valued above all else, Boyd and others like him sought to survive free on the streets of Philadelphia as best they could, without completely surrendering themselves to the control of the prison or almshouse authorities.[108]

The almshouse could provide a variety of resources for the poor as they headed back into Philadelphia. Having received clothing, Leah McGee "borrow'd several things among the People & then ran off," a rare recorded instance of theft from other inmates. Appropriation of almshouse property was another matter. Archibald McGowan, a "Notorious one handed Villain" whose injury was sustained during the War for Independence, regularly "robs the House of blankets &c.," which he and his wife Elizabeth then sold. Margaret McLean "lacerated her leg" in climbing the fence "with shoes, hose & other necessities," hoping "to spend those things & then return again." The trade in such items was lively, and Marsh recorded his suspicions that many residents resorted to such institutions as the illegal tavern of Mary Carroll, a former resident whose "most infamous place of Rendezvous" was popular with almshouse residents who entered "with the Publick's Cloathing &c. *all for Rum.*" John McKinley, together with his wife and child, took "bread and also Tea & Sugar" from the almshouse, having "avow'd among the People an intention or design of not returning."[109] It was only by leaving the almshouse that McKinley could be sure of keeping his family together, for in the almshouse they would be separated and the child quite possibly bound out.

There were other welfare strategies employed by those within the almshouse. Some residents were in receipt of pensions, usually as a result of service in the Continental Army. Such pensions were required to be turned over to the Overseers of the Poor in order to help defray the costs incurred by the resident. Few, however, willingly surrendered such precious funds. The lame shoemaker John Cooney "continually finds means to obtain & make [a]way with his Pension," beyond which "he continually purloins and makes [a]way with more leather, Tools &c. than all his Earnings would amount to." Cooney and his wife and child success-fully retained his pension while actually making money out of the almshouse, as he used the institution's raw materials to manufacture shoes sold for his own profit. Like Cooney, Archibald McGowan "always finds means to dispose of his pension & then spends the whole Produce," and Marsh and the almshouse authorities clearly despaired of such char-acters.[110] Perhaps, however, men who had lost a hand or gone lame in the struggle to secure American independence believed that they had earned the right to spend their small pensions as they saw fit.

Alcohol was forbidden within the almshouse, but this did not prevent residents from escaping to find solace in taverns and grog shops. Like their early modern European ancestors, the almshouse residents re-garded "all Holly [day] times or festivals" as occasions for celebration, which inevitably involved drinking. On such days residents were "remark-ably Drunk disorderly & irregular . . . *All with impunity.*"[111] Clearly, almshouse authorities did not enjoy sufficient power to eliminate such traditional practices. Thus Cornelius Buckley "ran off on Christmas Morning," only to return three days later with a bottle of rum, while Harry Musgrove endeavored to ensure that work in the almshouse did not interfere with drinking outside its walls: he "has long been in the Practice of going over the fences for Rum in the night with which he got intoxicated & behaved very riotous & disorderly," after which "he would lay in bed all the next day, indulging himself, with reading and Sleeping, and *then* out & Drunk again at Night." When the authorities finally ended this pursuit, Harry "jump'd the fence," leaving Marsh to record "a good riddance of bad Rubbish, as long as it lasts."[112]

Thus, for all the suffering within the almshouse, and despite the best attempts of authorities to instill order, deference, and a work ethic among those who were fit to work, there were many who resisted. For them, the almshouse provided a means to continue living life on the streets as best they could, and their community had its attractions. It was with approval that Marsh recorded how Elizabeth McClinch's mother had secured a suitable post for her in the nearby countryside, and then later with amazement that he registered her return to the community, "meerly for the sake of being among the fellows here." He could do no more than dis-miss her as "a very worthless Idle body."[113] These records resonate with the frustration of civic authorities and those of the middling sorts and elite who sought to control the poor, ignoring the friendships, family ties, and community that bound together members of the city's lower sort, both in and out of the almshouse.

The attitude toward London's undeserving poor expressed by William Hogarth in such vicious caricatures as "Gin Lane" was shared by those who organized and ran the Philadelphia Almshouse. Parts of the rapidly growing city, especially the waterfront and the fastgrowing ghettos of Southwark and the Northern Liberties, must have appeared to middling and elite Philadelphians as bearing a marked resemblance to Gin Lane, whether it was parents like those of eight-year-old John Yard, who "Neglect to provide for him," or ragged and even naked drunken men and women such as Thomas McCain and Mary Ann Lawrence.[114] As the Daily Occurrence Dockets demonstrate so vividly, there were poor folk in the streets and alleys of early national Philadelphia and even within the almshouse who might not have seemed out of place in Hogarth's nightmarish vision. This deeply concerned elite and middling sort Philadelphians, who earnestly believed that such lower sort folk had no place in William Birch's rather more idyllic street scenes, and city authorities employed the almshouse and the prison both to remove undesirables from the streets and public places of the city and to refashion their bodies and lives.

Chapter 2

Villainous Bodies

George Washington was the very embodiment of republican respectability, and in dress, demeanor, and stature the Virginian displayed "a perfect good breeding." For Washington, control of his body, his words, his emotions, and his actions had all been integral to his very being ever since he had copied out and begun practicing rules of civilized behavior at the age of sixteen. It was with their bodies that members of the early national elite displayed material wealth and power, thus demonstrating class and status in the most visible manner. The body—how it was dressed, how it was employed, how it moved, and how it interacted with others—furnished tangible evidence of both moral and material well-being.[1]

In stark contrast to Washington and his ilk were the bodies of Philadelphia's vagrants, a general term employed by their betters to categorize lower sort folk whose appearance and demeanor suggested that they might be unemployed, homeless, and unable to provide for themselves. For generations such people had been dealt with in and by the almshouse, but as the new republic grew and the ranks of the urban poor exploded, the prison was reinvented in part to deal with the increasing bodies of more and more socially threatening, impoverished men, women, and children. Vagrancy was, quite literally, criminal, and the bodies of villainous vagrants were read by contemporaries as connecting and embodying both poverty and immorality. While Washington's appearance epitomized bodily control and thus symbolized moral purity and even political virtue, the undeserving poor "offend thy view," for such "wild beasts" were "idle and vicious" people, who were "addicted to vice . . . corrupt in principles or conduct . . . depraved . . . wicked," and "habitually transgressing the moral law."[2] The English writer William Harrison had condemned such "thriftless" poor, including "the riotour that hath consumed all . . . the vagabond that will abide no where . . . the rog[u]e and strumpet."[3]

Middling and elite Philadelphians agreed with Harrison, interpreting the bodily condition of certain members of the lower sort as the result of choice rather than circumstance, and consequently they usually held such folk responsible for their bodily and moral condition. Often civic authorities all but refused to differentiate between vagrants by choice and vagrants by necessity. Thus, among those arrested during July of 1796 were two men and one woman who were taken up while "lurking about the Market in High Street" as "drunken, idle vagrants"; another trio who were charged "with being notorious vagrants . . . Drunk, beging [sic] & abusing the Citizens"; two more women described as "Vagrants found drunk & Idle in the New Market"; and a group of two men and eight women who were "drunken fighting Idle disorderly Vagrants & Vagabonds."[4] The reasons for the poverty or drunkenness of such folk were irrelevant, for their situations and actions were interpreted as evidence of immoral and dissolute lives.

Such criminally impoverished folk appeared 'masterless,' in that they were neither in proper control of their own bodies nor appropriately controlled by others. Categorized as "vagrants," they were treated by their betters with suspicion and fear as "vicious," "vulgar," "useless lumps of clay," who could not or would not adhere to normal civilized rules of behavior. Vagrants might well steal food, clothing, or other goods, rendering property insecure, and their shoddy appearance, their soiled countenances, and their noisy and disrespectful demeanor meant that the bodies of the poor seen on the streets and in the public places of Philadelphia appeared to the well-to-do as problematic, dangerous, and as ever threatening to run out of control. John Alexander has demonstrated that the supposedly idle poor inspired fears that without proper discipline and control they might threaten the very fabric of society. Rather than deserving pity and warranting charity, the "thriftless" poor were to be taken up, incarcerated, punished, and corrected.[5]

Such "masterless" men and women were nothing new in early modern society, but what most frightened the middling and upper sorts in early national America was the enormous expansion in the number of impoverished vagrant bodies in the towns and cities of the new republic. The nation's population—including the impoverished lower sorts—was growing extremely fast, as President Thomas Jefferson made clear in his State of the Union address to Congress in December 1801, in which he laid before Congress the results of the second national census. "You will perceive," he told members of Congress, that if "the increase of numbers during the last ten years" continued at the same rate, the nation's population would double within just over two decades.[6] Jefferson was merely articulating what his fellow Americans knew and experienced on a daily basis: during the years following the War for Independence, their republic was enjoying spectacular growth in population, geography, trade, and economy. While farms and plantations spread westward, increasing numbers of immigrants were pouring into the United States, and as the nation produced more crops and goods, American ships and commerce were reaching out across the globe. During the late eighteenth and early nineteenth centuries American cities grew rapidly, as crops and migrants from the countryside, and imported goods and immigrants from abroad, poured into these fast developing centers of trade, commerce, and manufacturing. New York City expanded from a city of just under 22,000 in 1770 to a bustling metropolis of over 60,000 by 1800, the population of Baltimore doubled between 1790 and 1800, and the city of Philadelphia grew from 15,000 in 1760 to over 41,000 in 1800 (over 61,000 if the districts of Southwark and the Northern Liberties are included).[7]

On the one hand American expansion generated enormous excitement, and one can sense Jefferson's enthusiasm when he asked his countrymen to "contemplate this rapid growth and the prospect it holds up to us . . . [of] the settlement of the extensive country still remaining vacant . . . to the multiplication of men susceptible of happiness, educated in the love of order, habituated to self-government, and valuing its blessings above all price."[8] On the other hand, while many shared the president's vision, their enthusiasm was tempered by the fears engendered by the rapid expansion of the nation, and especially by the unbridled growth of their small, orderly towns into large and riotous cities.

Late colonial Philadelphia had been little bigger than an English market town, stretching about eight blocks from north to south and no more than about six blocks inland from the Delaware River. Even in the center of the colonial Quaker capital, Philadelphians had been little more than a five-minute walk from open fields (see Figure 5).[9] It had been, at least in the rosy memories of some inhabitants, an ordered community in which each individual—whether slave or servant, apprentice or journeyman, a wife or child—belonged to a household and was responsible to the head of that household. Just as in early modern Europe, this was an idealized organic society of orders and ranks in which those without independence worked for and deferred to the independent head of their household, and those of limited means and property deferred to those with wealth and power.

Traditionally, when people had fallen out of this regulatory social structure—such as those who had been orphaned or widowed or who were prevented by injury or disease from supporting themselves and their dependents—the community came to their aid through a system of poor relief, often within the institutional framework of the almshouse. Such men, women, and children who were poor through no fault of their own inspired sympathy and charity, for, as the *Philadelphia Minerva* noted, "virtuous poverty is no crime."[10] But as Philadelphia was transformed from a colonial town into a large and populous national city, the numbers of the masterless poor swelled, filling the streets and public places of Philadelphia with the impoverished bodies of immigrants from Europe and the Caribbean, migrants from the countryside and other towns, and the poor who were native to the city. Walking the streets, the city's middling and upper sorts saw more and more bodies of visibly poor men, women, and children who were not subject to the normal social controls of work and household. Moreover, the democratic sensibilities encouraged by the War for Independence and the difficult task of keeping oneself and one's family out of poverty combined to lessen the deference of many lower sort Philadelphians, and those who ruled the city began to recognize that the idealized organic society of colonial Philadelphia was disintegrating in the face of the enormous social and economic changes of the post-revolutionary era.[11]

The vagrants, strollers, and ramblers who wandered the streets of Philadelphia appeared to many as outsiders, people who leeched from society rather than contributing toward it. As a result, the upper and middling sorts of the city were increasingly likely to make moral and legal judgments about the impoverished bodies surrounding them.[12] The tone and language employed by Joseph Marsh, Jr., as he recorded the admission of vagrants into the city's almshouse, reveals something of the depth of resentment such bodies inspired among the civic officials responsible for their discipline and incarceration. William Ofrey was "an impudent Vagrant Stroller from Jersey," while Daniel Murphy and his family were "Noted Vagrants & beggars & infamous former Customers."[13] When Elizabeth Shipheard, "a worn out worthless Stroller," died two months after her admission, Marsh recorded the event without sympathy.[14] Whether it was Mary Allen, the "naked Distressed Rambler swarming with vermin," the "Vagrant Pockey Negro" James Willis, who died shortly after his admission, or any of the other homeless and jobless women who entered or left the almshouse, Marsh had no kind words for them.[15]

Night watchmen and civic officials, even including such men as the mayor himself, did not hesitate to act personally against masterless bodies rendered suspect by their impoverished condition. The nature, presence, and appearance of such folk ill suited the mores of respectable republican society; they appeared to their betters as bodies out of control, and as such they were approached, questioned, and taken into custody. Vagrancy was a crime, and the Vagrancy Dockets and criminal records illustrate a comprehensive attempt to control, punish, and forcibly remake the bodies of the "masterless" lower sort. Whether they were slaves or servants, those who lived and worked on the streets of Philadelphia or those passing through the city in search of work and a home, vagrants were people whose bodily existence and appearance could visibly disrupt the smooth running of daily life in an organized and hierarchical society.

The crimes and offenses associated with vagrancy, together with imprisonment in Walnut Street Jail, allowed those with power and property to
assert control over the bodies of the lower sort (Figure 8).

For many who were incarcerated, vagrancy was a condition over which
they had little control. In an age of rising expectation, during which the
city and commerce grew rapidly, building and manufacturing expanded
as never before. This did not necessarily improve the lot of workers in the
city, however, for such factors as seasonal fluctuations and bad weather
could leave unskilled workers standing idle. Moreover, more and more
skilled workers no longer served craftsmen in a system designed to help
workers acquire and develop skills that would help them improve their
material conditions and social standing. A rapidly growing proportion of
bound labor was unskilled, and even much of this was irregular, casual
labor. Consequently a great many impoverished Philadelphians, including
many Irish and black men and women, found it extremely difficult to secure
enough well-paid work to meet their needs. Yet rarely did contemporaries

Figure 8. William Birch, Goal [sic] in Walnut Street, Philadelphia, 1799.
Courtesy of the Library Company of Philadelphia. This engraving shows the
moving of a small building that became the first African American church in
the city. In the background is the Walnut Street Jail, a building employed to
incarcerate the bodies of troublesome lower sort men and women, both black
and white. Only the worthy working poor appear in this illustration.

recognize the precariousness of their lives. Joseph Gale was one of very few to observe that "the most afflictive and accumulated distress" in Philadelphia existed among such Philadelphians as "the *Irish Emigrants* and the *French Negroes.*" He went on to declare that more thorough investigation of their condition and the "many acts of depredation, and many scenes of horror" for which they were held responsible, would be shown to be due "to the extreme poverty of this distressed class of people."[16]

Uncertain employment, poverty, and want were thus major factors in the lives of many of early national Philadelphia's lower sort. Middling and elite Philadelphians often interpreted these conditions not only as evidence of dubious nature and troublesome disposition but as criminal conditions, and many vagrants were incarcerated as criminals in the city's prison. The Walnut Street Jail lay close to the center of the city, a few dozen yards south of the Pennsylvania State House. The cold, gray walls of the prison contrasted sharply with the warm, red brick building that had housed the colonial government before becoming the new nation's first capitol. Just as different were the people within. The well-dressed and well-educated farmers, planters, lawyers, and merchants who lived and worked in and around the Pennsylvania State House appeared to hail from a different world from the people with ragged clothing, "pock marked" faces, "slender" bodies, "thin visage[s]," and scars who entered and exited the prison.[17] The buildings of the city's other main institution of incarceration, the almshouse or the bettering house, were even larger and certainly more striking than the State House, spread out as they were over half a city block in the open fields that lay a mere five blocks west and two blocks south of the Walnut Street Jail. As two of early national Philadelphia's most striking buildings, they represented the awesome power of the middling and upper sorts to control and correct the bodies of the troublesome poor.

Vagrancy was significantly different from crimes against persons and property. To civic authorities, the idle poor were illegitimate bodies, neither fully and gainfully employed nor subordinate to proper social control by their betters. By not working these folk were de facto criminals, a status that appeared to be confirmed by the petty crimes committed by many. The motives for such crimes were of little import to those who imprisoned them, yet the bodies of the unemployed and often homeless all told their own stories of life on the margins of the republic. Without doubt many broke the law because they had little choice, and their theft of food, clothing, or money helped keep them alive. Vagrancy records were defined by the attempts of the state to inscribe patterns of behavior on the imprisoned, and the tension between the lived body of the individual and the body controlled and inscribed by authority lay at the very heart of life both in the Philadelphia Alms House and the Walnut Street Jail.[18]

Those arrested and imprisoned as vagrants might include not only those without a residence or legitimate employment, but also runaway servants, slaves, apprentices, and sailors; disobedient or violent servants and apprentices; those found drunk and incapable on the streets or in public places; prostitutes; and men and women found to be behaving in a "disorderly" fashion. All such individuals could be classified as vagrants because they were "masterless": this vaguely defined, catch-all category allowed Philadelphia's civic authorities to clear the streets of offending and undesirable bodies. However, while the Vagrancy Dockets show those with power and influence exerting control over the jobless poor, they are also a record of lower sort dissent and opposition, chronicling resistance against masters and mistresses and the persistence of a popular culture of drinking and carousing that appeared all but impervious to official restraint.

Just as in the prison population as a whole, black Americans accounted for approximately one-quarter of the incarcerated vagrant bodies. However, while only 22 percent of the prisoners tried and convicted were women, 46 percent of vagrants were female, most likely because the kinds of offenses committed by impoverished women were more likely to appear in the vagrancy dockets than in the prison dockets, even though the result was often the same, namely incarceration in the Walnut Street Jail. The combined total of vagrants, vagabonds, and strollers comprised the single largest category of offenders in the Vagrancy Dockets, accounting for 201 of the 500 cases (40 percent). A total of 53 percent of white female and 11 percent of black female offenders were incarcerated as vagrants, as opposed to 51 percent of white men and 2 percent of black men.[19]

In many cases, the particular nature of vagrancy was implied rather than stated, as when the white woman Sarah Harrington was "Charged with being a Vagrant to be kept at hard labour for the space of thirty days." Identical language was used to describe the condition and consequent punishment of two black women, Violet Rogers and Rosey, while

TABLE 3. Race and Gender of Prisoners, Philadelphia, 1790, 1796–97

Race/gender	Prison Sentence Dockets		Vagrancy Dockets	
Black men	33	(13%)	86	(17%)
Black women	20	(8%)	36	(7%)
White men	110	(44%)	177	(35%)
White women	27	(11%)	196	(39%)
Indian men	1	(0%)	0	
Unknown male	50	(20%)	5	(1%)
Unknown female	9	(4%)	0	

Source: Prison Sentence Dockets, March 1795–December 1797; Vagrancy Dockets, 31 May 1790–9 November 1790, 1 June 1796–26 October 1796, Philadelphia City Archives.

the black man James Walker received the same one-month sentence after being charged "with being a disorderly Vagrant Person."[20] In other cases, more qualitative judgments found their way into the Vagrancy Dockets, as when Sarah Gault was charged "with being an Idle disorderly . . . woman" or Margaret Simons was accused of "being a Vagabond following Idle disorderly and dissolute Courses of Life."[21] It was with evident disgust that the record-keeper noted the incarceration of Eleanor Bryan and Jane Brady, two white women who in the late summer of 1796 were charged "with being notorious Vagrants found drunk & Idle in the New Market."[22] Perhaps most pointed of all were the accusations leveled against Philip Skamp and John Stuart, whose vagrancy charges were supplemented by the observations that Skamp "appears able to work, but through intemperance has no place of abode," while Stuart was "lurking about the City & refusing Employ when offered him."[23] Philadelphia's civic authorities condemned men and women who refused or by their own dissolute lifestyles were rendered unable to work as criminally immoral and offensive.

Vagrants represented a divisive and even dangerous threat to the order and hierarchy of early national society. At times the threat was rendered more obvious by the actions of the vagrants themselves. The white man Joseph Kelly was charged "with being found lurking about the Market and giving Contradictory accounts of himself"; unable to establish that Kelly had committed any crimes, the civic authorities condemned his masterless state and suspicious demeanor and incarcerated him as a vagrant.[24] Francis McMarron resorted to begging, and was imprisoned for "being a Vagrant Asking for Alms about the City & Abusing the Inhabitants."[25] James Ross, another "notorious Vagrant . . . and a common disturber of the peace," went further, "throwing stones in the Street." Like many of the homeless in modern American cities, those treated as vagrants in early national Philadelphia were poor, and quite possibly some of these were hindered by learning disabilities or mental illness and were at best barely able to fend for themselves. However, outside the Pennsylvania Hospital or the almshouse, only the prison was available to house them, and such people were quite likely to find themselves incarcerated in the Walnut Street Jail as vagrants.

In an attempt to rid the streets of the increasing numbers of evermore threatening vagrants, constables, night watchmen, and city officials, made occasional sweeps resulting in the incarceration of entire groups of these poorer Philadelphians. On October 11, 1790, for example, Mary Gorman, Lawrence Gorman, Patrick Dalton, and Cornelius Ridley were all dealt with in this manner, each labeled "a lazy idle Vagrant"; four days later William Tholley, John Reily, John Brown, and Thomas McKean were all incarcerated as vagrants; ten days later later a further nine men and two women were imprisoned, each as "A disorderly Vagrant person."[26] Such sweeps may have been occasioned by popular or political pressure, at times when the streets of the city appeared to be overwhelmed by the bodies of the impoverished masterless poor.

Some form of community and culture may well have been shared by many who found themselves among the ranks of vagrants, and "lurking about the Market" appears to have been common among vagrants, prostitutes, and others who ended up in the almshouse or prison.[27] Included among several of the rounded-up groups of vagrants were men and women whose shared last names suggested that they were married, such as Mary and Lawrence Gorman, Alexander and Lydia McKinsey, and Rosanna and Jacob Spry. Poverty and vagrancy in the early republic were not necessarily solitary or individual affairs, and on the streets, in the almshouse, and in the prison, community surely existed among men and women—whether family or friends—who ate, drank, and slept together and who knew the best places to beg food and shelter and the most likely ways to avoid the unwelcome attention of city authorities. Such communities of the vagrant lower sort horrified their betters, and incarceration in the Walnut Street Jail was intended to punish and eradicate such behavior.

Although homeless and unemployed vagrants comprised the single largest category of people in the Vagrancy Dockets, they were far from alone in seeking to elude civic officials. Runaways constituted the second largest and other major category. Under the general rubric of vagrants were 120 (24 percent) escaped slaves, indentured servants, apprentices, and seafarers. Once again, the tension between legal authority and individual autonomy is suggested by the many men, women, and youths who sought to steal their own bodies from bondage and bound labor in order to create some kind of new life for themselves in Philadelphia. Many of those who sought such freedom were black, and even more were male: the Walnut Street Jail housed approximately three black runaways for every white, and four male runaways for every female.

Slaves comprised at least one-quarter of all runaways and one-third or more of all black runaways. Only when city officials and record keepers were sure that a black man or woman was a slave did they record such status in the Vagrancy Dockets, as in the case of Toney or Tom, who has concealed "himself on Board the sloop Prince William . . . from St. Kitts."[28] Others, too, had sought to escape bondage in the Caribbean by hiding aboard ships bound for the United States. Perhaps when Anthony had run away from his master James Musfour on Bermuda, he had specifically sought out a ship bound for Philadelphia, given the port's reputation as the first American city to begin the process of ending slavery and the related development of an important free black community into which refugees and runaways might hope to blend. Unfortunately for Anthony, he was able to breathe the free air of Philadelphia for only a short time, and after nine days in jail he was delivered to Captain William Newbold for delivery back to Bermuda.[29]

Other black runaways were refugees from enslavement in the southern United States. The African-named Minga had run all the way from South Carolina, while Tom was secured in the jail to prevent his running away from his owner Bernard Marchison, whose schooner *Sunberry* had recently arrived in Philadelphia from Georgia.[30] Significantly, Tom had not actually attempted to escape enslavement, but was incarcerated in order to prevent such an attempt. While it is possible that the slave had revealed a desire to achieve freedom and mastery over his own body, it is equally possible that his master had realized the impossibility of keeping Tom away from freedom and its attractions and had feared that the temptation would be too much. In either case, the appeal of the city was obvious, and on occasion groups of Southern slaves banded together in an attempt to find their way to Philadelphia: Peter, Tilbry, and James, for example, confessed that they had run away to Philadelphia "from their Masters in Northampton County in Virginia."[31]

On many occasions, prison officials were unable to determine the status of masterless black bodies taken up on the city's streets. Bob was "taken up as a Vagrant and from circumstances he is strongly suspected of being a Runaway Slave," and so he and others like him were incarcerated for periods of a month or longer while newspaper advertisements attempted to locate masters who could prove their legal ownership of the unfortunate prisoners.[32] Even if no owner came forward, the freedom of black men and women was by no means certain, since they would be required to meet the costs of their incarceration; failure to meet these costs, the likely outcome for most impoverished blacks, meant that their labor would be sold to a new master for a period of several years, thus ensuring that they would not continue in a masterless state. Simply being black and masterless qualified men and women for prolonged incarceration.

The ending of slavery in Pennsylvania resulted less in a sudden and dramatic rise in the number of free blacks than in a gradual transformation

TABLE 4. Runaways Recorded in Vagrancy Dockets, 1790, 1796

Status	White male	White female	Total white	Black male	Black female	Total black	U/K male	Total male	Total female	Total
Servants/ apprentices	21	7	28	38	17	55	3	62	28	86
Slaves	0	0	0	30	2	32	0	30	2	32
Sailors	2	0	0	2	0	0	0	2	0	2

Source: Vagrancy Dockets, 31 May 1790–9 November 1790, 1 June 1796–26 October 1796, Philadelphia City Archives.

of lifelong slavery into a finite period of servitude. Thus many runaway blacks, most especially those from Pennsylvania, were former slaves who were identified as servants. Nelly was recorded as the runaway "Indented Servant" of James Brown, while Phyllis had absconded from the service of Hugh Moore in Philadelphia: it was not sufficient to record that she had stolen her own body, for she had also taken the clothes that she wore, and this theft was recorded in the Vagrancy Dockets.[33] Another runaway Pennsylvanian was Cuff, who had chosen freedom over service to Samuel Jenkins. Cuff was a West African name, and this man's desperate search for a more complete freedom than servitude allowed had led him to prefer this name to that of Jethro, a name given to him by others and cited in the record of his imprisonment.[34]

Included among the ranks of runaway whites were apprentices and even sailors. Most apprentices had been bound out to learn a trade while still very young, and often they had enjoyed little if any choice in the matter of their future work. While some were bound out by parents anxious to ensure that their sons would master a craft and therefore be able to provide for themselves and their families, others were orphans or the children of indigent or ill parents in the almshouse, hospital, or even prison, and in such cases neither parent nor child enjoyed any control over the apprenticeship. It is scarcely surprising, then, that some apprentices preferred running away to laboring under a demanding or undesired master. Jacob Drummer, for example, absconded from his master, Philadelphian Richard Allen, and was kept in prison for a week at hard labor with only bread and water as his punishment. Other apprentices ranged from further afield, sharing with runaway slaves the hope that Philadelphia's bustling community would provide sanctuary. Peter Smilie had absconded from an apprenticeship in New York City, accompanied by another runaway. Unfortunately for him, his masterless status attracted attention, and he was imprisoned for just over three weeks, after which his master arrived in Philadelphia to claim him.[35]

Seafarers, too, sometimes had contractual obligations to the captains of the vessels in which they sailed, although with the exception of occasional slaves, these were contracts made by free adult men, rather than by those with the power to buy and sell their bodies and labor. The freedom of such men may have been somewhat illusory, of course, since seafarers were the poorest workers in early national Philadelphia, and their poverty and lack of opportunity may have forced them into unwelcome voyages. On occasion, sailors might even find themselves in debt from prior voyages, having been advanced salary, clothing, and supplies. Similarly, their debts to an innkeeper at whose institution they lived while in port may have effectively been "sold" to a captain in need of hands. In such cases, seafarers may have felt as trapped by their contracts as other bound workers. Such may well have been the case with Peter Dickson, who had been paid an advance by the master of the sloop *Nancy*; his attempt to leave without fulfilling the terms of his contract led to his imprisonment " 'till the sd. Vessel be ready to proceed to Sea," at which point he would be returned "in order that he may perform the Voyage agreeable to Contract by him made." William Carey was charged "with running away from the brig *Louisa*," whose master, Samuel Moore, left the seafarer in jail on bread and water rations before retrieving him for the voyage. Thus could the jail be employed by middling and upper sort Philadelphians to chastise and control the bodies of disobedient and troublesome servants and employees.[36]

The large majority of runaway whites were, however, indentured servants. While the ethnicity of these people was seldom recorded in the Vagrancy Dockets, it is likely that many had come from Ireland and Great Britain and some from continental Europe. Michael Van Keek and Maria Van Keek, who absconded from the service of the stone cutter James Fraquain, were probably a Dutch couple who had secured a new life in the United States by selling their labor for passage. Others were impoverished Americans, a group that included the children of men and women who were lodged in the almshouse, for such children might well be taken from their parents and bound out as servants by the almshouse authorities.[37]

The motives that inspired indentured servants to run away varied. Some may have found a half-decade of service to another person frustrating or even unbearable; others may have fled from a harsh and unsympathetic master or mistress. Still others, no doubt, simply sought to escape a burden they did not enjoy. Mary Smilie, the indented servant of Lewis Bergery, ran away from her master and was "found in an infamous disorderly House." Jane McElroy, quite possibly an Irish immigrant, was imprisoned after "absconding from the service of her master Charles Pryor & associating with idle disorderly people." The disapproving tone of these sparse records imply that Smilie and McElroy were lazy, good-for-nothing servants. It is also possible, however, that such men as Bergery and Pryor were demanding masters who allowed their servants little time for themselves. Young men and women, in the prime of their lives, often rejected such restrictions, especially if like McElroy they were Irish and subject to an ethnocentrism second only to the racism experienced by black Americans. In such circumstances the records of the incarceration of Smilie and McElroy may actually say much about a desperate search for companions and community and an unwillingness to return to service.[38] Other records give no evidence of the motives of runaways, but whatever the causes, the disobedience of would-be masterless men and women threatened all masters. When David Humpskill ran away from his master Alexander Dallas, or when Lewis Simon absconded from the service of Doctor Caspar Wistar, they illustrated that even the most respected men in Philadelphia faced servants who could not or would not serve them.[39]

The remaining cases in the Vagrancy Dockets include drunks, those accused of disorderly behavior and of running disorderly houses, and prostitutes, which together comprise 24.6 percent of the record. Mary Evans was "found in the Market intoxicated, with strong Liquor," for which offense she was imprisoned for thirty-six hours. Edward Serjeant, too, was "found drunk & Lying in an indecent manner in the market." Unwilling or perhaps unable to give any "account of himself or his abode," Serjeant was treated as a vagrant and imprisoned at hard labor for thirty days.[40] Evans and Serjeant provide further evidence that the market was a place of rendezvous for the lower sorts, a place where they assembled to drink and carouse, to beg work, food, and alms, and even to steal food.

Members of the lower sort might be confined for a variety of reasons. Joseph Kennedy combined drunkenness with disorderly behavior when he was "taken up Yesterday in the Street Drunk, striped to fight & behaving outragiously." Two white women, Mary Ray and Elizabeth Griffiths, were imprisoned at hard labor for thirty days after "being excessively abusive, disorderly Women, whose behaviour in the Market in high Street was disgraceful to the City."[41] Any form of lower sort public behavior that did not meet the standards of propriety demanded by civic officials might be defined by the latter as vagrancy and result in the imprisonment of the offenders, as Jane Peck found when she served a month for "being a Drinking disorderly Woman and a common disturber to the Neighbur hood." Catherine Courtney was guilty of little more than "being in bad company," while Ann McDonald was charged "with profane Swearing." Beyond the pale was Dubain, a black American charged "by Divers Witnesses with having frequently voided his Urine in the Public Pumps in Race Street."[42] Sarah Thompson and Martha Patterson were typical of the prostitutes who were treated and punished as vagrants: the former was charged "with being an Idle dissolute & Notorious Prostitute," the latter "with being an Idle dissolute Person and common Street Walker."[43] In these cases, prostitution appeared as simply one element of the dissolute and masterless state of vagrancy. Thompson was one of six prostitutes imprisoned on the same day, suggesting that, like other vagrants, prostitutes were cleared off the streets by occasional sweeps conducted by city officials.

The imprisonment of large numbers of vagrants was in part the result of a late eighteenth-century debate about the nature and purpose of the jail in a republican society, a debate that resulted in a series of significant reforms. For centuries prisons had functioned as little more than holding cells, housing those awaiting trial, convicted felons awaiting physical punishment, and persons unable to discharge contracted debts. In short, prisons were not in themselves places or indeed instruments of punishment, but were rather the places where those accused of crimes might be housed before trial or punishment. Throughout the colonial and revolutionary periods, the prison confined the bodies of vagrants and other criminals who had been seized by the state, before they were publicly marked or even destroyed in punitive ways that ranged from incarceration in the almshouse to whipping to branding to execution. Thus had the rule of law been inscribed upon the bodies of the poor who disobeyed.[44]

As the new federal government assumed shape, republican incarceration and punishment underwent a revolutionary transformation in Philadelphia's jail. Rather than seizing and breaking the bodies of convicts, the prison assumed long-term control of convicts in general and vagrants in particular in order to set about refashioning them. The *Rules, Orders, and Regulations for the Goal [sic] of the City and County of Philadelphia* laid out precisely how criminal bodies would be "washed and cleansed" on first admittance, and then "cloathed according to Law." Male and female convicts were kept separate, as were different types of vagrants such as runaway slaves and servants, disorderly apprentices and servants, and the often homeless and jobless strollers and ramblers. Virtually all aspects of the bodily lives of the prisoners were controlled by prison authorities, who banned alcohol, forbade conversation, and strictly regulated diet and sleeping arrangements. Most important of all, vagrants and indeed all prisoners were made to work, and they spent their days picking wool, oakum, and hair, spinning, sewing, washing, shoemaking, weaving, clothes-making, sawing wood and stone, or making nails. In attempting to reform criminals, lawmakers and prison authorities hoped to produce prisoners who would "distinguish themselves by their attention to cleanliness, sobriety, industry and orderly conduct."[45]

Thus the *Rules, Orders, and Regulations* of the prison sought to transform the very bodies and souls of such criminals by means of a uniform regimen of labor, built upon the reformative foundations of solitude, silence, cleanliness, and a "simple diet."[46] Upon arrival in the jail convicts could expect to be

placed among the rest; their clothes are taken away, and if necessary exposed to heat in an oven, and the common dress of the prison put upon them. They are made acquainted with the regulations of the house, and interrogated with respect to the labour they are willing to perform . . . The work assigned them is adapted to their strength and capacity. There are in the house looms for weavers, workshops and tools for joiners, carpenters, turners, shoe-makers, and taylors; the convicts who possess such trades, are allowed to practice them; the remainder are employed in sawing and polishing marble, in cutting logwood, in pounding and grinding plaister of Paris, in carding wool, or in beating hemp. The weaker and less skillful are busied in picking wool, hair, or oakum. The inspectors have lately added to these establishments a manufacture of nails, capable of affording employment to a great number of prisoners, and bringing considerable profit to the house. Every one is paid in proportion to his labour.[47]

Women, too, were put to work, "spinning, sewing, preparing flax and hemp, and in washing and mending for the house."[48] However, men and women now labored, ate, and slept separately. Accommodation was communal and basic:

> The rooms in which the prisoners sleep, are on the second story. They contain each about ten or twelve bedsteads, on which are mattresses stuffed with cedar shavings, sheets, and coverlids, or rugs. Each person has a separate bed. The room is well aired, and well lighted, though in such a manner as to prevent every communication with the street.[49]

The disciplining of imprisoned bodies began—and continued—with ritualized cleansing and the imposition of standardized clothing. Communication with the outside world, and indeed with other prisoners, was all but eliminated, and while "at their work, the prisoners are permitted no singing or laughing, nor indeed any conversation, except such as may immediately relate to their business. This prohibition of all unnecessary converse is relied upon, as an essential point for the complete administration of the prison."[50] With a strictly regulated work day that stretched from dawn to dusk, prison life had changed enormously. If successful, the Walnut Street Jail would imbue prisoners with the ideals of "cleanliness, sobriety, industry and orderly conduct," thereby preparing them for useful lives within early republican society.[51]

In colonial America, the body of the convict had publicly displayed the cost of breaking the law, which ranged from scars inflicted by the lash, to mutilated ears and noses, to branded cheeks and hands, to the destruction of convicted bodies on the gallows. With the reforms of the late eighteenth century such public displays all but disappeared. Now the criminal body was hidden from public view by high walls and locked doors, behind which the convict would labor in silence, dressed in common with other prisoners. Thus, it was supposed, would discipline be imposed on the bodies of those who had broken the law, with thoroughgoing regulation of the time of prisoners and the strict governance of all aspects of their lives.[52] The informal jail of the colonial era gave way to a highly ritualized regimen within a prison regulated by strict written rules and regulations. No longer were the bodies of prisoners restrained by pain and by shame; rather, prisoners were refashioned as productive republican citizens through the well-regulated reformation of their bodies, from the clothes they wore to the food they ate to the work at which they labored.[53]

With the transformation of prisons into institutions of reformation, life within the Walnut Street Jail changed enormously. The prison was now to become a refuge, of sorts, filled with "that perfect quietude, in which it is intended the prisoner should be kept, and converted, as it were, into a new being."[54] Spurred on by a republican impulse to refashion a better society, which was in turn premised on a belief in the natural virtue latent in every human breast, reformers hoped that the reformed prison would provide citizens with a general and very visible example of the cost of law-breaking, while at the same time would train convicts in the virtues of labor and discipline. Visitors to the prison were not slow to realize that reformation of prisoners' bodies was linked to the health of the body politic. Robert Turnbull, for example, thought of crimes in terms of bodily ailments, describing them as "disorders of a state." Following the analogy to its logical conclusion, Turnbull suggested that treatment and cure should be applied to such social ills, and that only as a last resort should amputation "of the infected limb" occur.[55]

How prisoners experienced the new regime and its lofty objectives was, of course, another matter entirely. Cheap, standardized clothing was not only uncomfortable but also a denial of individuality that was contested by some prisoners. I "took the detested garments," recalled one, "which I modelled to suit my taste."[56] Food was at best bland and usually insufficient to the dietary requirements of adults, and many rooms were too cold in winter and overrun by vermin in summer. Although prisoners were usually able to undermine the ban on unnecessary conversation, the prohibition of alcohol and the "liveliness and animation which such liquors might induce" was far harder to overcome. In a culture in which the consumption of significant amounts of alcohol was not only common but socially acceptable, its complete withdrawal may have had traumatic physical and psychological effects on those whose bodies had become dependent on rum and similar beverages.

In a very real way, the prison records illustrate civic authorities' attempts to remake the bodies of vagrants and the "masterless" poor, and in their pages the bodies of those incarcerated appear as the focal points of both punitive and reformist impulses. In this process, and thus in these records, the bodies of those imprisoned were mere objects, and much of the actual experiences, lives, and condition of the people who inhabited these bodies remain hidden.[57] There are hints of larger life stories, and sometimes of resistance, however, in the spare and often impersonal records, from which can be gleaned some sense of the lives and characters of the Philadelphians who found themselves incarcerated in Walnut Street Jail.

If the prison served as a place to imprison and reform the bodies of vagrants who broke the law and threatened republican order, the incarceration records also tell stories of the culture and community of the lower sorts who found themselves on the wrong side of law and order. Although objectified as criminal bodies by the authorities who imprisoned them, vigorous assertions of individuality and agency appear in the records of imprisoned vagrants. The prison regime required deferential submission to authority and the acceptance of a new code of individual and communal behavior, but the records occasionally hint at a variety of forms of resistance to this regime and its objectives. Peter Grant, an African born on the Guinea coast and imprisoned for theft, was recorded as speaking "very Bad English" and having "long hair combed up very high before," an unusual style that may well have represented a vivid assertion of the styles of his homeland.[58] Henry Holmes, a black American from Staten Island who had stolen food and clothing, wore "his hair cued behind & some small plats about his head [and] ears," a style that is not uncommon among contemporary African Americans.[59] Along similar lines, when Jack Smith and Jethro each insisted on being called Cuff, and when other blacks faced imprisonment with names such as Minga and Phebe, they did so with African names.[60] While it is impossible to know exactly what such names meant to their bearers, they were not the names of those who sought to abandon their past and its sense of family and heritage; these are all instances of prisoners retaining and even celebrating a culture separate from the world view and values championed by prison authorities.

Those American, African American, and European servants who disobeyed, resisted, or even assaulted their masters risked incarceration as vagrants. For some, like Flora, such resistance meant "being stubborn & disobedient," while for others like the white man William Moody, it involved "attempting to strike his . . . master."[61] Disobedience had always been a form of behavior available to servants and slaves, but what had changed in the 1790s was context. Both for masters and for those bound to serve them, the American Revolution and the social and political chaos of the late eighteenth century all meant that resistance was more loaded than ever before: freedom and popular rights seemed more attainable to those in service, while law, order, and property—the basic props of civilized society—appeared to more affluent Americans to be in mortal danger.

For some of those whose bodies were bound in service to others, resistance proved more practical than running away. Disobedient and misbehaving servants and apprentices account for almost 10 percent of the cases recorded in the Vagrancy Dockets, illustrating the ways the prison was used as a disciplinary tool by those with the power and money to own the bodies and labor of others. Walter Rosalio was charged "with

Misbehaving himself toward his Master John James," and as a result was imprisoned on a bread and water diet. Similarly the "mulatto" Elizabeth Johnson was accused of "very bad behaviour to her Master Hugh McCollough," while John Hazle was charged "by his Master Doctor Jas. Biglow with being an incorrigible wicked Boy."[62] In such cases the misbehavior is not specified, but is condemned in language that makes clear the moral imperatives of a hierarchical society: children, slaves, and servants were to obey parents and masters, and those who did not were—almost without exception—regarded as behaving in an immoral and illegal fashion. Motives for such misbehavior seldom appear in the Vagrancy Dockets, meaning that we are reading the interpretations of slighted masters and prison authorities. But while the words and the motives of the rebellious servants elude us, their bodily defiance speaks loudly through the records.

In some cases the actions of misbehaving servants are cited, as with William Kennedy, whose Master George Weed charged Kennedy with "greatly misbehaving himself & getting drunk, & also with committing several dishonest Acts to the injury of his Sd. master."[63] But even here the motives of the servant are far from clear. On other occasions, servants employed physical violence against the property or persons of their masters. What is perhaps most interesting about these cases is that they appear to have involved the exercise of power by those with the least power of all, for in many cases it was bound women and black Americans who reacted with the most force and even violence against their masters and mistresses.

Moreover, these were generally not covert acts of resistance but open acts of defiance: these male and female servants were telling their masters and mistresses that they found labor and their position, on present terms, unacceptable. In some cases, the record of resistance is rather vague, as in the case of the black American Peter. "Charged with being guilty of disorderly and turbulent conduct towards his Mistress," he was imprisoned at hard labor for thirty days in an attempt to cow him into better behavior. Phebe Bowers, a young "Mullato," was accused of "threating the Life of her Mistress Rebecca Greenay," while the "negress" Eve was actually accused of "Assault & battery on the body of her Master John Walker." John Kirkpatrick, an Irish servant, was imprisoned by his master John Wharton, who charged him with "insolent behaviour & also calling his mistress a dam'd Bitch." In the case of Claude, a black American, one can sense the frustration of a master who charged him "with being guilty of such attrocious & passionate behaviour that he cannot with safety keep him longer in his House."[64]

Perhaps it is in this last record that some clues about possible motivations for such misbehavior can be found. Running away represented a radical form of resistance, but it was both difficult and dangerous, especially for black Americans and for women of either race. Moreover, it could mean abandoning not only one's master but also friends and perhaps family. Other forms of resistance, however, enabled those in servitude to attempt to renegotiate the terms of their labor. Those consigned by their masters to the Walnut Street Jail often were accused of the most extreme acts of resistance, men and women who in their anger, their frustration, or even their desperation had resorted to bodily violence or the threat of such violence. Many other smaller acts of resistance must have taken place that did not find their way into such records, and indeed such contemporary sources as the diary of Elizabeth Drinker, filled as it is with everyday details of life within the Drinker household, contains many of her complaints about the behavior of recalcitrant servants. The law mandated that masters owned the labor—and thus, to all intents and purposes, the bodies—of male and female servants, and they did not hesitate to employ the prison to discipline those who employed their bodies to resist the lawful authority of their masters. That the prison should be used to correct the misbehavior of servants and dependents says much about its value to society as an institution for the correction of illegal lower sort bodies. At the same time, however, the continued existence of vagrancy and disobedience among the lower sort illustrate a willingness to contest such correction. The Vagrancy Dockets show that the bodies of servants, slaves, and apprentices were contested and that masters could not expect to easily enjoy full and complete control of their human property.

The vagrants who spent time in the Walnut Street Jail were often members of communities of the poor, communities that existed both inside and outside the prison (Figure 9). Under the new prison regime, alcohol was often hard to come by, but the white clay pipes unearthed by archaeologists show that prisoners were able to smoke together, while rough dice fashioned from beef shank bone illustrate that prisoners were able to socialize together—in defiance of prison rules—much as they had outside of the jail.[65] Much to the horror of Ann Carson, such gatherings in the jail were often comprised of congenial groups of black and white prisoners, who "promiscuously, without distinctions of age or colour . . . pursue their daily avocations; and also, at one table, take their scanty meals."[66] When visiting the prison Robert Turnbull observed the same lack of racial distinctions, recording the relative absence of "shameful, degrading distinctions."[67] Racism existed, of course, inside and outside the jail, but at the same time communities existed that transcended color lines. Poverty and crime brought men and women of different races and backgrounds together. Thus the black woman Phebe Mines and the white woman Catherine Lynch were together accused of "committing divers Larcenys." While Lynch escaped imprisonment, Mines, the apparent ringleader, was sentenced to serve two years in jail. A little over two months later, however, Mines had teamed up with two white women, Margaret Field and Joan Holland, with whom she escaped "by getting into the Dungeon through the Arch and over the Wall into Sixth Street."[68]

Such communities and friendships were surely forged in places like the notorious Philadelphia market place, and in the disorderly houses that the city authorities tried so hard to close down. At the center of such institutions were Philadelphians like Margaret Jeffreys, who was imprisoned as a vagrant in November of 1790 for "being a common disturber of the peace and harbouring Vagrants."[69] In homes such as Jeffreys' the poor could meet and even sleep, purchase the cheapest of food and drink, and perhaps exchange information and even stolen goods. Vagrants, criminals, servants, and runaways imprisoned in the Walnut Street Jail were not a group apart from Philadelphia society at large. Rather, the large majority were drawn from the ranks of Philadelphia's

Figure 9. William Birch, Goal [sic] in Walnut Street, Philadelphia, 1799. Based on the original at the Library Company of Philadelphia, with additions by Anthony King. The Walnut Street Jail lay close to the center of the city, facing the Pennsylvania State House (Independence Hall) to the north and a large paupers' cemetery filled with the bodies of revolutionary war soldiers and yellow fever victims to the west. People milled around the building constantly, including those on their way in and out, those who visited the prisoners, and those who worked in the jail or who furnished supplies.

lower sort, little different from many outside the walls of the prison, but seen by affluent Philadelphians and civic authorities as examples of a dangerous deterioration in the social order. The Walnut Street Jail provided one of the most tangible reminders of the ever-widening gulf between rich and poor in early national Philadelphia, serving as it did to remove, seal off, and control the illegitimate and immoral bodies of any of the poor and lower sort who were not properly controlled. The lower sort were not, however, so easily controlled.

Chapter 3

Hospitalized Bodies

More than anything else, the records of the Pennsylvania Hospital for the Sick Poor reveal a great deal about the illnesses and injuries most commonly suffered by all of Philadelphia's lower sort. But while the hospital promised expert medical care, it was as much an institution of social control as were the prison and almshouse, and its services were available only to those who fashioned and managed their bodies appropriately as the deserving and deferential poor. Although some feared the hospital as a place where the sick and injured might easily die, it was certainly preferable to the rudimentary health care available in the almshouse, but no more than a fortunate few of the sick poor were able to have their bodies treated and cared for in the Pennsylvania Hospital.

While the institution's records reveal a great deal about the illnesses and injuries afflicting all lower sort Philadelphians, they also speak volumes about the power of hospital authorities to judge impoverished bodies and furnish life-saving treatment based on these assessments. The annual accounts, published each year as a broadside by the Managers of the Pennsylvania Hospital, along with the manuscript Book of Patients and Admission and Discharge records reveal the kinds of treatable illnesses and injuries endured by the city's lower sort, while various notes and manuscript records kept by attending physicians provide a more rounded picture of individual cases. Together these records reveal the range and nature of treatable medical conditions afflicting the bodies of Philadelphia's working poor, the ways they were treated both in and outside the Pennsylvania Hospital, and the judgment and control of certain folk embodied in their hospitalization and treatment (Figure 10).[1]

No more than a small minority of lower sort Philadelphians were admitted to the Pennsylvania Hospital, because in most cases medical care for the sick and injured remained a domestic concern, handled by friends and family within the home. Only the wealthy could see or call for doctors on a regular basis, and thus the poor were generally unfamiliar with professional medicine. The differences between medical treatment at home and in the hospital were, when compared to the differences in modern America, relatively small. Drawing on centuries of accumulated folk wisdom and practice, it was ordinary folk who treated the large majority of injuries and ailments. All communities and many households contained people who knew something of the medical properties of various herbs and plants and others who knew how to drain blood, and together these men and women would have practiced a rudimentary yet often effective form of medicine that was as familiar as the

Figure 10. William Birch, Pennsylvania Hospital in Pine Street, Philadelphia, 1799. Based on the original at the Library Company of Philadelphia, with additions by Anthony King. The majority of the sick and injured poor were treated at home by friends and relatives. Many more were placed in the sick wards of the almshouse, where they were clothed and fed but not treated. Only a few, deemed as members of the "deserving poor" by their betters, were admitted to the Pennsylvania Hospital, which was intended for lawabiding, hardworking, and deferential poor people whose illnesses and injuries could be treated, allowing them to return to a useful and productive role in society. They came and went on a daily basis, with many more visiting for what was effectively outpatient care, while visiting family and friends brought in provisions. The injuries and illnesses that brought them to the hospital were common among the lower sort. Many were treated and cured, but in an age when infection was little understood the hospital could be a dangerous and often deadly place, and some left the institution in old and rough sheets on their way to the paupers' graveyard. Yet the medical attention afforded to hospital patients was far superior to the rudimentary care given the sick and injured residents of the almshouse.

conditions it treated. Only in rare cases, if the sufferer's condition failed to improve, would family and friends consider employing the services of a doctor, if one were available.

When their bodies were laid low by disease or by injury, or rendered worthless by old age, debility, or insanity, and when family or friends were unavailable or unable to furnish care within the home, the lower sorts who lived in larger towns and cities were far more likely to be consigned to the medical wards of the almshouse than to a hospital. Within the almshouse the sick and infirm were sorted and housed according to medical conditions, with large rooms set aside for the insane, those suffering from venereal diseases and from alcoholism, women advanced in pregnancy, and those who were too old and feeble or too badly injured to work. However, while the almshouse provided accommodation, it gave relatively little in the way of actual medical care and treatment; the sick and injured poor were inadequately nursed, and rarely were they cured. For them, the almshouse could be a terrible place, as much a prison as anything else, and continued ill health, poverty, and misery shaped the lives of many—if not most—of the unwell people incarcerated within its walls.[2]

Only the largest cities had dedicated hospitals for the treatment of the sick and injured poor. Philadelphia led the way with the Pennsylvania Hospital for the Sick Poor, founded in 1752, while New York City's hospital only began admitting patients in the 1790s, and Boston's Massachusetts General did not open its doors until 1821.[3]

The Pennsylvania Hospital was a "fine, elegant, and well kept building" in the southwestern corner of the city, no more than a few hundred yards from open fields, the Pennsylvania State House, and the densely populated environs of Southwark.[4] Yet whether or not they were admitted and treated, for Philadelphia's lower sort the Pennsylvania Hospital was as much an instrument of class and social order as it was a refuge for the ill and injured. Although the hospital marked an improvement over the almshouse in that it was intended to cure and mend rather than simply house the sick and injured, such care was available to precious few of Philadelphia's poor. No more than a small proportion could hope to receive the necessary written testimonial from one of the institution's financial contributors or one of the hospital managers, who were entitled to recommend servants and impoverished neighbors for admission. Thus it was only those regarded by their betters as the deserving poor who were intended to receive preferential treatment in the hospital, and the large majority of lower sort Philadelphians knew that ill health or serious accident was more likely to land them in the almshouse. In most cases, it was not doctors who made decisions regarding admission on the basis of medical condition, but rather laymen whose decisions about ill and injured bodies were moral and financial rather than medical. It was only by positioning oneself within a deferential network of social relations, by belonging to the correct church, serving a particular family, or working long and hard to maintain oneself and one's family, that an impoverished Philadelphian had any hope of securing admission to the Pennsylvania Hospital.[5] Little of this world appears in the records, for the tenor of exchanges between those admitted to the hospital and the people who recommended or treated them is all but lost to us.[6]

Access to the hospital was not only restricted by the worthiness of the impoverished person seeking admission, for the hospital had a relatively small number of beds, nowhere near enough to deal with all the city's sick and injured poor. By the early nineteenth century over 40,000 people lived in Philadelphia, with more still in the Northern Liberties and Southwark, yet while the almshouse contained an average of some two hundred sick beds, the hospital has less than one-third this number. Moreover, financial pressures forced the directors of the hospital to limit the number of "free" beds made available to nonpaying poor people, and by 1796 this number was set at thirty. A large portion of the hospital was set aside for the care of mentally ill patients. While a dwindling proportion of these were members of the "deserving poor," more and more came from wealthier families who were not able or chose not to care for them in their own homes and were willing and able to pay for the relative comfort of private rooms and medical care in the hospital.

There were other restrictions on access to the hospital. The directors and medical staff of the hospital sought to exclude those suffering from infectious diseases, as well as many others who could not easily and quickly be healed or cured (with the exception of mentally ill patients). Diseases could quickly spread and wreak havoc on weakened hospital patients, and so they appear far less frequently in hospital records than they did within the population as a whole. One unfortunate white man was admitted in September 1791 with a wounded hand, but before this was healed he displayed symptoms of a deadly infectious disease and was promptly "sent out with the Smallpox."[7] Those suffering from such diseases as smallpox or yellow fever were unlikely to gain admission, for the hospital was intended for hard-working and socially useful members of the deserving poor who had been laid low by an illness or injury that could quickly and easily be treated.[8] Once cured, the person would then return to productive life and work in the city with deferential gratitude for the charitable care he or she had enjoyed. Just as the almshouse was intended to refashion the bodies of the undeserving poor into hard-working and respectable members of the community, the hospital was designed to reward the deserving poor by restoring their bodies to health.

Admission to the hospital was thus based on a combination of moral worth, as judged by their betters, and a treatable condition, as judged by the professional doctors, who seldom initiated but rather endorsed the recommendation of admission.[9] Some of the referral forms still exist, and the objectification of the bodies of even the deserving poor is made clear in the words and writing of their betters. Thus one "free Negroe" suffering from remitting fever was recorded as "a proper Object for the Pennsylvania Hospital."[10]

The creation and growth of the Pennsylvania Hospital did not, then, change medical care for the large majority of indigent Philadelphians. The care of the sick and injured remained a largely domestic affair. Although in certain instances doctors could provide expertise and medical or surgical procedures unavailable outside the hospital, the majority of injuries and illnesses were treated at home in much the same way as they were treated by medical professionals within the hospital. Moreover, such treatment was furnished by family members and friends, and as such was almost always seen as preferable to the impersonal care provided by hospital employees such as Elizabeth Trudy, a housemaid turned nurse, or Elizabeth Brown, who was promoted from cowherd to nurse, or even Ann Gillispey, who went from cooking to nursing and then back to cooking.[11] The Pennsylvania Hospital was chronically underfunded during the early national era, and conditions—while preferable to the almshouse—were often far from desirable. One hospital resident, for example, complained of the "House Ratz" that ran over his face every night, while the Reverend Ezra Stiles Ely's diary entries of his visits to New York City's hospital are colored by his deep-seated fear and loathing of the conditions he found and even of some of the people within.[12]

Nonetheless, the hospital was able to provide a higher quality of food and shelter than the almshouse, together with far superior medical care and attention, and without the necessity of laboring for one's keep. Indeed, the hospital purchased a wide variety of foods for those in its care, who might expect a basic diet of grain and rice, supplemented when possible by meat, poultry, fresh fish, and shellfish, root and green vegetables, fruit, dairy products, and such extras as sugar and molasses. Moreover, since alcohol was regarded as having valuable medicinal properties, the hospital sick might enjoy hard cider, beer, wine, or rum as part of their daily regimen.[13] For some, then, the hospital was a relatively attractive prospect, and hospital managers sought to avoid rewarding the undeserving poor with free food, lodging, and care, which was meant to mend their bodies and thus prevent them from becoming dependent on their betters. The managers were glad to encourage the development of a dispensary that provided out-patient services for far more indigent

Philadelphians than were admitted into and treated within the hospital itself.[14] Between 1786 and 1791, the first five years of the dispensary's operation, it provided advice and medication to nearly 8,000 Philadelphians, during which time the hospital admitted and treated fewer than 2,000 people.[15] The hospital was thus a last—though often best—resort, which is perhaps best illustrated by the fact that those admitted were required to provide or have others provide a security of approximately five dollars, which sum was intended to cover burial costs should the unfortunate person die.[16]

While drawing on traditional folk medicine in many of its procedures and treatments, the Pennsylvania Hospital was nonetheless emerging as the new republic's most advanced center of medical practice. Doctors like Benjamin Rush had been trained at Edinburgh University, and hospital physicians administered drugs and treatment and undertook surgical procedures in accordance with both traditional and newly developing medical theories and practice. The hospital was becoming a leading center for the education of American physicians, and medical students supplemented medical care and helped finance the institution through their payments "for the privilege of attending the practice of the Hospital, and for the use of the books in the medical library."[17] Yet many of the ideas that governed the treatment of a wide variety of ailments, illnesses, and injuries had changed little for centuries, although during the early national era these were being transformed by "the therapeutic revolution."[18]

Both doctors and lay people had little beyond their physical senses with which to diagnose a patient's condition, and thus they tended to focus on what went into and out of the body. In often vague and sketchy records of the condition and treatment of their patients, the hospital's doctors made clear that they continued to regard ill health as a result of pathological imbalances in the four liquid "humors" of the body—blood, phlegm, yellow bile, and black bile—or in the internal organs themselves. Doctors interpreted the symptoms of patients as evidence of such imbalances, and then prescribed drugs and treatments such as bleedings, laxatives, emetics, enemas, and even the use of heated instruments to create blisters in order to counteract them. Thus, in both medical texts and practice, drugs were categorized by their effects, and diuretics, cathartics, narcotics, emetics, and diaphoretics were intended to flush poisoned or excessive quantities of humors from the body.[19]

For many centuries, the people of Europe and colonial America had shared these kinds of beliefs, and the therapeutic medicine practiced in the Pennsylvania Hospital was as much premised on familiar foundations as it was a new departure. Disease, illness and injury were as much cultural as they were physical states and experiences, for they were known and interpreted according to a variety of accepted theories and practices.[20] Accordingly, the bodies of sick and injured lower sort Philadelphians were objectified in that they were effectively reduced to an interrelated series of symptoms and conditions, and, once categorized, an appropriate therapeutic treatment began.[21] Secure in their belief that all parts of the body were related to one another, early national doctors accepted that an imbalance in one part might well have been caused by problems within another. In order to restore good health, the doctors sought to equalize the humors and restore bodily equilibrium. So deep and pervasive was this sense of how body and medicine worked that, even when treating physical injuries or common diseases whose course and effect were sadly familiar, doctors tended to employ therapeutic regimens, carefully regulating what went into and came out of the body in order to achieve balance and a return to good health.

Thus, when a young man attempting suicide had plunged a chisel between his ribs, the sutures and dressings of his wound were complemented by regular bleedings, all intended to help restore mind and body.[22] Similarly, a man who had been paralyzed by a fall of some 40 feet, and whose pulse was "scarcely perceptible," was "ordered to be bled."[23] In another case, the skull of an unfortunate young man traveling from Delaware to Philadelphia had been fractured by a falling mast. In order to help his body heal, the attending physician not only had a "soft bread & milk poultice" applied to the wound but also prescribed regular bleedings and the "lowest diet," bland and simple fare that would excite neither mind nor body.[24] For an African American man who had fallen from a ladder and fractured his ribs and injured his head, there was more of the same, including five bleedings, saline laxatives, and occasional enemas.[25]

Therapeutic medicine emphasized the ways a body was constituted of interdependent elements, all kept in a delicate balance. One result of therapeutic theory and practice was that the maintenance of one's body assumed considerable significance, and those who were believed to have abused or improperly cared for their bodies were, to varying degrees, held responsible for the ailments they suffered. Such intemperate folk were thus more likely to be incarcerated in the almshouse than treated in the hospital. A variety of ailments and even injuries and epidemic diseases were regarded as resulting from an unbalanced state within the individual. When administrators and doctors decided which members of the sick and injured poor merited admission into the hospital, social attitudes and medical belief and practice merged in a comprehensive approach to ill health. Ideally, those members of the undeserving poor whose condition was their own fault would end up in the almshouse, while those whose lives and work had rendered them more worthy of help might find themselves in the hospital, where their bodies would be nursed back to health.[26]

While far fewer sick and injured Philadelphians found their way into the Pennsylvania Hospital than into the almshouse, hospital patients suffered from a representative array of injuries and illnesses, thus allowing us to see the ways in which illness and injury were inscribed upon the bodies of Philadelphia's working poor. The accounts published annually by the managers of the hospital included a table labeled "Abstract of Cases," which recorded the number of patients admitted, the general nature of their ailments and injuries, whether they were "poor" or others had paid for their care, and the disposition of their cases. The largest single category of resident patients, generally slightly more than one-third, were "lunatics," a catch-all category covering a variety of forms and degrees of mental illness, but most of these were long-term residents.[27] The proportion of newly admitted patients suffering from insanity, mania, or related conditions was significantly lower: only 5 percent of the seafarers, 8 percent of those recorded in the Admission and Discharge records, and 25 percent of the men and women listed in the Book of Patients. The disparity is a reflection of both the nature of mental illness and the long-term treatment it often required, and the purpose and nature of the records themselves. The annually published abstracts of cases recorded all the patients who were treated in the hospital over a given year, and the Book of Patients consisted of a similar although far more detailed listing of all patients. Those suffering from more serious cases of mental illness would often spend years and even decades in the hospital, and these men and women would appear in such records, whereas the Admissions and Discharges and Seafarers' Records listed only those admitted over a short period while ignoring others already in the hospital. In most years, well under one-quarter of the people admitted to the hospital were "lunatics," although the insane comprised half or more of the hospital's resident population.[28]

Derangement, depression, and mania afflicted rich and poor alike, and just as with illness and injuries, such conditions were often dealt with at home. Unusual behavior and activities were countenanced by family and friends, and allowed by the community as a whole, until a person became violent, dangerous to self or others, or in other ways undermined community norms. Ever since the 1730s the almshouse had, in the tradition of the hospices of medieval Europe, provided a home for insane men and women who were no longer able to live at home. The hospital, however, promised a far more hospitable environment, treatment, and even the possibility of a cure for at least some of those suffering from mental illnesses.[29] The "Abstracts of Cases" record that around one-fifth of those patients categorized as lunatics were "cured," while a further 10 percent or more were "relieved." Others died, eloped, or were taken out by family members or friends, but each year around half of all lunatics remained in the hospital, and many spent large portions of their lives within its walls.

There was enormous diversity among the "lunatics" who populated the lower floor of the hospital, and eventually a whole wing. In his manuscript record of such patients, Doctor Samuel Coates recorded that their mental illnesses took very different forms and had radically different effects. One aged Quaker woman had lost her reason following the death of her husband, after which she had commenced public preaching in a manner that shocked her Quaker friends, before announcing that she was the child of George II and the rightful ruler of America. For years this woman was well known in Philadelphia, inhabiting a tiny one-room stone building in Willing Alley that she called her Castle, "defending it valiantly with her broad sword, a silver cane, which she would brandish against the Trade boys, Who often attacked her." Clearly, the medieval tradition of taking pleasure by the taunting of those who had lost their reason was alive and well in the new republic. Eventually this woman was admitted into the Pennsylvania Hospital, which she called her Palace, and for years she held court within its walls, adapting her clothing to give it an appropriately regal appearance.[30]

A case such as this provided amusement to hospital staff and visitors, including Governor Thomas Mifflin, who spent time talking with her, and the woman herself appears to have enjoyed a decent existence, helped no doubt by the daily allowance of one gill of rum. Coates recorded that the "infirmities she laboured under required" this allowance, and that over the last twelve years of her life she consumed approximately 110 gallons of rum, which would have functioned as a soporific.[31] Other patients, however, were rather less fortunate in their condition. One, a nurse at the hospital, "became melancholy" after her husband died during the yellow fever epidemic of 1798. After a year of treatment

TABLE 5. Resolution of Cases Involving Lunatics, Pennsylvania Hospital, 1796, 1797, 1801

	1796		1797		1801	
Total	95		98		92	
Cured	20	(21%)	16	(16%)	19	(21%)
Relieved	15	(16%)	12	(12%)	9	(10%)
Taken out	3	(3%)	1	(4%)	2	(2%)
Eloped	3	(3%)	3	(3%)	0	
Died	12	(13%)	13	(13%)	7	(8%)
Remained	42	(44%)	49	(50%)	55	(60%)

Source: "Abstracts of Cases," 1796, 1797, 1801, Archives of the Pennsylvania Hospital.

she was deemed "improved both in body and mind" and released, yet she immediately walked to the river and jumped off Thomas Penrose's wharf, "& was drowned, before any Assistance could be given to her." That harsh existence and the fragility of life could adversely affect the mental health of impoverished Philadelphians is hardly surprising; when this unfortunate woman's suicide was communicated to her family, "her intimate friend and Companion . . . became fixed in a state of melancholy and despair," and although a year of treatment in the hospital enabled her to "recover her reason," she "never resumed her Accustomed cheerfulness, but gradually fell into a consumption of which she finally died."[32] For the poor of Philadelphia, physical and mental health were closely related.

Others were apparently driven mad by such experiences as disappointment in love or alcoholism. Coates records the case of a strikingly beautiful young woman whose dementia was caused by a failed love affair. On one occasion she tried to stab one of her attending physicians while on another she broke out of the hospital "without Shoes or Stockings on, her Bosom bare, and her ringlets of beautiful black hair flowing in wild disorder," in order to prevent the slaughter of a bull being baited by packs of dogs and watched by a large crowd. The young woman succeeded, in part because she calmed a large and angry bull that no other spectator dared approach, and she was allowed to return to the hospital. While the taunting of lunatics may have remained common, with wealthier Philadelphians even paying to enter the hospital in order to view and bait the insane patients, perhaps other medieval traditions survived too, such as the beliefs that some of the deranged might have enjoyed special relationships with God, and perhaps even special powers.[33]

It is unclear what prompted the attempted suicide of a twenty-one-year-old carpenter, admitted in April 1803. Intent on "destroying himself," the young man had employed the tools of his trade and "plunged a chisel into this left side, between the 4th and 5th Ribs." Admitted within two hours of the injury, this unfortunate man did not live long enough to be treated as a victim of melancholia, a significant category of lunatics, for despite regular bleedings and careful dressing of the wounds he died three days after his admission.[34]

One of the reasons for the relatively large number of lunatics within the hospital is the fact that, for the first time in the city's history, an institution existed that was designed to provide a certain degree of specialized care and possibly even a cure for those suffering mental illness. For those whose families enjoyed the means, the hospital thus provided an extremely useful service, and soon at least half of lunatic patients paid or had family members pay for their treatment. Wealthier Philadelphians paid for private cells with additional food and fuel, good clothing and attentive service, which made institutionalization of relatives suffering mental illness a relatively attractive proposition. In contrast, no more than 15 percent of the sick and injured paid or had family, friends, or, in the case of servants, employers pay for their hospitalization.[35] Moreover, the high proportion of insane patients, many of them paying customers, decreased the number of beds and the amount of resources available to the sick poor, whatever their condition.

The "Abstracts of Cases" routinely lists about thirty different conditions, including lunacy, suffered by the patients admitted. These include a wide variety of treatable complaints, from whooping cough to epilepsy, burns, and cancer. However, the large majority of non-lunatics fell into six categories: those suffering from venereal diseases, sore legs and ulcers, fevers of various kinds, broken limbs, dropsy, and rheumatism.

All these were potentially serious and even fatal conditions. In both 1796 and 1801, the hospital managers reported that over 10 percent of those admitted with venereal disease had died, while 27 percent of those admitted with fever in 1796 and 30 percent of those with broken limbs in 1801 did not survive their illness or injuries. Yet what is most striking about the records issued by the hospital is the successful treatment of so many patients. In most years at least one-third and as many as three-quarters of these impoverished men and women were either "cured" or "relieved." Perhaps this striking success rate was in part because the hospital was intended as a place for the treatment of the curable deserving poor; those who were undeserving of such assistance, or whose condition was too serious or beyond the abilities of the hospital staff were left to suffer and perhaps die at home or in the almshouse.

While the "Abstracts of Cases" reveal something of the general medical profiles of the men and women admitted to the hospital, they record neither gender nor race, but the databases compiled from other hospital records provide a rather more nuanced record, while the actual bodies of the people admitted and treated appear in the pages of the Book of Patients. White men constituted the large majority of patients, in part because so many seafarers and soldiers were referred to the hospital. Of the 500 patient records employed in the Book of Patients database, only

TABLE 6. Major Categories of Patient Admissions into the Pennsylvania Hospital (percent)

Time period	Venereal disease	Sore legs, ulcers	Fevers	Broken limbs	Dropsy	Rheumatism
1795–1796	12	14	16	4	3	2
1796–1797	15	12	4	5	4	9
1800–1801	11	11	4	4	1	5

Source: "Abstracts of Cases," 1796, 1797, 1801, Archives of the Pennsylvania Hospital.

9 (2 percent) were of black women, and 32 (6 percent) of black men, while a further 77 (15 percent) were of white women: the remaining 382 (76 percent) were white men, including 17 soldiers. Race is harder to determine in the Admission and Discharge Records, but the gender disparity is even more striking, for only 9 of the 100 patients recorded were women.

In other regards, the ailments, illnesses, and injuries listed in these records echo those published annually by the hospital managers. "Lunacy" accounted for 124 (25 percent) of the cases in the Book of Patients database: 22 percent of black female, 22 percent of black male, and 21 percent of white male patients. Interestingly, however, fully 45 percent of white female patients were admitted with this condition. By this time, doctors had already begun to define certain kinds of female behavior as "hysterical," and perhaps the institutionalization of women for what men regarded as insane behavior had already begun. Venereal diseases struck across race and gender lines, accounting for roughly one-sixth of each group of patients, although no black female patients were recorded as being thus afflicted.[36] Similarly, 18 percent of patients in the Admissions and Discharges records were suffering from venereal diseases. It is perhaps not surprising that such diseases had struck down 55 (27 percent) of the sailors admitted. For all that many seafarers may have developed monogamous relationships that some celebrated with tattoos, others may have had no long-term partners, or they may have been unfaithful to them during the long voyages that took them to many different ports and gave them wages to spend in brief periods of riotous excess.

Beyond lunacy and venereal disease, however, the record becomes rather more complicated than the simplified tables published by the hospital managers. Sore and ulcerated legs accounted for 45 (9 percent) of the Book of Patients database, fevers laid low 58 (12 percent) of the patients, and broken limbs a further 45 (9 percent); beyond these, patients were recorded as suffering from a wide variety of conditions. It is hardly surprising, for example, that injuries and a wide variety of infectious diseases affected so many of the seafarers whose cases were recorded in the U.S. Seamen's records. Work at sea was probably more dangerous than any other single job in the early republic, and two men admitted into the hospital in 1802 were typical: one entered with fractured ribs and a recommendation as "a steady man" from his captain, while another was suffering from a diseased arm injured by an "accident at sea."[37] Other injuries included contusions on the head or body, wounds (including sword and gunshot wounds), all manner of fractures, and even a dog bite. Long hours spent on and above the deck in all weathers affected the sailors' health in other ways, for rheumatism struck down far more of them than the population as a whole, and fully 48 (24 percent) suffered from a condition that must have ended the career of many older workers. Moreover, sailors were the unwitting vehicles for the transmission of myriad germs and infectious diseases, many of them picked up in the ports that were the focal points for the spread of disease. From diarrhea to a whole variety of fevers, disease was the other great threat to the sailors who worked the trade lifelines of the nation.

The range of illnesses and injuries recorded in the Book of Patients is remarkably broad, and it is in this very diversity that the threats to the bodies of lower sort Philadelphians become apparent. Beyond lunacy, venereal disease, and so forth, one finds the African American woman suffering a pain in her breast, or the white man suffering from frostbite. The woman was listed as "poor," but had managed to find the all-too-necessary sponsor who pledged security for her burial, and she died a week following her admission.[38] Another African American to die in the hospital was a young "negro Lad," and it is quite likely that he was a servant and that the man who provided security for his burial was his master. Admitted in August 1791 with bad burns occasioned by scalding, he lingered for three painful weeks before succumbing to either his injuries or subsequent infections. Whether his injuries took place in a kitchen or in another work place is unclear.[39] Other accidents and work-related injuries brought impoverished Philadelphians into the hospital, some to recover and others to die. One white man was admitted late in 1791 with a "fractured head occasioned by a fall." Listed as "poor," he was presumably brought in as an emergency case, since nobody was listed as guaranteeing security and payment for his treatment and for the burial that was required when he died three days later.[40] Others who died were often suffering from the common maladies and illnesses of their era, such as the "poor" white man admitted with "Fever & Ague," with one of the Overseers of the Poor guaranteeing payment for his clothes and, if necessary, his burial. In a case such as this, it was hoped that proper medical care and attention would restore the patient to health, but this particular man survived Christmas and the New Year only to die after less than three weeks of care.[41]

However, while some died in the hospital, many more lived, with their conditions either relieved or cured. For the masters of servants and apprentices, the hospital provided a vitally useful service, allowing them to pay to have the bodies of sick or injured workers restored to health, rather than having to devote precious resources to their care in the master's own home. The master of one young woman, a "Taylor," paid eight shillings and four pence for each of the three weeks that his female servant spent in the hospital recovering from a "Sore Arm."[42] In another case, an African American suffering a wounded arm was treated for two weeks, with his master, a merchant, providing payment. Once healed, the servant was "Taken out by his Master."[43] Another African American, whose condition was not recorded, was entered into the Book of Patients with just a first name. Quite possibly he was a slave and his labor was owned by the captain of a ship, who paid for the care of his property and then came to the hospital to retrieve him.[44]

For others who had no masters or whose masters found it cheaper to secure a new worker, the best they could hope for was a testimonial from one of their betters and admission to the hospital as a "deserving" poor man or woman, one of the few who were judged worthy of free medical care. Fortunate indeed was a white man admitted in April 1790 with both of his legs and one of his arms broken, for his recovery took eight months. Another was admitted two years later, after having been "badly wounded in his head" by the captain of the ship on which he served; he was, however, admitted as a poor man, for the captain took no financial responsibility for his actions. One "poor sailor" spent nine months in the hospital recovering from "Leprosy," before being discharged "Cured & Relieved in May of 1793.[45]

Occasionally, it was family members rather than employers who paid for hospitalization, as in the case of a young white man admitted with "Venereal & lunacy," the latter presumably a symptom of a particularly bad case of venereal disease, with his father paying for the almost two months of treatment required before he could be discharged "Cured."[46] With the exception of lunacy, this was not an era when the middling sorts or elites would commit family members to the hospital, preferring the ministrations of family members and professional doctors within the privacy of their own homes. It was more often those with fewer resources who employed the hospital, and the expense of such treatment together with the loss of the income of a sick or injured person could help push a family into poverty. On rare occasions, people paid for their own care, which involved paying for medical care and treatment and furnishing security to cover the cost of burial, a realistic but hardly encouraging prospect. A particularly interesting example of this occurred in the late summer of 1791, when two young women were admitted together for treatment of the venereal disease they were both suffering. Both women were very unusual in that they furnished their "own security," and both left the hospital, their condition relieved, some three weeks later. It is quite likely that these were two prostitutes whose diseased condition was an occupational hazard that injured and killed many of their profession. In most cases, as the disease progressed such women would be incarcerated in the less hospitable almshouse, but in this case the women had seized the initiative and saved money for their treatment in the far preferable surroundings of the hospital.[47]

Along with seafarers, one of the largest groups of workers in the hospital was soldiers. Since Philadelphia was the national capital during the

1790s, wars and military actions against the western Indians and the Whiskey Rebels were conducted from the city, and it is hardly surprising that the government chose to employ the hospital to restore some soldiers to health. On occasion, such men appeared to have been injured at work, as in the case of one soldier "hurt by a fall," who was admitted early in 1792, only to die four days later, and another who had injured his finger but was then "Discharged Cured."[48] More commonly, soldiers were admitted with the diseases and illnesses that always killed far more of their number than did the bloodletting of war itself. As with seafarers, venereal disease was the most common complaint, accounting for 53 percent of the soldiers in the database. Others suffered from much the same ailments that struck down the civilian population of Philadelphia, such as pleurisy, fever, and epileptic fits.

In the case of one soldier, who entered the hospital in June 1793 suffering from venereal disease, a notation in the Book of Patients recorded that five days after his admission the man was "taken out by order of his security." Another man who had been treated for fever was "taken [out] by the Capt." What these records suggest is that, having paid to have men treated, military authorities were eager to have them return to their duties. Some 24 percent of all soldiers in this sample were recorded as having "eloped," and it would appear that the hospital provided sick and injured soldiers with an opportunity to avail themselves of free health care before leaving both hospital and army.

Civilians, too, occasionally eloped from the hospital, and 4 percent of white men and women in the sample left the hospital in this manner. On occasion these escapees were lunatics, men and women who were not in full command of their sense. Others appear to have been servants, as in the case of one young woman whose expenses had been paid by her master, who fled the hospital two weeks after her admission.[49] Just as with soldiers, the hospital healed servants and furnished them with the time and space to consider and effect an escape from their servitude. In such cases as these, we find rare examples of the inversion of the logic of a hospital intended for the deserving poor, with men and women taking advantage of hospitalization but then refusing to return to the life of service and labor that had entitled them to hospital treatment in the first place.

Others were taken out of the hospital by friends or family members. In some cases, it is possible that there were no longer funds to pay for hospitalization, while in others it may have become more practicable to provide care at home. It is difficult to know what happened in the cases of such patients as a black woman suffering from rheumatism, who was "Taken out by her friends," or "a Free man" recorded as poor, suffering from diarrhea, who again was "Taken out by his friends."[50] Others in the hospital were new to the city, as was the case for an unusual group of three African American men, all admitted in the spring of 1793 suffering from scurvy. An unusual condition on land, it is likely that these men, all of whom had French names, were slaves, former slaves, or free mulattos from Haiti, who had fled or been taken from the violent revolution engulfing that island and had suffered from malnutrition on the voyage to Philadelphia. All were poor, and one needed a full two months to recover.[51]

The manuscript record of a "Collection of Cases" reveals more details about the condition of ill and injured lower sort bodies and the treatment that they received. By definition, the cases recorded by hospital doctors in painstaking detail described conditions or medical procedures of unusual interest to the attendant physicians. As such they were not necessarily typical, yet they remain useful in fleshing out the kinds of men and women who came to the Pennsylvania Hospital and the injuries and illnesses that brought them there. On occasion, patients found themselves in the hospital because of the inadequate treatment they had received at home or in the community. Thus a twenty-five-year-old white woman who had been "slightly indisposed" had done what many of her contemporaries would have considered natural: she attempted to have her natural humors balanced by bloodletting. She had gone to a local farrier who was supposedly expert in the procedure, but unfortunately the wound that he created continue to bleed, and even when it had healed a swelling developed, which throbbed painfully.[52] Something similar had happened to a young seafarer, who had been bled by a fellow sailor in a manner that caused "an Aneurism of the left arm from a puncture of the artery," a condition that was treated successfully over the course of ten weeks in the hospital.[53]

A good many of the cases that interested the hospital's physicians were the result of accidents and injuries, providing further evidence of the day-to-day risks facing the bodies of Philadelphia's working poor. The harsh and dangerous conditions of work at sea and on the docks meant that seafarers furnished the doctors with a good many of these injuries. One twenty-eight-year-old seafarer had suffered a broken arm "by a heavy Sea breaking over the ship." The conditions meant that the injury was not treated until the following day, "when the Captain and Mate bound it up, and applied splints over it." Since a good proportion of seafaring injuries occurred on the open sea, sailors must have developed knowledge and skills for dealing with such injuries, but three weeks later, when the ship arrived in Virginia, a doctor examined and "told him that the ends of the bone were not in a proper situation." Once admitted into the Pennsylvania Hospital, an operation to break and reset the arm was postponed by "the Weather becoming very hot," and a subsequent bout of bilious fever, but eventually, over two years after the original injury, the relieved seafarer was discharged.[54]

Other sailors were admitted after falling from the masts or rigging of their ships. A week after Thomas Jefferson's reelection as president, one such sailor fell "from a height of about forty feet upon his head and back," and was brought into the hospital with a barely perceptible pulse. Bleeding did not help this unfortunate mariner, who died a day later. Another sailor, only nineteen years of age, was rather more fortunate. Having "fallen from the main-top-gallant-mast head" while at sea, he had suffered a compund fracture of the tibia. Surely in some considerable pain, perhaps relieved by grog, the sailor "had been drest, under the direction of the captain, with two large cloths, wrapt around the limb, including two pieces of split hoop-poles." Ten days later the ship arrived in Philadelphia, and the sailor was immediately transferred to the Pennsylvania Hospital. The doctors were impressed by the treatment he had received, noting that the "dressings and attention afforded had retained the limb perfectly straight, and there was no retraction." Most medical knowledge was shared by doctors and lay people alike, and it was only specialized procedures that set medical professionals apart. However, an ulcer had developed on the patient's leg, laying "a considerable surface of bone entirely bare, including the whole of the fracture on that side of the tibia." Placing the sailor "on a low diet" to calm him, the attending physicians applied a poultice to the ulcer and a specially constructed splint to the leg. The resolution of the case is unclear, but it is not hard to imagine that for the remainder of his life the sailor would have shown the injury in his gait.[55]

Workers on land were also subject to a variety of injuries. One such man was a thirty-five-year-old blacksmith, troubled by an aneurism in the left leg, which he first became aware of when struck by "a violent pain in the ham" following a long walk. A painful tumor then developed, and by "the time of his admission into the Hospital, it projected 5 Inches from the Ham." The tumor was removed, the patient recovered, and he "returned to his usual business and continued working at it."[56] The very fact that the attending doctor chose to record this illustrates the moral imperatives at work in the Pennsylvania Hospital. It was not universal care of the sick and injured that motivated the managers and physicians, but rather the recovery of the gainfully employed members of the respectable poor whose illnesses and injuries could be treated.

In another case, an African American man of forty who was employed in the construction of a building in the city was "climbing a ladder with a hod" when knocked off by a falling piece of timber. The fall was a serious one, and the unfortunate man was brought to the hospital with fractured ribs, an injured skull and shoulder, and a "fractured . . .

thorax." His pulse was low, his breathing labored, and his hearing all but gone, so the doctors "bled nearly 20 ounces," a treatment they repeated four times, accompanied by saline laxatives and occasional enemas. More than these treatments, however, it appears to have been a month of constant care that allowed this body to heal, although when the man was discharged "cured," the attending doctor recorded that the man's shoulder was now "much more nearly of its natural shape than before," suggesting that here was another impoverished Philadelphian whose body would forever show the cost of hard and dangerous physical labor.

The inability of the hospital to do more than relieve the condition of some patients is demonstrated by the case of a forty-five-year-old Irish laborer who had spent eighteen months in the hospital being treated for rheumatism. Even after his discharge, the laborer's limbs "remained considerably stiff"; unable to cross the street in time to avoid "a 5 horse waggon," he was knocked down and run over by "the whole machine, to the wight of 3 tons." His condition was so serious that those at the scene immediately bled him, before rushing him to the hospital. Holding out little hope, the physicians prescribed "Forty five drops of laudanum," but admitted that he might "require the immediate presence of a priest of his own religious persuasion." While the resolution of this case is not recorded, it is hard to imagine that such serious internal injuries could have resulted in anything but death.[57]

A particularly interesting case is that of a thirty-year-old African American woman who sought admission to the hospital for the removal of a very large tumor "produced more than ten years before by a kick upon the pudenda." Over the years the tumor had grown considerably, extending from three inches above the pubis to within two inches of the anus, and then hanging "almost twenty inches, and its lower part almost reached the knees." Not surprisingly, the "patient walked with great difficulty," and before students and fellow doctors the tumor was removed in the operating theatre that remains to this day beside the Library of the Pennsylvania Hospital. Three months later the patient was discharged "well."[58] Quite how the original injury was sustained or whether indeed it was the cause of what those present defined as a tumor is unclear, although it is apparent that this woman believed the original injury to have been severe enough to cause her debility, and the doctors recorded this without critical comment or question. The *Oxford English Dictionary* records that between the sixteenth and nineteenth centuries the word "tumour" could refer to any "abnormal or morbid swelling or enlargment in any part of the body.[59] Perhaps, like many black Philadelphians, this woman may once have been a slave, and a brutal kick to her groin may have been inflicted by her master or another white man. What is abundantly clear is that all white masters enjoyed the power to inflict such injuries on the black women they owned, and some of the injured and deformed African Americans walking the streets of early national Philadelphia owed their physical condition to slavery and to their slave masters and mistresses.

It was not just the workplace but life in their homes and on the streets that could injure impoverished Philadelphians, and the medical records of the hospital underline the fragility of life. One fourteen-year-old boy was admitted after falling from a horse, and although the bones in one leg were badly broken the physicians were able to set them. The boy's open wounds, however, did not heal, and ten days after the accident he began to experience difficulty in moving his jaw. Tetanus set in, and despite the use of laudanum and regular blistering, the unfortunate boy soon died.[60] An even younger child, a six-year-old boy "of a delicate Constitution," suffered terribly after running barefoot in the street and treading on a broken glass bottle. The wound would not stop bleeding, and when the doctors came to clean it they were forced to reopen it in order to remove "a parcel of dirt and small stones that were forced in." Still the bleeding would not stop, and the doctors were forced to improvise a mechanism designed to reduce the flow of blood to the boy's leg. Six weeks after the injury he was discharged, "cured," fortunate not to have contracted the tetanus that would surely have killed him.[61] One boy, only eight years old, had two of his teeth knocked out by an axe. It was not his mother but another woman, probably his mistress, who brought the child to the hospital, bringing the teeth with her, and over the course of three months the doctors were able to reset the teeth into his mouth.[62]

Any kind of blow might threaten serious injury. One man was accidentally struck by "the shaft of a Carriage, which struck directly over his liver." At first he was treated at home and attended by a physician, but following his apparent recovery the patient "exerted himself too much" and found himself in the hospital, where "he complained of rigors, succeeded by febrile heats." His liver was much inflamed and very tender, and as with many internal injuries the doctors could do little more than make his condition comfortable and attempt to heal his body through regulation of what went in and out. Unfortunately, such care was insufficient, and the patient died.[63] And there were other hazards, as experienced by an unfortunate young black woman bitten by a rabid dog. At the dispensary "the parts penetrated by the animals teeth . . . were completely excised," but infection and the accompanying symptoms set in and she was admitted to the hospital. Aware of her situation, she "readily consented to be secured in the straight jacket, though it seemed to distress her that this precaution was necessary." Soon even this was insufficient, and "Dr. Rush's tranquilizer was substituted for the jacket," an electric-chair like apparatus designed to hold still and calm the patient. It was not long, however, before "she terminated her miserable life."[64]

For women, pregnancy remained as potentially dangerous as any illness or injury. One expectant woman was admitted to the hospital during the first trimester, "in consequence of abuse from her husband." His physical violence may have had both physical and mental effects, however, for although "she was delivered of a fine healthy child," following the birth she began experiencing "extreme pain in the umbilical region," and "her countenance was dejected." Her body rejected all food and medicine, and by the third day of her illness the unfortunate woman's "strength was nearly exhausted, eye ghastly & face cadaverous, pulse scarcely perceptible." That evening she died, and the city had another impoverished motherless child, less that two weeks old.[65] In another case, a thirty-three-year-old woman was admitted while pregnant and suffering from dropsy, a disease in which watery fluid collects in the body and causes swelling, today known as edema. Regularly "tapped" to draw off fluid, the woman found that her doctors could do little else for her; a day after her child was stillborn, "death released her, from all her sufferings."[66]

On occasion, patients were admitted whom the hospital managers and doctors judged to be unworthy of the hospital, men and women who did not appear to be drawn from the ranks of the deserving poor. That such moral judgments were important becomes clear in the way they color the otherwise objective medical records found in the Collection of Cases. Thus the record of a sixty-year-old man admitted "for a mortification of his left foot, which was brought about by the kick of a horse," refers to the patient as "an intemperate man having been accustomed to drink freely of Whiskey."[67] Similarly, "a Porter aged 31 Years, who has been in the habit of drinking large quantities of ardent Spirits," was judged and labeled according to his fondness for alcohol and not by the fact that he worked and that alcohol had no apparent connection with the injury to his leg that led to its amputation.[68] When Irish birth and venereal disease was added to excessive drinking, the doctors were not slow to record them, as in the case of an Irish laborer who, while employed digging earth, was trapped by a landslide. Unable to evacuate his bowels or bladder, the unfortunate laborer had suffered internal injuries that the attending physicians were unable to heal, and a day later he expired.[69] In such cases, even though these men were all working for their living, they were judged as less than fully fit for the Pennsylvania Hospital. Many like them would have been less fortunate, and found themselves placed in the almshouse, where little in the way of medical care and healing was available.

Such judgmental records as these furnish further evidence of the ubiquity of a culture of drinking among the lower sorts of early national

Philadelphia. On rare occasions, other injuries suggest other cultural forms and expressions, such as the case of "a young black woman, otherwise healthy," who was admitted because the "perforating" of her ears had led to the growth of two large tumors, one hanging from each ear. Quite possibly the woman's ears had been pierced with an unclean instrument, and infection had set in. In a relatively simple procedure the tumors were removed and the ears healed, and she was discharged "cured." The piercing of ears "for rings" remained rare, although perhaps rather more common among seafarers and African Americans, who sought to decorate and make their bodies distinctive in a variety of ways, from tattoos to colorful clothing to earrings.[70]

Overall, however, the hospital records reveal more about the dangers and hardships of life and work among Philadelphia's lower sorts than they do about culture and sociability among such folk. A combination of moral imperatives and financial exigencies meant that relatively few of the poor were able to enjoy the preferable conditions and superior medical care of the hospital when compared to the almshouse. Most of the time, the managers of the hospital succeeded in their mission of restricting access to the deserving poor. It was generally only those whose work, behavior and demeanor, and membership in a deferential network of social obligations were apparent to their betters who could hope for a chance of securing admission to the hospital.

But the injuries, illnesses, and ailments suffered by these patients were ubiquitous among the city's lower sorts. Although the dispensary provided drugs and some treatment to a far greater number of lower sort Philadelphians than were ever admitted into the hospital, the costs involved meant that many who required residential care had no option but to join the large groups of sick and injured poor in the almshouse. While both the hospital and almshouse housed the bodies of injured and ill impoverished Philadelphians, there were significant differences between them. The hospital was an institution dedicated to medical care and treatment, a far more gentle and peaceful environment than the almshouse, which functioned more as a prison and workhouse. Philadelphians who required medical attention, both rich and poor alike, hoped to receive it in their own homes. But for those impoverished Philadelphians for whom such domestic care was not an option, the hospital was the best they could hope for, albeit an option available to few of them. It was, indeed, the Pennsylvania Hospital for the Sick Poor, and thus the very act of hospitalization marked the bodies of those admitted—in moral and qualitative as much as medical fashion—as poor, as "deserving," and as sick or injured.

Chapter 4
Runaway Bodies

In the fall of 1793, an indentured white American servant named John Collins ran away from his master's iron works in Chester County, Pennsylvania. Collins's master Dennis Whelan placed an advertisement in the *Pennsylvania Gazette*, offering twelve dollars reward for the capture of his valuable skilled worker. Whelan described his servant as being "above 20 years of age... of a fair complexion, about 5 feet 7 inches high, tolerably square built, his head rather small, his chin peaked and inclines upwards toward his nose, which is sharp." Furthermore, Whelan observed that Collins "chews tobacco profusely, and is fond of strong drink, [and is] peevish and quarrelsome when intoxicated." The runaway "may be easily discovered to be a Forgeman by the inside of his hands being black or blue, and the skin being perforated with a number of small holes." Noting that Collins's clothes "are uncertain, as he may exchange what he took away," Whelan nonetheless described these items as "one coattee of second cloth, a lead coloured sailor fashioned jacket, one red under jacket, Russian sheeting shirts, tow trowsers, one pair of olive green coloured trowsers of foreign manufacture, commonly called royal rib, [and] a beaver hat, remarkably shallow in the crown and very large in the brim."[1]

Two years later "a Negroe man, named Dick" ran away from his master Abraham Hunt in Trenton. Convinced that Dick had crossed the Delaware and entered Pennsylvania in the company of Ned, another black runaway, Hunt also placed an advertisement in the *Pennsylvania Gazette*. His master described Dick as being "about 28 years old, 5 feet 5 inches high, tolerable black smooth skin," with "a bunch of bushy hair behind, and had his fore-top lately cut off; has scars on his back, having been several times flogg'd at the whipping post; if attacked closely will stammer in his answers; had on, and took with him, an old fur hat, with a remarkable high crown and narrow brim, a blue surtout, and homespun trowsers."[2]

The advertisements for runaway men and women that appeared in the *Pennsylvania Gazette* and other early national newspapers constituted the era's most complete and detailed descriptions of lower sort bodies. The advertisements were all about bodies, and comprised both affirmations of power over slave and servant bodies, and protestations of resistance against such power.[3] By describing runaways in terms of property, often alongside advertisements for livestock, and by caricaturing them in ways that degraded African Americans, Irish, German, and native-born white Americans, masters defined, evaluated, and objectified their slaves and servants.[4] Yet the advertisements and the descriptions they contain serve to illustrate that impoverished men and women who did not enjoy legal ownership of the labor of their bodies or even their very bodies, nonetheless strove to refashion and redefine their bodies, thereby reasserting control over them. More than anything else, runaway advertisements tell stories about battles over the bodies of lower sort men and women who owned next to nothing but who sought to own themselves.[5]

In early national Philadelphia, the differences between advertisements for runaway blacks and runaway whites were far smaller than they had been earlier in the century. With Pennsylvania moving toward gradual abolition, and slavery declining in popularity throughout the Middle Atlantic and even parts of the Upper South, a good many black runaways were servants rather than slaves. While the language and tone of advertisements for runaway whites changed little over time, the masters of runaway blacks were ever more aware of their audience, and some took pains to point out that their charges were servants rather than slaves, or that they had been promised liberty. Thus Jacob Rush protested that twenty-two-year-old Joe's "time of servitude will end in 7 years and 7 months," while Andrew Lowrey grumbled that he had "intended to set said slave [free] at a reasonable period."[6]

Philadelphia, more than any other early national city, acted as a magnet for all manner of runaways. As the capital of the first state to begin the process of ending slavery, and the home of a growing free black community, the Quaker City of Brotherly Love appeared to promise freedom to runaway black slaves and servants hailing from the city and its suburbs, rural Pennsylvania, New Jersey, Delaware, Maryland, and the Upper South. Indentured white servants, many of them Irish and German, were also attracted by the city's ethnic diversity and rapidly expanding economy. Both black and white runaways passed through or settled in Philadelphia, in search of friends and family, shelter, work, and freedom, and among the lower sorts who thronged the city's streets were a good many men and women whose bodies had been stolen from their legal owners.[7] Consequently, the masters of indentured servants and slaves who had absconded published advertisements in Philadelphia newspapers. This chapter is based upon a survey of all the runaway advertisements that appeared in the *Pennsylvania Gazette* between 1784 and 1800.[8]

Runaway advertisements were descriptions of a specific class of the lower sort, men and women who owned little or nothing and whose bodies (or the labor of their bodies) belonged to other people. By running away these folk had reasserted complete control over their own bodies, yet many of the advertisements illustrated that running away was actually the last of a series of skirmishes fought by owner and owned on the battleground of the body. As such, early national runaways embody the experiences of the poor in a real and vivid fashion, demonstrating both the ways power inscribed itself upon poor bodies and the ways the poor resisted such power and sought to fashion and control their own bodies for their own ends.[9] No other men and women so vividly demonstrated the tension between the power of more affluent Americans to control the bodies of the lower sort and the ability of the poor to resist such control and retake possession of their own bodies.

As a result, runaway advertisements often hint at starkly different constructions of individual bodies and general bodily types.[10] Gesture, stance, and countenance are all interpreted according to a value system that attributes positive or negative qualities to the ways a person stands, looks, and communicates with another.[11] A master may well have believed his servant or slave to have been typically black or Irish, and displaying many of the characteristics that were assumed to be inherent to people of that ethnicity, race, and class. Yet while descriptions of attitude, mannerisms, language, and clothing might reinforce such assumptions, they could also betray the ways individuals resisted such easy categorization. This was clearly true of Dublin, a twenty-five-year-old African-born slave who had run away from his master Gabriel Davis in Lancaster County. Either Davis or another white man had named the slave for a major British city, marking his movement away from an African into an Anglo-American world, while yet setting him apart from white Europeans, who enjoyed surnames and who did not take place names for their given names: Dublin was a slave of the British Atlantic world rather than a citizen of it. His master recorded that the slave spoke "good English" and was "a tractable fellow either on a farm or in a tanyard," suggesting that he had worked well and hard, and implying some surprise that Dublin had absconded. Yet the advertisements also recorded that Dublin had been badly scarred on one cheek "by the kick of a horse," suggesting that his labor for Davis may not always have been pleasant or willing. Going on to admit that "it is likely he may change his name and perhaps some of his clothing," and then listing fourteen items of clothing that Dublin had taken with him, Davis acknowledged that the slave had been injured by his work and that he was ready and willing to escape it and strive for a free and independent existence.[12]

The clash between owners and owned was even more apparent in the case of Ben, a slave who ran away from his Maryland master in 1791. Micajah Merryman was fulsome in his praise for Ben's skills, describing him as "a good waggoner and plowman" who "can do any thing of plantation business, as well as any man." This skilled and hardworking slave was also, however, "a very artful fellow, a great thief and dreadful liar," and Merryman conceded that "it is likely he will change his name and cloaths."[13] Like Dublin, Ben had demonstrated his ability to live and act the part of the hardworking and skillful slave, while also betraying to his master a vigorous spirit of independence that made running away more than possible.

Runaway advertisements reveal that the struggle between owners and owned for control of the bodies of servants and slaves was played out in a variety of ways. This was a struggle over the meaning and significance of the ways servile bodies appeared, for the body itself was the single most important battleground between masters and their human property. The age of the runaway body reveals something of personal history and motivation, while the struggles implicit in the naming of black bodies tell stories of power and resistance. The ways servants and slaves spoke and their powers of literacy could on the one hand serve to illustrate the power and control of masters, while on the other hand they might constitute powerful assertions of spirited independence. Bodily markings could reveal the ways discipline and work had scarred runaways, yet such injuries might also indicate the motivations behind a bid for freedom. Moreover, some bodily markings were the work of the runaways themselves, and as such were perhaps the most physical way a slave or servant could assert power over his or her own body, in symbolic defiance of the power of masters to mark slave and servant bodies with the lash and the branding iron. Finally, the styling of hair and the use of clothing reveal a great deal about personal independence and motivation on the part of the runaway, for they bear witness to statements of personal style and the ways runaway servants and slaves could prepare their bodies for a life independent of the controlling authority of their master.

One of the identifying characteristics of the runaway servants and slaves who inhabited early national Philadelphia was age, for most were young. There are a number of reasons for this, not least the fact that the effects of many years of hard labor made both escape and then the independent struggle for survival increasingly difficult as bondsmen and -women grew older. Many of the men and women who had sold their labor as indentured servants (or whose labor had been sold by parents or guardians) were in their teens or early twenties. White female runaways' ages ranged from twelve to twenty-eight, with a mean of 19.2; white males were between the ages of thirteen and forty-five (although very few were older than their late twenties), with a mean of 22.6. Ethnicity was a factor here: American-born white males in indentured servitude or apprenticeships tended to be very young, with a mean age of 19.7, whereas Irish and German male servants had an average age of 22.1 and 26.8 respectively. European-born servants were often young men with no opportunities in the land of their birth, while a good many of the American-born white servants were children or youths whose parents or guardians had apprenticed them out or indented them.

Black men who ran were relatively young, ranging in age from twelve to forty-three, but with an average age of 25.6 and with most clustered in their mid-twenties. Black female runaways were significantly older, with a mean age of 28.2. Of even more import is the fact that a good many black women who ran from servitude were far younger or older than the average: almost one-third were older than thirty-five while another third were twenty-one or younger. Some black women appear to have sought an escape from servitude early in the years during which the sexual exploitation of their bodies inherent within slavery was more likely, while older black women hoped to steal both themselves and their children away from such a system. Thirty-five-year-old Rachel, for example, took her nineteen-year-old daughter Jemima and her fourteen-year-old son Jem when she ran away from her Maryland owner in the spring of 1794. A lifetime of slave labor meant that Rachel was "troubled with pains, and her ancles and wrists frequently swell," yet she ran. Perhaps she feared that her children would be taken from her, or that her daughter might suffer as it is possible she had suffered: Rachel was black, but her daughter Jemima was a "likely bright mulattoe," and the possibility of rape was as real for her as it had been for her mother.[14]

Similar fears may have motivated younger black women to run away. Twenty-three-year-old Dinah's owner described her as "a likely wench" and offered £6 for her return: such women had no protection against their white masters or other white men in the communities in which they lived.[15] Other young black women already had children: Dorcas was only twenty-one when she ran in 1794, but she took with her two sons, one aged four and the other sixteen months. Perhaps persistent sexual exploitation prompted her attempt to escape slavery, or maybe she sought to protect and keep united her young family.[16] Such motivations had far less relevance for white women or for either black or white men. White female servants were almost always young and unmarried, and in fact were liable to be penalized by an extension of their term of servitude should they become pregnant. Although sexual exploitation by their masters was possible, indentured white women were less vulnerable than were black female slaves. For black men, sexual fear operated in an altogether different fashion, and although some ran with wives, partners, and children, neither black men nor white men were likely to have experienced the motivating fears that drove some black women to run away.[17]

The bodies of most of the runaways in Philadelphia and indeed throughout the early national United States were, then, fairly young, although European-born male servants and African American women were often older, sometimes well into their forties. Philadelphia's civic and judicial officers would have known all this, and as they walked the streets of the city the ages of the bodies of lower sort men and women would have betrayed them as possible runaways. In an age when men and especially women needed to prove either independent status or dependence on a male head of household—most likely a father or husband, or an employer or master—those who walked the streets without such proof were liable to be taken for runaways. As a result, a good many newspaper advertisements were placed by jailers who had been given custody of men, women, and children taken up on the streets and then incarcerated as suspected runaways. The poor were not, in the most literal sense, free to walk the streets of Philadelphia.

Virtually all the runaway advertisements in the *Pennsylvania Gazette* gave the name of the person who had absconded, although masters were not slow to note that names might be changed to avoid detection. For white servants, names might well reveal ethnicity, as in the case of servants from Ireland like Peggy Daley and John Boyle or Germans like Frederica Goettle and Johannes Gunen.[18] The naming of the body is an exercise in power, identifying and in very real sense marking the body, and these Europeans and other white runaways had almost certainly been named by parents with whom they shared a surname that marked their membership in a family. For black runaways, however, names were not always parental expressions of love and identity.

When masters and owners referred to and described black runaways in their advertisements, they usually gave only a first name. None of the black women in this sample, and only 26 percent of the black men, were referred to by both a first name and a surname. Although fifty years old, with "hair or wool somewhat grey with age," John Smith's slave was known simply as Dinah, just as another Maryland slave—this one a skilled male craftsman in his mid-thirties—was described to the world as Isaac.[19] Either whites did not know the surnames of their black slaves and servants or they chose to ignore them. In either case, the employment of only first names belittled black Americans, treating them as little more than children and as wholly and legally dependant bodies with no rights or identity outside their master's household.

Many slaves—and not a few of the men and women from the middle Atlantic and upper South whose slavery had been transmuted into servitude—had been given their names by white masters. The naming of these bodies constituted a theft of the love and power that would normally have been employed by their parents, and often this power was exercised by white masters in a manner designed to reaffirm white power and black impotence. Few if any white boys would have been christened by their parents with such names as Caesar, Jupiter, or Sambo, but white masters did not hesitate to employ racially specific names that ridiculed their bearers.[20] What slave could even dream of the powers of a classical ruler or god, and what slave could ever escape the racist slurs of a name given by Anglo-American whites only to Africans and African Americans? While white owners laughed, however, their naming of black bodies, with all that it symbolized, may have been yet another of the myriad grievances that motivated slaves and servants to run away.

What few white masters knew or cared to acknowledge, however, was that an increasing number of their black slaves and servants did have surnames, and that these names allowed black men and women to shape their own and their children's identities independently of their masters. At its most basic, the employment of surnames gave black Americans a sense of dignity that many whites may have thought inappropriate. More fundamentally, however, black adoption of surnames, which very often differed from the family name of the present master, revealed a strong attachment to slave families and to fathers and husbands, and thus represented an assertion of paternal rights and a disavowal of the lack of freedom entailed in and by the matrilineal nature of racial slavery. Naming one's own body and the bodies of one's children was a kind of freedom, a freedom that slaves asserted quietly in servitude but then more loudly when they ran away, an expression of identity that transcended white ownership. Owners and masters may have suspected that their black slaves and servants had surnames, but even when they knew this to be the case there was not a lot that they could do about the situation.[21]

When masters advertised that their black slaves and servants might change their names, they were acknowledging not only the likelihood that runaways would seek to disguise themselves, but also that a dual system of nomenclature existed. This is abundantly clear in the case of Caesar, the runaway slave of James Anderson of Chester County, Pennsylvania. When Anderson noted that Caesar "calls himself Jacob Holy," the white man was acknowledging that even before running away his slave had already declared a nominal independence for his body.[22] Interestingly, none of the black female runaways in this sample were recorded by their masters as having other names, whereas over 10 percent of black males were thus described. Given that the lack of a surname and the imposition of demeaning first names was an emasculating process, perhaps black male servants and slaves were more vigorous in asserting the right to name their own bodies and thereby resist their lack of power in a matrilineal slave system that empowered white men.

Regardless of the means by which they secured freedom, black Americans immediately asserted complete possession of the naming process, acquiring or publicizing surnames and then naming their own children accordingly. Eschewing the demeaning classical and place names bestowed by white masters, and abandoning the African names of their ancestors, almost all Philadelphia's free blacks had British first and last names that asserted their status as free and independent men and women.[23] All the black male runaways in this sample whose masters recorded them as having surnames had anglicized names, such as Daniel Gift, Moses White, and Jeffrey Butcher.[24] The appropriation of Anglo-American names by African Americans may well have bothered many whites: when in 1790 West Chester sheriff Charles Dilworth incarcerated a young black male as a suspected runaway, he noted that the "Negroe man calls himself JOHN RUSSELL," as if unsure whether this information might help identify the hapless black American or actually help him to assert his freedom.[25] What is beyond doubt, however, is that had the man reported his name as Dublin or Monmouth or Caesar, both the sheriff and newspaper readers would have had no doubt that he was a runaway.[26]

When composing runaway advertisements, masters often gave thought to their slaves' or servants' manner of speech as an expression of the ways in which they dealt with white men and women of power. Runaways who sought to establish a new and independent life would need to negotiate and interact with employers, and distinctive modes of communication might readily identify runaways who posed as free men and women. Many runaways had assumed sufficient skills and familiarity with Anglo-American language and culture to seek a free and independent life or, at the very least, a radical change in their lives and work. Masters were not slow to recognize these talents and abilities, resulting in a tension within many advertisements between praise for the hard work and skills of the runaway and condemnation of the motives that had driven such a valued and competent worker to seek his or her freedom.[27]

How slaves or servants communicated with their masters and mistresses spoke volumes about their abilities and their relationship with the men who owned their labor and even their bodies. The extensive powers masters enjoyed over the bodies of their slaves and servants had an enormous impact on these laborers, and confrontations or even normal day-to-day interactions between master and laborer could be a dangerous and frightening ordeal for the latter. In their runaway advertisements masters recorded a variety of effects, including stuttering and other speech defects, that occurred when their slave or servant was verbally "attacked," or subject to "sharp" questioning.[28] Isaac Stidham noted that when questioned twenty-four-year-old Sam "will frequently have one of his hands in his breeches." Nineteen-year-old Ned, "if attacked closely is apt to stammer in his answers," and twenty-eight-year-old Dick who ran with Ned "if attacked closely will stammer."[29] Such reactions appear to have been far less common among runaway white servants; they were not rooted in an inability to speak English, but rather in the power that white masters enjoyed over enslaved black bodies and the fear such power inspired. Dick's master, New Jerseyan Abraham Hunt, recorded that his slave bore "scars on his back, having been several times flogg'd at the whipping-post," rendering Dick's verbal confusion during encounters with whites all the more comprehensible.[30]

Some servants and slaves reacted rather differently to the power exercised by their masters, with verbal and physical actions that appeared to express resentment and anger. According to her owner James Allen, thirty-five-year-old Nancy was "somewhat addicted to spasmodic affections, upon sudden fits of anger"; Allen was clearly confused by these outbursts, lamenting that his slave "understands farmers kitchen work very well" and that she "was indulged with very good cloaths." He was unsure as to whether her fits were the result of a physical affliction, or her inability to shield the outpourings of resentment and rage that had presumably encouraged her to undertake the ultimate act of resistance by running away.[31] Other slaves had courageously risked punishment by "back talk," by which means they had expressed their own opinions and even dared to disagree with their masters.[32] Peter Jacquett clearly didn't believe anything that his slave Peter said, describing him as "a smooth tongued artful fellow, a noted liar, [and] a great villain," while the master of twenty-year-old Nancy angrily referred to her as "very artful, and of impudent speech."[33] For some slaves and servants, verbal proficiency provided a means of quite literally renegotiating the terms of their bondage, for smooth-tongued men and women could attempt to manipulate their masters and mistresses and talk their way out of trouble.

Alcohol played an important role here, and was mentioned in a good many runaway advertisements. Not only might liquor provide a temporary solace for the slave or indentured servant, but it might also loosen inhibitions and encourage otherwise obedient and even docile servants and slaves to articulate anger and resentment. Masters showed little interest in the detrimental effects that alcohol might have had on the health or even the work habits of their servants and slaves, but were concerned instead by they ways in which drink eroded the deferential pose of servile bodies.[34] Thus Cain was a skilled "currier and tanner by trade," who "understands all sorts of farming business," but his skills and hard work were undermined—according to his master—by the fact that he was "fond of strong drink, and very talkative and saucy when in liquor." Irish servant David Miles was "very quarrelsome when intoxicated," while his compatriot George Russell was "very talkative and abusive when in liquor." Similarly, indentured servant Reuben Loring was "rather impudent when intoxicated," and indentured iron worker John Collins was "peevish and quarrelsome when intoxicated."[35] Even sixteen-year-old John Clerk, an indentured servant in Princeton, New Jersey, was "very much given to drinking," and his master had seen him "groggy" and consequently "so rude as to throw his shoes through the window." There was, perhaps, more to this encounter than is revealed in the runaway advertisement, for two weeks later the young servant's father placed his own notice in the *Pennsylvania Gazette* protesting the innocence of "his injured Son."[36] Whatever the case, here and in numerous other instances, alcohol loosened the bonds of servitude by encouraging slaves and servants to articulate discontent and even anger, thereby raising their master's control of their bodies as an issue, and even challenging such control. Given that these men and women had then run away, the master's acknowledgment of prior instances of verbal resistance suggested a history of anger and resentment: though some men and women were prompted to run away by a specific incident, all were motivated by the longstanding subjection of their bodies to the authority of their masters.

Whites may well have enjoyed easier and more frequent access to alcohol than blacks, but the fact that significantly more white servants than black servants and slaves were prompted by alcohol to articulate their feelings suggests that black Americans were rather more skilled at concealing their true feelings, even when drunk. White masters judged their servants and slaves by the interactions they shared, and some black Americans were careful to reveal as little of themselves as possible in these interactions. Jeremy Black, the Delaware master of Ben, described his man as "an excellent ox waggoner," but apparently knew little more about him, recording that Ben was "not very talkative." This may well have been precisely what Ben wanted, and perhaps he was in fact willing and able to be far more talkative and sharing of himself when in company with others than his master's family. Similarly, when twenty-year-old James was apprehended as a suspected runaway by the Salem County jailer in New Jersey, the young black man was careful to keep to himself, giving jailer Jonas Smith little to insert in his advertisement beyond a description of clothing and the observation that he "laughs but seldom, talks but little, and appears to be very sulky."[37] If James was indeed a runaway, his best chance at avoiding identification by his master was to employ skills perfected by many slaves and servants—the ability to hide as much of their personality and their beliefs and attitudes as possible from the white men who held power over their bodies.

Written speech provided another avenue for expressions of power and resistance by black servants and slaves. Masters rarely mentioned the literacy of runaway white servants, except in the cases of European-born men and women—especially those from Germany, but also those from Ireland and Scotland—for whom literacy in a language other than their own was a notable fact. However, literacy among African Americans had very different connotations, both for the runaways and for their masters. It was extremely rare for a black woman runaway to be described as enjoying the ability to read and write, but well over 10 percent of the black men in this sample were recorded as partially or fully literate. In early national America, as education spread and became increasingly accessible to and valued by all manner of white Americans, black slaves were systematically denied literacy and the power that such skills conferred. Literacy and illiteracy thus functioned as bodily markers, with slaves, servants, and even free persons who were forced to live illiterate lives symbolically limited to the life of the body. In contrast, whites with access to literacy were free to transcend the body and enjoy the life of the mind.[38]

Runaway advertisements for literate black men were thus imbued with the suspicion of masters who knew that their servants and slaves had mastered a skill that enabled them to think, act, and live beyond the world of servility their status demanded. It was not simply that literate runaways were able to forge passes that might enable them to elude recapture. Rather, literacy represented an attempt to escape the world of the body and physical labor in which black slaves and many black servants were expected to spend their entire lives. Thus, after recording that his slave Damon "has been learning to read," Robert Goldsborough, Jr., described the runaway as "extremely artful . . . [and] capable of any fraud." Similarly, the fully literate mulatto slave Barney was "an artful fellow," while the "very active and ingenious" Cain was likely to "forge a pass."[39] It was rare for the master of a literate runaway black to omit such loaded accusations and descriptions, for the very act of literacy represented an assault on an American racial divide that elevated whites to the enlightened life of the mind while consigning blacks to the bestial work of the body.

Servants and slaves were defined and identified by their bodies, by the work these bodies could do and the ways such work marked them, but also by the ways they chose to present their bodies in interactions with other people. Given that white servants and black servants and slaves were kept and valued for their physical labor, it is hardly surprising that masters referred to them in much the same way that they might describe livestock, and runaway advertisements appeared alongside notices for the sale of cattle, horses, and other animals. Labor defined the bodies of runaways, and the work they did and the ways it shaped their bodies were often integral to the advertisements that described them. To her master, German-born Anna Louisa Moeller was "a strong thick girl," while Jesse James described his "Negro servant girl" Jude as "strong and well made," and Abraham Larue, Jr., commended Tobias as "a stout able Negroe man . . . well acquainted with all kinds of plantation work."[40] Runaways were often credited with a wide variety of skills and crafts, and even on occasion complimented for their skills. By thus acknowledging the abilities of their servants and slaves, masters were both affirming the servile status of men and women whose labor belonged to them, and also warning others of the skills a runaway might employ in his or her efforts to create a free and independent life.[41] As such, the master was recognizing the potential of the runaway to pass as free.

Runaway advertisements were often quite detailed and subtle in their descriptions of the ways slaves and servants presented their bodies during interactions with their masters. Posture was important, in that it spoke volumes about status and attitude. The gentleman—as a person of wealth, power, and influence—was expected to hold his body upright in a dignified manner, for "slumped shoulders and a hung head" were emblematic of servility.[42] However, while this meant that what elite men and women would have regarded as undignified bearing may have characterized the bodies of many poorer men and women on the streets of Philadelphia, a confident pose and stature did not necessarily mean that the person walking through the New Market was actually entitled to the freedom that he or she was enjoying: runaways knew better than most how the status of freedom or servility marked stature.

Such knowledge had profound effects on the ways servants and slaves held their bodies. Through kinesics—gestures, bodily movements, facial poses, and expressions—these men and women were able to communicate nonverbally, and masters were sufficiently aware of the import of such characteristics to note them in runaway advertisements.[43] Whether indentured servants and slaves appeared appropriately meek and respectful or were unbecomingly bold and assertive was readily apparent to their masters, who sought in runaway advertisements to convey these mannerisms and even the attitudes that underlay them.

The "down look," for example, referred to the ways servants and slaves would look down when communicating with their masters and mistresses, resolutely refusing to make eye contact. Masters were not always certain whether the "down look" communicated deferential respect and submission to or insolent disregard for their legitimate authority. For both whites and blacks, the "down look" may have been as respectful as it was secretive. Looking anyone in the eye, especially a superior, implicitly communicated trustworthiness, truthfulness, and sincerity. Moreover, such direct eye contact may also have indicated a presumption of equality by servants and slaves, a presumption that would not have been welcomed by their masters and mistresses. Thus by making eye contact with their masters, servants and slaves could both affirm and undermine the master-servant relationship.[44] On the other hand, masters were not slow to perceive the down look as a means by which true feelings could be hidden. Thus Ben had "a down look when attacked with guilt," while Joe's abilities as a skilled and capable house servant were undermined by his "propensity for running off," a kind of dissatisfaction and disobedience well hidden by his "down look when spoken to." Sambo, too, was noted for his "downish look," but his refusal to show his true feelings may well have been attributable to the fact that this boy had been separated from his mother in Philadelphia, to whose tender care he had presumably run. [45]

White servants, too, especially those from Ireland and Germany, were often recorded as avoiding eye contact and the communication it entailed. Irishmen Thomas Godwin and John Shae both shared the down look, as did the Germans Frederick Kabelmacher, who had "a pale and down look countenance," and Christian Van Phul, who hid behind "a down look whilst speaking to any person."[46] John Henderson, a nail-maker in Philadelphia's Third Street, gave a rather more complete and very evocative description of the down look of Alexander Anderson, a "round shouldered" boy "pretty much pitted with the smallpox." According to Henderson, young Anderson "has something of a condemned look with him, appearing afraid to look you in the face," and one senses on the part of the white servant either real fear or a heartfelt desire to keep his feelings to himself, or perhaps a combination of the two.[47]

What is perhaps most interesting about the 'down look' is that it appears to have been more gender than race specific.[48] Males runaways were far more likely to be described as having a "down look" than were female runaways. Perhaps this explicitly submissive stance was so common among laboring women, trained from birth to defer both to men and to their social superiors, that it was not considered worthy of note. This seems unlikely, however, given servants and slaves who eschewed the down look in favor of a more assertive and potentially aggressive stance included women as well as men. In some cases, it appears that a servant or slave knew the protective value of the down look, but on occasion could not prevent a show of bitterness, anger, or resentment. This may well have been the case with the "Irish servant lad" John Boyle, who—according to his master—"when spoken to appears bashful or dissident." Similarly contradictory was the description of John Christopher Gill, a

German-born cooper with "a surly down look."[49] Clearly Gill had failed
to hide behind a down look that communicated deferential submission
or hid anger and resentment, just as twenty-five-year-old Bob's "surly
countenance" undermined the mask of his down look.[50]

Others were less cautious and betrayed their true feelings in defiant
postures. William Tod described Primus as having "a very black and surly
countenance," explicitly linking his color with a rebellious disposition.[51]
Sixteen-year-old Catherine McCormack chose not to hide behind a submissive stance, and Jeremiah Barnard recorded this runaway servant as
having "a bold disposition," just as Joseph Ashton described runaway
Charlotte Page as having "a very forward countenance, and . . . a very
surly temper."[52] In such cases as these, masters appear less than surprised
that their servants or slaves had run away, since these men's and women's
bodies had long betrayed rebellious inclinations.

While runaway advertisements contained objective information about
sex, race, height, and age, and often detailed information about skills
and abilities, they also featured far more subjective descriptions and
analysis of the ways servants and slaves held themselves, moved, and
acted, and the tenor and style of their communication. By definition,
such descriptions were based on observations of interactions between
master and servant, and they were composed after the servant had rejected the legal authority of their master by running away. Thus owners
and masters sought to find clues in their recollection of the very bodies
of runaways, attempting to find hints of beliefs and attitudes that ex-
plained the actions of their property. In short, masters looked to the
bodies of their runaways for clues as to what was going on in their minds,
implicitly acknowledging the very thing that servitude attempted to
negate, namely, the existence of an independent mind and a spirit that
would be free. In recording Nancy as having been "very artful, and of
impudent speech and behaviour" her master presented her as an easily
identifiable rebel, while John Christian Huber was more confusing to
his master, for the German servant had appeared "a civil well behaved
fellow" yet had demonstrated that he was "averse to servitude" by running away.[53] While the nonverbal communication of servants and slaves
hinted at their thoughts, beliefs, and motivations, it also provided them
with a potential shield: masters were destined to spend many hours trying to decipher the bodies of their workers.

The ways the bodies of runaways were scarred, maimed, and otherwise
marked revealed much about their ancestral lives and work in servitude,
as did the ways they sought to fashion their physical selves. But the
human body can function as a canvas, a form and surface to be molded
and inscribed in a wide variety of ways.[54] As a result, whereas their sub-
jected status could be marked on their bodies, slaves and servants could

also seize some small measure of personal control by personalizing their bodily appearance. Yet again, the very appearance of the body could relay a tension between the body as property and the body as a free and independent entity.

In the case of African-born slaves, bodily markings might provide evidence of the cultural values and practices of their ancestral societies, and as such bear constant witness to lives of freedom that predated their servitude in North America. By the late eighteenth century, only a small number of blacks in the Middle Atlantic and the Upper South were African-born, making such markings rather more rare than they may have been fifty years earlier. For some West African men, ritual scars on the face signified their passage into manhood, marking their ascent to a particular role and status within their communities in the most vivid and permanent fashion.[55] Such scars might be placed on the forehead or the cheeks, and almost 10 percent of the black men in this sample were recorded as having scars in these areas, although often it is unclear whether these were African ritual markings or simply the result of an accident or injury. On occasion, however, the evidence is more clear, as in the case of William Liggins: "marked on each cheek, which appears to have been burnt in," Liggins's appearance caught the attention of James Ash, the sheriff of Philadelphia, who thought it more than likely that the man had run away from his master.[56] African markings were increasingly uncommon, and among legally free blacks they must have been all but unknown.

Far more common were the scars, injuries, and markings that were the result of hard labor in servitude, and which inscribed the bodies of many runaways.[57] The bodies—or the labor of bodies—belonged to masters who must have regarded such injuries as analogous to a broken plough or a maimed horse. As such, masters recorded the scars and effects of such injuries with dispassion, commonly regarding them as no more than identifying features. William Trainer, "born in this country of Irish parents," could readily be identified by "some red marks of burns by the smith's fire," just as the runaway forgeman John Collins had hands turned black and blue by his work.[58] The labor of these men had been owned by masters, and this labor had marked them as effectively as a brand or the lash.

In other cases, the cause of identifying injuries was less readily identifiable, although work was often the most likely cause. Nineteen-year-old black servant John Farmer was recorded as having "lost one joint from the finger of his left hand," quite possibly the result of a farming accident incurred as he worked for his master Amos Cooper in Gloucester County, New Jersey. John Peak, an English-born indentured servant, had also "lost one finger." Such an injury might easily have occurred during Peak's years of skilled work "at the blacksmith's business," or even during his more recent stint of agricultural labor on his master's farm. It was almost certainly work for his master, Samuel Westcott, that had marked the body of his eighteen-year-old slave for life: Cuff was described by Westcott as having run away with a limp in "his left leg, owing to a cut with an axe, which appears by a considerable scar in his ancle."[59] Female runaways were less likely to be scarred and maimed in quite this fashion, although their work, too, could mark their bodies. Thus, seventeen-year-old black Jude had "a scar on her arm, and a white mark on her face, occasioned by a scald," most likely the result of an accident in such domestic labor as cooking, washing, or soap-making.[60]

In some cases, the bodies of black slaves and servants had been permanently marked and deformed by masters who had displayed power and ownership over these black bodies in the most violent fashion.[61] However, in the aftermath of the American Revolution and with slavery gradually ending in Pennsylvania and other northern states and in question as far south as Virginia, owners seeking the return of black slaves and servants appear to have been increasingly reluctant to advertise the power and violence at their disposal and the ways it marked black bodies, perhaps sensing that such an approach might well promote more sympathy for the runaway than for the master. During the final two decades of the eighteenth century, readers of the *Pennsylvania Gazette* would only rarely have read of such runaways as Phil, who had escaped from his Virginia owner James Coleman bearing "the marks of the whip on his back," or the New Jersey runaway Dick, who also wore "scars on his back."[62] Even more unusual were such men as Dave, the mulatto slave of Henry Miller in Augusta County, Virginia: an easy escape was unlikely for Dave, since he was "branded on the forehead with the letter M." His owner's mark was seared into his flesh and was far more visible than the scars of the lash that might be covered by a shirt and jacket. Just as his violent master had hoped, Dave's only hope of escaping him and slavery was "to burn or cut out" the brand, further marking and damaging his own body to eliminate the stamp of slavery.[63]

If bodily markings might effectively brand a runaway while simultaneously displaying a struggle between owner and owned, so too might clothing identify a man or woman as the property of another, while yet allowing that individual to personalize his or her appearance, as well as giving the easiest means by which to finance escape. Lengthy and detailed descriptions of clothing were the most vital components of a great many runaway advertisements: in the absence of distinguishing marks and scars, or anything unusual about the body of the runaway, the clothing he or she wore was often the most distinctive feature.[64] Thus the advertisement for the runaway slave Sampson passed briefly over his height, stature, complexion, age, and smallpox scars before devoting four times as much space to the following description of his clothing:

Sampson . . . had on a new high crownded hat, maker's name in the crown Jacob Hollingshead, of Philadelphia, one coat, waistcoat and overalls, all new, made of elastic cloth, one white linen shirt, thread stockings, good shoes and steel buckles; he had with him a bundle of clothes, consisting of two ruffled shirts, one marked with the letters I.C. [the initials of his master, John Crapper] one pair of cotton stockings, marked I.C. one pair of black worsted, never wore, one pair of black velvet breeches, one red jacket, three white cravats, one black ditto, one linen handkerschief, marked A.D.C. one pair of children's stockings, one pair of white yarn stockings.[65]

Not surprisingly, masters tended to buy cheap and simple clothing for their slaves and servants, clothing similar to that worn by lower sort men and women and doled out by the almshouse authorities. Wealthy men and women could be identified not just by the quality of the fabric of their dress, but also by the cut, for their clothes were tailor made, carefully matched, and intended to fit closely to the body. In contrast, the clothes of the lower sort were loose and ill-fitting, often mismatched, and designed to allow freedom of movement to men and women who performed arduous physical labor. Wealthy men wore stylish but impractical close-fitting, waisted coats, with skirts dropping below their knees; working men wore loose-fitting coats, known as loose coats, frocks, great coats and surtouts. Bought off the peg, these coats had been manufactured from coarse fabrics in fairly drab shades of brown, cinnamon, gray, or blue. Beneath these coats, workingmen commonly wore hip-length, sleeveless jackets, again designed to allow ease of movement. Most common of all was the "sailor's jacket," a style of double-breasted jacket, thick and warm, and available in a variety of styles and colors. A hat, shirt, trousers, stockings, and shoes rounded out the workingmen's wardrobe: for many runaway men, these were the kinds of clothes provided by their masters, and what identified them was the amount, style, quality, color, and age of these garments. Women, too, shared a variety of clothing that identified them as workers, usually in a domestic setting. Many wore a cap or bonnet of some kind, a shift and petticoat, and one or more gowns, together with aprons, handkerchiefs, stockings and shoes. While male and female slaves from the rural South may have been dressed rather more poorly and in a somewhat different style, most of the runaway advertisements in the *Pennsylvania Gazette* describe men and women who were dressed in the common garb of the middle Atlantic working poor.[66]

While the clothing of workingmen and -women was all of a type, it could be personalized by the wearer in a variety of ways that made it potentially useful to masters seeking to identify their runaway slaves and servants. Owners might dole out clothing in a mixture of styles and colors, perhaps including their own, higher quality cast-offs: James Gunn, for example, recorded that the clothing worn by his twenty-four-year-old runaway black servant included "some old silk stockings marked I. Gunn."[67] Moreover, slaves and servants often sought to make their dress more distinctive and fashionable, perhaps making or buying additional items of clothing or dying and altering other clothes.

Black American slaves and servants, drawing on a different cultural tradition and aesthetic code, were not slow to mix clothing styles and colors in ways that set them apart from whites.[68] Thirty-two-year-old Phil, for example, not only assembled a variety of cast-off and other clothes, but then dyed some of them in vibrant colors. His master described Phil as wearing "a purple twilled home-made coat, very large for him, fulled and dyed in the family, and is spotted by dying, with large yellow gilt buttons, white twilled breeches, not fulled, a striped cotton waistcoat, two new oznabrig and one white shirt, a new scarlet waistcoat, new drab overalls, [and] his shoes have soals nailed on."[69]

Such an assemblage would have looked unusual to whites, and may have helped them to identify him, but Phil quite likely cut a dashing figure in the African American community. Moreover, as a man scarred by his master with "the marks of the whip on his back," Phil's attempt to take control of this aspect of his bodily appearance assumes even greater significance. The use that Phil and other black slaves and servants made of bright colors clearly built on African traditions, and on occasion African or African American clothing styles were noted in runaway advertisements. Thus twenty-four-year-old Silvie was described by her owner as having run away "dressed in the West India Creole manner," with a "handkerchief round her head" and "ear-bobs" dangling from her ears.[70] Dinah, too, was recorded as having "ears bored for wearing rings."[71] In an age when earrings were worn only by a few, chiefly male seafarers, these bodily adornments decorated black female bodies in a distinctive fashion. Clearly, what a slave or servant wore on his or her body could constitute both a statement of individuality and an assertion of membership in a black American community, both of which represented a very real form of independence from the complete control of their masters.

Runaway slaves and servants often took a great deal of clothing with them, clothing they might have accumulated over a period of years, which might be supplemented by better-quality items of apparel stolen from their masters. While a runaway might expect to need extra clothing for the long and hard road to freedom, many advertisements describe large and unwieldy amounts of clothing that were surely supplemental to the needs of the fugitive. Thus Sam, in addition to his new felt hat, "sailor made jacket," waistcoat, trousers, shirt, shoes, and stockings, took with him "a wallet full of clothes of sundry kinds," while Honour and Peggy Daley ran with "several changes of apparel," and indentured servant Christian Ludwick Burger took two coats, several jackets, two pairs of breeches, numerous shirts, and many other items.[72]

No doubt some runaways hoped that a large stock of clothing would allow them to mix and match items and thereby fashion disguises.[73] In most cases, however, this would have been a dangerous strategy. Masters were often able to describe all their slaves' and servants' clothing in great detail, especially when items had been purloined from the master's own wardrobe, and this would surely have rendered adequate disguise almost impossible. Moreover, masters were not slow to point out that they expected runaways to quickly change their dress to items unknown to their master, surely the most effective form of disguise. Consequently, lengthy and detailed descriptions of clothing often ended with such laments as "but may change his clothes" or "but it is likely he will change them."[74]

Rather than using the clothing they ran with for disguises, many runaways appear to have regarded these items as a readily negotiable form of currency, a strategy that built on a traditional early modern market in second-hand clothing. For centuries, members of the European and American lower sort had bought, sold, and exchanged clothing, and a large and elaborate trade in such items had rendered clothing a form of street currency. Whether they were seeking to improve their appearance or raise a little cash, men and women of the lower sort regularly bought and sold used clothes, and after food clothing was perhaps the most sought-after and easily disposable commodity of its age. For poor men and women who could ill afford even the most basic new clothing, let alone higher-quality items of style and color, second-hand clothes were the next best thing. Moreover, since clothing could be bought and sold with such ease, clothes and fabric were common targets for thieves: in seventeenth- and eighteenth-century England, clothing was stolen more often than anything else, and plenty of the inmates of the Walnut Street Jail had been incarcerated for stealing or receiving stolen clothes. This trade in second-hand clothing was tremendously important to runaway servants and slaves, who sold the clothes given to them by or stolen from their masters, or exchanged them for other clothes. By this means, runaways were able to change their appearance and gain some ready cash, two strategies guaranteed to improve their chances of evading capture.[75]

However, while runaways may have adopted a very utilitarian approach to clothing, it is also likely that for some the ways in which they dressed and fashioned themselves were important bodily expressions of independence that predated and perhaps encouraged their running away. As such, individual style may have been tremendously important to these men and women, and it could have transcended the actual items of apparel that they took with them, and then perhaps bought and sold. While members of the lower sort struggled to feed, clothe, and shelter themselves and their families, some indentured servants and slaves—for all their lack of freedom—may have been able to spend time and what little cash they had to improve their self-presentation.[76] Dress allows one to project a carefully constructed image of oneself, transforming one's very body into a commodity for the display of coveted items and fashionable styles. People who were not servants and slaves outfitted themselves according to what they could afford, their tastes and preferences, and the norms for their region, their work, and so forth, in a manner expressive of "normality." It seems clear, however, that some servants and slaves self-consciously fashioned their clothing and appearance against mainstream culture; in this context, style may effectively function to communicate a visible subculture that stands in opposition to the mainstream culture of those who owned servants and slaves.[77]

A great many runaways were in their late teens or twenties, and the large majority (including almost all white indentured servants) were unmarried. Thus, although dependent on their masters for clothing, servants and slaves were of an age when style, fashion, and self-presentation may have been of considerable significance, and they used whatever opportunities they had to accumulate fashionable clothes.[78] Particularly stylish were men and women like twenty-six-year-old Christian Henry Malchowff, who according to his Philadelphia master "generally looks neat and makes a good appearance." Twenty-year-old Dinah, "a large comely person," wore earrings, and the clothes she took with her included "a large good muslin petticoat," a long-sleeved and ornately buttoned calico gown, a chintz jacket "bound with black," a blue and white striped gown, "a new chip hat," and a pair of leather shoes "with pewter buckles." Irish servant James Duffy, also twenty years old, was equally well dressed, sporting "a new brown coat, with carved silver washed buttons, a blue waistcoat with large buttons, a new round wool hat with silk loops, a light cloth jacket with sleeves and large buttons, striped tow trowsers, blue woolen stocking lately footed, strong shoes half worn, with yellow metal buckles, a pair of old buckskin breeches, and five new shirts."[79] On the other hand, servants like sixteen-year-old Catherine McCormack may have resented the fact that her master forced her to wear "a white shirting short gown, patched under the arms," an "old pair" of wooden heeled shoes, and other such unfashionable items, while Daniel Kennely cannot have enjoyed a vest that was "for him too slack," stockings that were too big, and other clothes that his master admitted "were not very new."[80] Masters faced a quandary when it came to clothing their slaves and servants:

providing good clothes gave men and women materials that could be exchanged or sold to aid escape, while shabbily dressed bondspeople may have been dissatisfied and provoked to seek better fortune elsewhere.

High-quality, fashionable clothing may have helped servants and slaves to carve out a time and space separate from that which belonged to their masters.[81] Francis Dunne was a twenty-five-year-old indentured servant in Philadelphia who according to his master "pretends to be some sort of preacher." Along with his "every day dress" Dunne ran away with his "Sunday cloaths," which included a large cocked hat, a dark blue overcoat, an olive-colored close-fitting coat and matching waist-coat of a style worn by more elite Philadelphians, black velvet and satin breeches, leather shoes with silver buckles, cravats, stylish handkerchiefs, and a variety of other items.[82] While the bodies of runaways were owned, marked, and defined by their masters, clothing allowed these slaves and servants a means by which they could redefine and repossess themselves. These were people who owned neither their labor nor their bodies nor even many of the clothes they wore, yet by fashioning an image for themselves they were able to feel and even appear somewhat independent. Thus clothing allowed these men and women to project assertive and subversive messages of individuality and bodily pride.[83]

For black Americans, not only clothing but also hair style furnished a highly personal and very visible means by which they might contest the hegemonic rule masters enjoyed over their bodies. References to and descriptions of the distinctive appearance of their hair marked many of the advertisements for runaway black servants and slaves.[84] In some West African cultures, the grooming and styling of hair had long been important social rituals, and white descriptions of runaways indicate that African Americans continued to style their hair in inventive and distinctive ways, affirming both individual identity and membership in a social group that transcended the power their master enjoyed over their bodies.[85] White masters were certainly aware of such practices and sometimes made note of them in runaway advertisements, as when Dinah's owner recorded that she had "long hair, which she dresses with great attention."[86]

However, while white Americans noted the care with which black Americans styled their hair, they sometimes had difficulty in adequately describing techniques for the presentation of a kind of hair that they derisorily dismissed as "wool."[87] Styles varied widely: some black men and women wore their hair long and bushy on top, while others cut short or shaved the back, front, or sides of their head. Alternatively, men like Dick, who had "a bunch of bushy hair behind, and had his fore top lately cut off," either cut short or shaved their crown while allowing hair to grow long at the sides and back.[88] Others combed and parted their hair, while some like John Johnson displayed "a high forehead, and hair combed back," combing their long hair directly up and away from their foreheads.[89] A few emulated contemporary white styles: Sam "had his hair tied" in a queue, and Mark appeared "very remarkable for the care which he takes in dressing and queuing his hair."[90] Perhaps others cared for their hair but did not style it, perferring to appear to whites as simply "black," thereby achieving an anonymity that must have served runaways well. For all black Americans, however, hair was as visible and tangible a measure of race and power as skin color, and especially for men and women who did not own their bodies, the styling of that hair might well assume no small significance. More than simply artistic expression, black hair styles defied the conventions of white society, exaggerating and even celebrating a sense of difference.[91]

The large majority of runaway advertisements were written by people who owned servants and slaves, and as such they reveal a great deal about their expectations of how servile bodies appeared and acted. Stature and gesture, the ways in which a man or woman spoke, the manner in which they communicated with social superiors, and the marks and clothing on their bodies might all reveal servile status, and masters were not slow to condemn runaways who had thought, acted, and dressed above their station. Such clear expectations of deferential civility made it possible for some runaways to pass as free by abandoning the bodily attributes and expressions of slaves and servants and adopting the proud and independent stance of free men and women. Others, cowed by years of submission to owners and masters, must have found such an act difficult, and their nervous stammering and overall appearance may well have betrayed them.

Yet while runaway advertisements articulated the beliefs and attitudes of masters, they also disclosed a great deal of information about the ways slaves and servants contested the control exercised by these masters. In their pride in names other than those used by masters, their willingness to argue against and even challenge their masters (especially when emboldened by alcohol), their "bold" and "surly" aspects, and their distinctive clothing styles, servants and slaves challenged the control over their bodies exercised by the masters who legally owned them. More than anything else, these runaway advertisements reveal a balancing act, a finely nuanced process of negotiation between masters and owned, with the bodies of these laboring men and women as the subject. Year in and year out, owner and owned had struggled to maintain control over these bodies. Philadelphia was home to many lower sort men and women who had sought to win this struggle once and for all, by running away and thus seizing and winning control of their own bodies.

Chapter 5
Seafaring Bodies

It was George Ribble's body that marked him as a man of the sea, the way he moved, his scars and tattoos, and the clothes he wore. As he walked through Philadelphia early in President Thomas Jefferson's second term, Ribble displayed the rolling gait of the man who spent as much time aboard ships as he did on land, and he wore the clothes of the seafarer, short working garments made distinctive by the use of oil and tar as weatherproofing. Ribble was almost two inches shorter than the average native-born adult white man, and the twenty-three-year-old had already been scarred by his work at sea. But more than anything it was this man's tattoos that identified him as a sailor and revealed something about his life, for they showed Ribble seizing control of his body and image in a manner unique to seafarers, writing his own stories and values on his very skin. Seafarers were the only white Americans to wear these emblems: the anchor emblazoned on his right hand emphasized Ribble's pride in his craft, the cross on his left hand indicated his religious convictions, and the spread eagle on his right arm celebrated the patriotism of a man born in Philadelphia during the final year of the War for Independence, a man who resented and perhaps even hated Great Britain and the Royal Navy for its continued impressment of American sailors like himself. Ribble most likely spent months and even years away from Philadelphia, yet his connections with the city remained strong, and on his left arm he wore a tattooed heart containing the initials of his young, illiterate partner, Mary Shippen.[1]

In early national Philadelphia, sailors were the lower sort's single largest occupational group and also its most easily recognizable. As they gathered in and around waterfront taverns, grog shops, and residences, their distinctive rolling gait, their tarred short jackets and trousers, their weathered complexions, and their unique songs, dances, jargon, and curses all marked them as men who worked at sea. Although many spent no more than a small portion of their adult lives as sailors, others formed a core of more professional, long-term sailors, and again it was their bodies that revealed them as such.[2] Tattooed arms and hands, scars and other injuries, a high incidence of disease and significantly shorter than average stature—together comprising what Herman Melville described as the "wens and knobs and distortions of the bark"—marked many of them as men who spent most of their adult lives at sea.[3]

Seafarers were the men whose labor made possible the trade and commerce upon which early national America depended. They were engaged in one of the hardest, most dangerous, and poorest paid of professions, and often historians have found it difficult to learn about the before-the-mast long-term seamen who were at the heart of the maritime community, for when they appear in such records as tax lists and militia rolls, it is all but impossible to differentiate them from short-term sailors. The relatively small number of professional seafarers, who worked at sea for longer than more casual sailors, had a place within and an impact upon the seafaring community out of all proportion to their numbers, as demonstrated by Table 7.

Figure 11. William Birch, Arch Street Ferry, Philadelphia, 1800. Courtesy of the Library Company of Philadelphia. This engraving shows the waterfront in the area between Philadelphia and the Northern Liberties. The bodies of the working poor, especially seafarers—far and away the single largest group of working men in the city—are presented in a sanitized form, with no sense of the condition of men whose bodies had been shaped and sometimes broken by work at sea, or of their lives among families and friends on or near the waterfront.

Thus, despite the fact that only 10 percent of these sailors served more than ten years at sea, these long-term seafarers accounted for as much as 37 percent of the total number of years served by all one thousand men in this example.

The bodies of professional mariners formed an alternative record that proclaimed their occupation and revealed a great deal about their backgrounds, experiences, attitudes, beliefs, and values. Like those of black slaves, the bodies of professional sailors were molded, scarred, and marked by their work in distinctive ways, yet at the same time these men sought to exercise some measure of control over their lives and bodies. With tattoos, a unique jargon and mode of expression, distinctive clothing, and their own culture of song, dance, and artistic expression, seafarers adorned and presented themselves as members of a self-consciously constructed subculture, standing on the margins of a larger culture and society that was completely dependent on seafaring labor.[4] Other urban workers sometimes sought to emulate the dress, style, and bearing of the elite, but seafarers appear to have reveled in their lowly work and status, using their bodies to proclaim membership in a fraternity of skilled seafarers. While it was true that the bodies of professional seafarers were shaped, bent, and broken by the rigors of life and work at sea, it is also true that such men took pride in their lives and work, a pride shown by their very bodies.[5]

The stories told by seafarers' bodies are found in a unique set of documents. In 1796, Congress passed "An Act for the relief and protection of American Seamen" in an attempt to protect American seafarers from impressment into the British Royal Navy.[6] The law entitled mariners who were American citizens and who paid a fee of twenty-five cents to receive "certificates of citizenship," a vocationally specific form of passport.[7] Completed on preprinted forms by public officials such as aldermen, notaries, and justices of the peace, each application for a "protection" was signed by the seafarer and witnessed by a friend or relative. The simple form documented the seaman's name, age, birthplace (or the date and place of his naturalization), race, height, literacy (as reflected in

TABLE 7. Length of Service at Sea

Years at sea	Sailors	Total years at sea
1–3	500	500–1,500
3–5	250	750–1,250
5–10	150	750–1,500
10–25	100	1,000–2,500

These are hypothetical statistics, designed to show the disproportionate significance of the relatively small number of professional seafarers.

the applicant's ability to sign his name), scars, injuries, marks of disease, and any tattoos on his body. Although many of these applications have been lost, 9,761 of the roughly 26,000 filed in Philadelphia between 1796 and 1819 are extant.[8] Long-term sailors were virtually the only white Americans of their era to wear tattoos, and 979 (10 percent) of the applicants were tattooed.[9] During the War of 1812, no more than eleven of the diverse group of almost 2,000 American soldiers held captive by the British were tattooed, and it seems likely that these men were or had been sailors. By contrast, hundreds of the American seafarers imprisoned in England during that war bore tattoos.[10]

Tattoos marked the men who made a career out of the sea, rather than occasional and short-term sailors. While their stature and illiteracy tell us of their lowly origins, and their scars, injuries, and marks of disease record the dangers of their occupations, it was the words and images engraved on their skin that reveal most about the beliefs and values with which they met their harsh circumstances. Some of the 979 surviving applications of tattooed seafarers are incomplete, containing little or no

Figure 12. William Birch, The City and Port of Philadelphia on the River Delaware from Kensington, 1800. Courtesy of the Library Company of Philadelphia. This illustration shows the waterfront where many lower sort Philadelphians were employed.

information about height, age, birthplace, or tattoos, and the following analysis is based upon the 500 fairly complete applications of sailors with tattoos filed between 1798 and 1816. These records reveal the bodies, and the stories they tell, of long-term sailors, for tattoos were among the visible indicators of long service at sea, and tattooing took place not on land but during extended ocean voyages.[11] A "pricker" used Indian or Chinese ink or prepared a dye from whatever materials were available, sometimes even urine and gunpowder. He bound several sharp needles together, dipped them into the ink, stretched the sailor's skin tightly, and then repeatedly pricked the needles through the epidermis so as to deposit the ink in the dermis.[12] This was a slow process: even a simple design might require several sessions, as pain and swelling made it impossible for the tattooist to keep working very long. Tattooing was dangerous; even today, men and women tattooed in a similar fashion risk infection, gangrene, tetanus, and lymphadenitis.[13]

Given the pain and peril, sailors were unlikely to mark their bodies with one or more tattoos unless they identified themselves and were willing to be identified by others as men who saw seafaring as a defining attribute of their lives. These 500 men had some 1,329 tattoos among them, almost 92 percent of which were inscribed on the hands and arms, allowing these marks to function as deliberately visible vocational badges. Since sailors were unlikely to accumulate slowly and pinfully acquired tattoos in quick succession, multiple tattoos strongly suggested long periods spent at sea.

The tattooed dates borne by thirty-five (7 percent) of these mariners provide further evidence that these men were long-term sailors. An average of nine years passed between the date tattooed on their bodies and the date on which they applied for a protection; for a few men such as William Story and Jacob McKinsey over twenty years elapsed.[14] While the applications fail to reveal the significance of tattooed dates, a roughly contemporary source suggests that seafarers employed them to register important dates in their lives. Thomas Ellison, one of the mutinous crew of H.M.S. *Bounty*, was recorded by Captain William Bligh as having the date "25 October 1788" tattooed on his right arm; Bligh recalled this as the date on which the *Bounty*'s crew first saw Tahiti.[15]

Tattoos, then, served to mark the bodies of many long-term seafarers. They were emblems of trade, experience, and proficiency, and they rendered the bearer instantly recognizable as a member of a proud and experienced cadre of professional sailors.[16] However, while tattoos were one of the most readily identifiable markers of men of the sea, the other material recorded on their applications for protection certificates reveals a great deal more about the bodies of the professional seafarers so prevalent in early national Philadelphia. The ages of all 500 men were recorded on their applications, and they ranged from thirteen to fifty-nine. Some 54 (10 percent) were in their teens, 355 (71 percent) in their twenties, and the remaining 91 (18 percent) between 30 and 59. Most were American-born; 486 recorded that they were born in the United States (including, after 1803, Louisiana). About one-tenth were New Englanders, another one-fifth were Southerners; the great majority hailed from the middle Atlantic region. Only two applications failed to record a place of birth; twelve were those of foreign-born seafarers who had produced naturalization papers to prove American citizenship.[17] Although the nation was overwhelmingly rural, over one-half of the native-born men had been born in urban areas, and other evidence contained in their applications for protections suggests that many had roots in the rapidly expanding urban underclass.[18]

These applications reveal that very few black Americans wore tattoos. Only 3 percent (15) of the 500 tattooed seafarers were black, all of them native-born—a surprise, perhaps, in view of the fact that 17 percent of the 9,761 sailors whose applications survive were black.[19] Other sources confirm that a good many African Americans, faced with limited opportunities, prejudice, and poverty on land, sought employment in the more egalitarian work of seafaring. By the early nineteenth century, as many as 22 percent of the men who sailed from Philadelphia were black, as were almost 20 percent of the American sailors imprisoned at Dartmoor, Chatham, and Portsmouth during the War of 1812.[20]

The most likely reason for the small number of black men bearing tattoos is that the blue or black inks used to create tattoos did not show up well on darker skin, giving blacks less reason to endure the pain and the risk of tattooing. Moreover, surviving African traditions of scarification may have been more familiar to black Americans than tattoos. However, while tattoos served as perhaps the most recognizable badge of long-term sailors, this does not mean that black Americans were not or were not regarded as being members of this fraternity. As W. Jeffrey Bolster has argued, tattoos "spoke to an occupational identity not dependent on race."[21] A good number of the non-tattooed blacks who applied for protections may have been long-term mariners, but given that tattoos provide some of the best evidence of lengthy service at sea, this study furnishes a far more complete picture of white seamen than of their black shipmates.[22]

Long-term seafarers were significantly shorter than other American men, a telling indication of the straitened circumstances of their upbringing. The protection certificate applications recorded the heights of 463 of the 485 white mariners, and all 15 of the blacks.[23] While genetics play the most important role in determining how tall a person grows, height can also be strongly affected by material circumstances.

Children raised in prosperous homes are more likely to achieve optimum height than children raised with insufficient nutrition in the stressful environment of an impoverished household. The result is a statistically significant difference in adult height between members of these two groups.[24]

Only 6 of the 15 black seafarers were old enough to have reached their full stature when they applied for protections; their average height was 65.7 inches.[25] Some 217 of the 471 native-born white mariners had achieved full adult height, and with a mean height of 66.4 inches they stood noticeably taller than these black shipmates, although the small number of black sailors does not allow for meaningful comparisons. White mariners were on average a striking 1.7 inches shorter than white male recruits to the Continental Army.[26] According to scholars who have analyzed their heights, the soldiers of the Continental Army were fairly representative of the native-born white male population as a whole, and their tall stature supports the conclusion that late eighteenth-century native-born white male Americans were generally far healthier, and consequently significantly taller, than their European counterparts.[27] The very substantial difference in heights between soldiers and seafarers indicates that the latter tended to come from the lower sort. Historians have demonstrated the ubiquity of multigenerational poverty in cities such as Philadelphia, and these applications provide compelling evidence that urban-born professional seafarers were drawn from the ranks of the poor.[28] Even those born in healthier rural areas may well have belonged to poor families that had migrated to urban centers and ended up in unhealthy areas such as Philadelphia's teeming Northern Liberties or Southwark.

The fact that many of the 500 seafarers were barely able to read and write strengthens the impression that they were of very low social status. Of the 486 white or black sailors who were recorded as native-born, 480 left some evidence of their literacy or lack thereof: 184 were unable to sign their names, and 207 were barely able to write their own names, making a total of 391 (80 percent) who were at best barely literate. In 88 cases, both the seaman and his witness were unable to sign their names.[29] On the whole, these professional mariners were far less literate than their countrymen who worked on land. Among native-born recruits serving in the army during this period, only 35 percent of those who had been craftsmen, 46 percent of those from the countryside, and 54 percent of those who had been laborers were illiterate or barely literate.[30]

Basic literacy was slightly more common among the rural-born sailors: 133 (60 percent) of those born in urban environments and 166 (70 percent) of those born in the countryside were able to sign their names.[31] The increasing concentration of population in late eighteenth-century urban environments spurred a republican drive for improved public education in the nation's towns and cities, but these improvements had not yet touched many impoverished urban-born seafarers. Given that it was not unusual for boys to learn to read but not to write, it is quite possible that many of these men were able to read on an elementary level, yet it remains clear that most long-term seamen were far less than fully literate. One who was, Samuel Leech, recorded in his autobiography that he was constantly employed "as a sort of scribe" by his illiterate shipmates.[32]

Just as illiteracy signified the lowly social standing of many of these men, their long years of arduous work at sea had scarred and maimed their bodies in quite distinctive ways. Long-term sailors faced years of labor in the sun and salt air, disease in foreign ports, backbreaking work, inadequate provisions, low wages, piracy, and impressment, all of which placed their bodies in stark contrast with the pale and soft-skinned countenances of the well-to-do.[33] Salem minister William Bentley was all too aware of the potentially deadly nature of seafaring life; he let hardly a day pass without prayers for a "Brother at Sea," a "fr[iend] at sea," or a "husband and friends at Sea"; grateful prayers of "thanks for the safe return of a Son from Sea" were altogether less frequent.[34]

Their arduous work and dangerous life left a literal mark on the bodies of professional seafarers, for 434 (86 percent) were scarred or disfigured.[35] The most common injuries were to the extremities. Broken or missing fingers, scarred or broken hands, wrists, arms, and elbows, and injuries to the legs, knees, feet, and toes were commonplace. Peter Hanse, a twenty-two-year-old seaman from New York City, had "crooked" or broken fingers on both hands and a large scar on his right shin, and Lawrence Hanson suffered from a common affliction among seamen, scarred or broken kneecaps.[36]

Injuries to the head and torso were far from rare. The head of William Travis of Maryland had been badly scarred by a "Craw Barr"; New Yorker Robert Andrews had a long scar on his left breast and an ear badly damaged by frostbite.[37] Other seamen were partially blind or had lost an eye, and several bore physical reminders of violent conflict, such as the scar on John Parker's left thigh caused "by the Cut of a Cutlass" and the "scar occasioned by a Musket Ball" on John Fullerton's right thigh.[38] Sailors who were too severely injured to continue working found themselves in hospitals or almshouses: such was the fate of Thomas Pain, who was lame, John Richards, who broke his thigh falling from the mast, Thomas Smith, whose feet were "mashed," and John Seaburn, who "broke his scull" in a fall from the rigging.[39]

None of the 500 applications mention scars caused by a whip. Given how full these documents are, this silence may indicate that very few American seafarers were lashed. It is also possible some of the white seafarers bore whip marks on their backs but that to have this recorded on a protection certificate might have suggested to a British officer that the bearer had seen service in the brutal British navy and was thus a Briton to be impressed. Similarly, some of the fifteen African Americans may have been scarred by the lash, but by choosing not to reveal these marks they were able to hide the wounds of slavery and lessen the possibility of reenslavement.

The incidence of contagious disease was far higher among seafarers than among the population as a whole, for every voyage exposed them to disease in foreign ports, and each arriving ship could bring another disease or a new strain into the maritime community. Disease marked their skins: the faces of close to one-fifth (85) had been ravaged by small-pox, a higher incidence than in the disease-ridden city of London.[40] Genteel Americans were constructing new standards of physical beauty, separating themselves from their forebears and their poor contemporaries by means of improved diet and inoculation against smallpox. But poverty and fear prevented many sailors from protecting themselves against smallpox. The procedure was expensive and required a quarantine of as long as two weeks, which workingmen and their families could ill afford. Consequently, inoculation scars were recorded on only seven of the 500 applications.[41] The urban poor suffered greatly from diseases such as smallpox and yellow fever, and often they resisted inoculation as a deadly innovation.[42]

The Reverend Nicholas Collin's detailed burial records confirm the dangers of disease for seamen. His parish, located close to the center of Philadelphia's ship-building district, was home to many mariners and their families; during his long tenure, Collin recorded deaths from a wide variety of diseases and disorders including smallpox, consumption, yellow fever, cholera, dropsy, pleurisy, hives, whooping cough, measles, bilious fever, distemper, dysentery, and apoplexy. He noted that Philadelphia sailor Thomas Dawson was only twenty-five when he fell ill and died in 1803 shortly after returning from a voyage to Canton, and his townsman John Stubbe was only twenty-six when he and several of his shipmates contracted "a mortal fever" in Wilmington, North Carolina.[43] Over 60 percent of the seafarers who died in Collin's parish were less than thirty years old; those who survived often had little choice but to display a disease-scarred visage that compounded other bodily evidence suggesting mean social origins and lowly profession.[44]

In fact it was disease and illness, far more than accidents and injuries, that marked the bodies of professional sailors. Among two hundred seafarers admitted to the Pennsylvania Hospital between August 1800 and November 1803, only sixteen (8 percent) were hospitalized for such injuries as "a Wound on his Foot," "a Fractured Leg," or a "Contusion of the head & fractured thigh."[45] Far more common were sailors suffering from a variety of diseases and illnesses including sore legs, inflamed eyes, consumption, pleurisy, a variety of fevers, and insanity. By far the most common complaint was venereal disease, which had laid low 55 (27 percent) of the hospitalized sailors, closely followed by 48 (24 percent) who were laid low by rheumatism, a broad and general category of complaint that could refer to any incapacitating pain in or inflammation of the joints and muscles. In different ways, both complaints revealed a great deal about the life of the long-term sailor. The former suggests the recreational nature of sex for sailors who had spent weeks or even months at sea, especially those who were unable or unwilling to form lasting monogamous relationships and who sought comfort and pleasure in port communities all around the Atlantic rim. The latter reveals something of the conditions of work at sea, and the ways mal- or undernourished bodies might falter after prolonged arduous work in cold and damp conditions.

In such chanteys as "Spanking Jack," sailors highlighted yet made light of the dangers of their profession. In this song the seafarers Spanking Jack, Bonny Ben, and Whiffing Tom are killed respectively by being washed overboard, attacked by a shark, and shot during an engagement with an attacking ship. Yet the rhythm and lyrics are upbeat, joyful, and proud. In such songs, seafarers celebrated their membership in a highly skilled and exclusive fraternity, and a working life in which they could be "manly and honest, good natur'd and free," and find brothers "Fond as pitch, honest, hearty, and true to the core."[46]

The tattoos of long-term seafarers provide far richer and more nuanced examples of the nature and significance of this professional pride and sense of separateness from the society and culture of men on land, yet at the same time they complicate this image by revealing something of a professional seafaring culture and *mentalité* that thrived on strong links with people and institutions on land. While their short stature, general illiteracy, scars and injuries, and marks of disease all furnish a strong impression of the poverty and harsh lives of professional seafarers, such circumstances did not mean that these men lacked strongly held beliefs, values, or pride. Their tattoos enabled them to articulate everything from religious faith to political principles to loving relationships, and we can employ the designs to learn more about the *mentalité* of those who worked at sea (Table 8). What is perhaps most surprising is that many of their tattoos reflected the deep-rooted and abiding significance of long-term seafarers' connections with people and life ashore.

Many of the men wore images that identified their profession and the work at which their bodies labored, for close to 22 percent of these tattoos were of such objects as ships, fish, the North Star, mermaids, or fouled anchors.[47] Hailing from New York City, William Gaines wore tattoos of "a brig [and] a foul Anchor" on his left arm, while William Adams and Thomas Milburn of Philadelphia had mermaids tattooed upon their hands and arms.[48] George Robinson of Maryland had "a star pricht near his left thumb"; fifty-nine-year-old John Williams bore "a fish on his left arm."[49] A long-term seafarer who wore a tattooed anchor trusted that this familiar symbol of hope would aid him in his hard and dangerous occupation. On another level these and other less talismanic representations of fish, ships, mermaids, and so forth—all of which were traditional and relatively common images within the seafaring community—suggest that these men took some pride in their profession, a pride that they proclaimed on their hands and arms. A good many early national Americans wore clothes, badges, and emblems that advertised their walk of life; with tattoos in general and maritime tattoos in particular, seafarers did much the same thing.[50]

The smallest category of tattoos displayed a similar pride in professional membership, while simultaneously proclaiming allegiance to an institution on land: five of the sailors in this sample wore tattoos of Masonic emblems. Particularly vivid were the tattoos of thirty-year-old James Henry of Philadelphia, who had "a Compass & Square, a Ladder, an hour Glass, and five points of fellow Ship, [and] the all seeing Eye" tattooed on his left arm, while twenty-eight-year-old William Watson was tattooed with a "Compass & Square, Ladder . . . Masonic arch, square & compass."[51] John Berry and James Henry went so far as to have their lodge numbers inscribed on their bodies.[52] Such images suggest that these men were no longer common sailors. Some of the men who made a career out of seafaring eventually acquired higher status as masters, mates, and supercargoes.[53] None of the 500 applications in this sample

TABLE 8. Subjects of Seafarers' Tattoos

	Number of tattoos	Percent
Maritime images	262	22
Sailor's name or initials	240	20
Name or initials of another	197	16.5
Religious images	110	9
Love and loved ones	89	7.5
Patriotic and political images	71	6
People, flowers, other images	66	5.5
Dates	33	3
Masonic images	13	1
Miscellaneous	111	9.5

Source: 500 Seamen's Protection Certificate Applications detailing tattoos, 1798–1816, Record Group 36, Records of the Bureau of Customs, National Archives.

make any mention of higher rank or status, and almost all these men appear to have toiled before the mast, but it is possible that these five seafarers had risen to higher rank and status, both on board ship and ashore, and had joined the Masons. While it is true that in the aftermath of the American Revolution, Freemasonry had become significantly more accessible to a broad crosssection of urban white males, the institution remained all but inaccessible to ordinary mariners. Only sailors of higher rank could have availed themselves of the opportunity to join this organization of skilled and relatively well-paid professionals and craftsmen.[54] By the mid-1780s, the cost of membership in Philadelphia lodges ran as high as $30—as much as a month's salary for a common seafarer or laborer—and most Masons hailed from the professional ranks of merchants, manufacturers, storekeepers, or skilled craftsmen.[55] With an average age of twenty-eight, the five sailors who wore Masonic tattoos were generally several years older than the seafarers in this sample, which suggests that these men had spent even longer at sea and that they might well have risen in rank and status to the point where they were able to join a Masonic lodge. The tension between the fact that these seafarers valued their membership in a society of men who lived and worked on land, while yet celebrating it with tattoos that marked them as men who worked the seas for a living, is a tension suggested by many of the tattoos worn by professional sailors generally.

The large number (21 percent) of tattoos that featured the name or initials of the bearer could function as proud assertions of personal identity within the seafaring profession, or as the means of ensuring correct identification should the sailor die away from home. John Fenton of New York City was one of the many sailors whose initials were tattooed on one of his arms, while others such as Francis Montfort had their full names recorded on their bodies.[56] Tattoos of initials or names furnished tangible evidence that the bearer was the seafarer named on the protection he carried; more significantly, perhaps, they showed the mariner acknowledging and making provision for the possibility that he might die at sea or in a distant land. Jeremy Bentham recorded that it was "a common usage among English sailors to trace their family and baptismal name upon the wrist, in distinct and indelible character . . . that they may be recognized in case of shipwreck."[57] Even in death, the seafarer marked with his own name had taken symbolic control of his own body's destiny. Tattoos that identified a mariner allowed him to hope that he might receive a Christian burial and grave should he die in foreign parts and that news of his death might reach loved ones at home. When Joseph Shourds of Tuckertown, New Jersey, applied for a "protection" in 1807, Justice Richard Palmer recorded that Shourds's initials were inscribed on his left hand and right arm, along with "his name in full length . . . done with Indian Ink." The initials R.R. appeared next to Shourds's initials on his right arm, while the initials R.S. were inscribed on his left hand, perhaps the initials of his companion before and after she married him. Should the twenty-five-year-old seaman have died away from her, his tattoo might have helped to save him from an entirely anonymous fate, and word of his demise might have reached loved ones.[58]

Like Shourds's a total of 197 (16 percent) of the tattoos were of the names or initials of other people. Both arms of Christopher Fenner, for example, bore the name "Elizabeth Deleur," while the right arm of John Peters of Philadelphia was tattooed with the name "Rachel Peters."[59] John Peters was literate, but Rachel may not have been, and during his long months at sea communication between them and thousands of similar couples was all but impossible. For men like Peters and John Hancurne of Charleston, on whose left arm the name "Ann Jackson" appeared over two interlocked hearts, the name or initials of loved ones indelibly inscribed on their skin served as a comforting reminder—perhaps the only tangible reminder—of a distant companion.[60] Philadelphia-born William Lane wore the same image on both his right shoulder and his right arm, a heart pierced by arrows and surmounted by the initials E.S., while Virginian Charles Davis had on his right arm "a double heart" containing the initials C.D. and P.M.[61] Some 89 (7 percent) of the tattoos of the 500 sailors directly addressed love and loved ones. Such images may well have meant a good deal to men who spent long periods at sea out of touch with the people they loved. In the absence of pictures and letters, tattoos of the initials or names of a partner, often accompanied by a heart pierced by "darts," affirmed and celebrated loving relationships. Simple hearts were the most common symbols of love: far more unusual were such images as the "Bleeding Heart" worn by John Slater of Delaware, which may have symbolized a lost love.[62]

Margaret Creighton has argued that by the mid-nineteenth century American sailors, "in distancing themselves from female relatives and women's work, sought to protect and enhance distinct masculine identities." Older sailors, according to Creighton, ridiculed green hands for their sentimental attachments to women on shore; acceptance "in the forecastle was contingent upon the shift of allegiance from home to ship."[63] While such attitudes may well have become common in the merchant marine of the mid-nineteenth century, in the early American republic virtue and sentimentality had yet to be reconstructed as feminine attributes, and professional sailors proved more than willing to employ tattoos to proclaim their participation in loving relationships. For all that it is possible that these emblems may have helped a sailor to affirm his masculinity and power over a woman, sentiments of affection and love appear to have characterized the tattoos of men like Joseph Golden of Frankford, Pennsylvania: Golden had "Mary marked on his right arm with India Ink and the words MGV my love" on his left arm.[64] The stereotype of rootless Jack Tars should be amended to accommodate those professional seafarers who maintained and indeed celebrated their bonds with family and friends on land.

Tattoos of the names or initials of people other than the seafarer himself suggest strong ties with loved ones on shore. This is borne out by the familial connections between some of the 150 Philadelphians in this sample and the witnesses to their applications, 22 percent of whom appear to have been relatives of the applicants.[65] Thus George White appeared as witness for his brother Francis, described in his application as a "Mulattoe."[66] James Walker's mother, Sarah, John Fenton's father, Thomas, and the husband of George Hyneman's sister all served as witnesses for these seafarers.[67] The names and initials inscribed upon their bodies, and the identities of those who accompanied them as witnesses indicate that many long-term seafarers, for all that they were part of a somewhat more permanent, professional core of sailors, in fact remained closely linked to families and loved ones on shore. Some sailors, far from their homes ports, could not have family members to vouch for them: Peter Sally and Lawrence Oliver, both from New Orleans, appeared together in Philadelphia on December 28, 1807, and each served as witness to the application of the other.[68]

At the same time that these tattoos recorded connections with people and communities ashore, they functioned as deeply gendered badges of professional identity, which proclaimed that those who wore them worked under harsh and dangerous conditions in a world from which women were almost completely absent.[69] Seamen depended on one another for their very lives, and the close quarters in which they worked and relaxed engendered an intimacy far more intense than in the workshops and farms of the new republic. Melville wrote often of the "loving and affectionate manner"[70] of sailors who aspired to live on board ship as a "happy family."[71]

Through male sociability and sexuality, sailors formed strong affectionate ties.[72] This raises the possibility that such initials as the MNS tattooed on the right hand of William Newark of Salem County, New Jersey, although they could have been the initials of a spouse or companion or even a parent, sibling, or friend, may have been those of another man.[73] In the late eighteenth and early nineteenth centuries, when homosexuality and heterosexuality were far less sharply defined and differentiated than they are today, some mariners may have recorded their homosexual unions on their bodies, just as others recorded the name and initials of the women they loved.[74]

The 110 (9 percent) religious tattoos show that some professional sea-farers shared the Christian faith of those on land, while at the same time suggesting that they fashioned that faith to fit their needs and circum-stances. Marcus Rediker, in a compelling account of life at sea in the first half of the eighteenth century, argues that "religion was in almost all respects a distinctly secondary matter." He suggests that the contingen-cies of seafarers' working lives, together with the "traditions of skepti-cism and disbelief within plebeian culture," combined to make irreligion a characteristic part of life at sea.[75] However, religious tattoos challenge this familiar image. An anchor, the "figure of Hope," was tattooed upon the left arm of George Gillespie and on the right arm of Bartlett Wrang-ham; James Head wore the same "mark of hope" on his breast.[76] Chris-tian iconography had long used the anchor to represent the cross of Christ, and thus as the mark of grace and salvation.[77] For seamen, the emblem served as both a badge of their trade and an expression of hope for safety and good fortune.

Crucifixes were by far the most common religious tattoos (75), testify-ing to the singular nature of seafarers' religious belief. Roman Catholic symbols and images were far from common in the stridently Protestant United States, and it seems unlikely that men such as John Hancurne of South Carolina, James Dixon of Boston, John Frazer of Pennsylvania, and John Brown of Norfolk, Virginia, were all Catholics, yet each had "the mark of Christ on the cross" tattooed on his body.[78] A total of 8 seamen from New England, 44 from the Middle Atlantic region, and 23 from the Southern states (including 12 from New Orleans) wore tat-tooed crucifixes. Professional seafarers saw crucifixes on visits to Cath-olic ports, and some would have seen them held high in holy day processions, but familiarity with crucifixes does not in itself explain why these men chose to wear the tattoo. Melville's short account of the aging seafarer Daniel Orme sheds some light on the phenomenon. Orme had the crucified Christ inscribed on his chest; the old man regarded the tat-too with deep reverence: the image brought good fortune and bestowed protection. Elsewhere Melville recorded seafarers' belief that tattooed crucifixes would guard them in even the dire circumstance of falling overboard into seas teeming with sharks.[79] Melville also recorded that some sailors bore tattoos of crucifixes in order to help ensure that they would receive "a decent burial in consecrated ground" should they die far from home.[80] Nicholas Collin recorded one Philadelphia sailor's pathetic plea for such a burial; the alternative that filled this mariner with such fear and loathing was to "be thrown into a pit like another beast without christian ceremonies."[81]

Often men at sea could practice religion only in an informal fashion; the illiterate among them even lacked the comforts of a Bible, unless a friend could read. For such men, religious tattoos were testimonials of faith, and even spiritual or magical talismans, comforting reminders of a benevolent deity. For many centuries the crucifix had represented suffering, and it is possible that this familiar symbol served a similar purpose for men whose bodies were exhausted or broken by the rigors of life at sea. While they may have functioned as a lucky badge, emblematic of vaguely defined religious beliefs, the cross and the crucifix may also have said much about how seamen identified with this archetypal symbol of pain.[82] Sixteen seafarers wore tattoos of plain crosses, as opposed to crucifixes, or anchors with their dual meanings.[83] Another eleven had tattoos of Adam and Eve under "the Tree of Life,"[84] and other religious tattoos included representations of the Virgin Mary and Saint Michael the Archangel, the patron saint of mariners. Like those who lived on land, seafarers drew on the complex heritage of pre-Christian folk beliefs, Catholic practices, and the broad sweep of Protestantism that informed popular religion in pre-industrial America, yet their marks of faith had unique significance and relevance for those who worked at sea.[85]

If some seafarers identified with the religious beliefs of men and women on land, their tattoos show that they also shared a profound sense of nationalism and a deep interest in the political contest between the Federalists and Democratic Republicans that characterized early national politics.[86] The maritime community articulated a vehemently anglophobic republicanism, and from the mid-1790s onward the Democratic Republican leadership was under constant pressure to represent the concerns of seafarers. From a play about American sailors imprisoned in North Africa performed in Philadelphia in 1794, to the Seamen's Protection Act of 1796, to a song celebrating them as "independent, Brave & Free," to seafarers' patriotic and political tattoos, we can find evidence of the political relevance of sailors.[87]

Some seafarers used tattoos to proclaim their patriotic and political allegiances, and 71 designs featured such images as eagles, American flags, the date 1776, and representations of liberty. Eagles were the most popular patriotic tattoos: Nathaniel Oliver of Philadelphia, Andrew Dodge of Poughkeepsie, and Charles Spinel of New Orleans were among the forty seafarers who bore tattoos of eagles and spread eagles.[88] Often the eagle appeared in conjunction with other patriotic symbols: twenty-one-year-old William Sweeny of Baltimore had "a Spread Eagle & 15 Stars" on his right arm, representing the fifteen states of the union in the mid-1790s.[89] Seafarers' ardently patriotic tattoos reveal an anglophobic patriotism born of a deep hatred of impressment and the cruel treatment many American sailors suffered at British hands; it was, after all, British abuses that prompted the legislation that mandated the protections for which these men were applying.[90] It would be absurd, however, to reduce the patriotism of sailors to no more than an enduring hatred of the British. In their songs and badges and in their patriotic demonstrations, these men developed anti-British sentiment into their own patriotic ideology, which featured defiant and exultant assertion of their place within and their support for the new American republic.[91]

Nor did this kind of seafaring patriotism disappear after 1783. During the War of 1812 the British captured and imprisoned many American sailors, the large majority of whom were prepared to endure harsh conditions at Portsmouth and Dartmoor prisons rather than break ranks and secure their freedom by volunteering to join the British Royal Navy. When two sailors did seek to escape their imprisonment by responding to these British invitations, they were forcibly tattooed by their fellow inmates: the letters "U.S." on one cheek and the letter "T," on the other marked these men as traitors for the rest of their lives.[92] Clearly, tattoos spoke loud and clear about patriotism and loyalty, and they spoke forever.

Seafaring patriotism transcended simply loyalty to the nation, for it had deeply partisan implications: the sailor strolling the streets of an American port town with an eagle, American flag, or liberty tree tattooed on his arm was no friend to the Federalist gentleman wearing a black cockade who walked past him. The Bostonian William Carson wore tattoos of "the Flag of the United States" and "the word Liberty," while twenty-six-year-old Samuel Anderson, who hailed from Maryland, had a Spread Eagle and thirteen stars on his left arm and "1776" on his right arm.[93] Anderson had not been born in the year America declared its independence, but his decision to have the founding date inscribed on his body marked him as a man who sympathized with the Democratic Republicans who celebrated electoral victories by singing "Jefferson and Liberty" and by toasting "1776," "Liberty," and "the Spirit of '76."[94] Other seamen such as Bostonian William Carson were marked "with the Flag of the United States" and "the word Liberty." Twenty-six-year-old John Whyman's tattoo of the Stars and Stripes was unusual in that it was rendered in red and blue, for the vast majority of tattoos were either black or blue. Philadelphia-born John Thompson, his face "very much pitted with the Small pox," had "the figure of a Spread Eagle, Stars and flag," his initials, and the date 1801 all tattooed on his left arm. These patriotic symbols, inscribed in the year of Jefferson's inauguration, illustrated Thompson's patriotism and the political sympathies that informed it.[95]

The patriotic eagle tattooed on the left arm of John Alexander acquired added partisan significance from the representation of "Liberty" on the same limb, and six seafarers wore tattoos of liberty trees, poles, or caps, designs that fitted the partisan character of the other patriotic and political tattoos.[96] Throughout the 1790s, particularly during the

Whiskey and Fries rebellions, opponents of the Federalists rallied around liberty poles with liberty caps on them.[97] Such was their symbolic power that by the end of the decade Federalists condemned them as "sedition poles" and used the Sedition Act of 1798 to punish those responsible for erecting them.[98] By the time Jefferson became president, the liberty cap and tree had become Democratic Republican symbols, found on coins, tavern signs, newspaper mastheads, and the banners of craftsmen or militia companies.[99]

The overwhelmingly Democratic Republican sympathies suggested by the political and patriotic symbols tattooed on these men are confirmed by other evidence of seafaring politics. Sailors joined in the Democratic Republican societies that played a vital role in constructing opposition to the Federalists.[100] They also took their politics out into the streets. When in 1798 President John Adams's secretary and several companions walked along the Battery in New York City singing the Federalist song "Hail Columbia," they were confronted by a large group of sailors "from the wharves and docks" who began singing the French revolutionary anthem "Ça Ira" before setting upon and routing the Federalists, injuring several of them in the process.[101]

Men who worked at sea were at the heart of the age of revolution, witnessing or participating in the American, French, and Haitian revolutions and in the aborted British revolution that began with the naval mutinies of 1798 at Spithead and the Nore.[102] The maritime community gave strong support to the French Revolution, for a while a radical Democratic Republican cause célèbre. When the people of Boston mounted a huge festival in celebration of the French victory at Valmy, "a number of citizen seamen" affirmed their own support of revolutionary French republicanism by taking the horns of the roasted oxen on which the townspeople had feasted, marching to the liberty pole, gilding the horns, and placing them atop the pole.[103] Liberty poles, often fashioned out of old ship's masts, appear to have had special relevance for sailors. By the mid-1790s, sailors' use of such symbols as the eagle, the American flag, and representations of liberty—both in popular political rites and tattooed on their bodies—indicated their support for the ideals of the American and French Revolutions, as articulated by the Democratic Republicans.

For generations, sailors had been in the forefront of urban protests against impressment or various imperial policies, and they carried this tradition into the new republic. On the eve of the 1796 elections, for example, a large group of them joined together in Philadelphia; wearing French Revolutionary tri-colored cockades, they marched to the beat of a drum behind a banner proclaiming "Jefferson the Man of the People." Such political activity by lowly mariners drew the wrath of Federalist authorities, who forbade the display of the banner and forcibly broke up the procession. By the end of the day "near 40 of these Rioters" were in custody, and "2 or 3 of them [were] much hurt."[104]

Seafarers' support for the Democratic Republicans was conditional, however, and in the face of Jefferson's disastrous embargo the foundering maritime community rebelled. They took to the streets in every major urban center, drawing attention to the suffering of their families and demanding either an end to the embargo or relief for their sufferings. In Philadelphia sailors paraded through the streets, lining up before the State House and then petitioning the mayor for relief; in Boston a similar procession "waited on the Governor" in order to relate "their distress and to obtain his advice"; New York City seafarers publicized their meeting in local newspapers, and they too petitioned the mayor, asking him how he expected that they and their families would survive the winter; in Baltimore hundreds signed a petition demanding relief.[105]

While sailors participated in the street politics of the early republic alongside laborers, mechanics, and other working men and women, more than any other group of American workers seafarers had witnessed and experienced revolutionary transformations, and they participated in American politics within that context. Their enthusiasm for the French Revolution, their general dislike of Britain, and their enduring loathing for the Royal Navy nuanced their support for the Painite and Jeffersonian ideology of the Democratic Republicans in distinctive ways. Once again, seafarers' patriotic and political tattoos illustrated the tension between the distinctive experiences and goals of sailors and their membership and participation in communities and institutions on land.

Long-term seafarers worked for years before the mast in one of the lowliest and poorest paid professions, and short stature, relative illiteracy, and the scars of work and disease all marked and differentiated their bodies from those who labored ashore, and from middling and upper-class men. Yet these sailors self-consciously displayed their pride in their craft and their country on their bodies, the very bodies that were scarred and even maimed by that work. The tattooed designs on these sailors' hands and arms proclaimed their profession, while at the same time articulating and affirming their connections to people, places, and institutions ashore. Pride is one of the most striking characteristics of the tattoos: patriotic pride, pride in craft, pride in relationships with loved ones, and pride in religious beliefs. During much of the twentieth century, tattoos functioned as proud and defiant assertions of working-class identity or consciousness, and much the same appears to have been true for the early national professional seafarers, who perhaps originated this aspect of working-class culture.[106] The workshops of the new republic fostered the creation of a distinct culture and *mentalité* among craftsmen and journeymen, and these men celebrated their professional and political identities in parades, carrying flags bearing emblems of their craft. The ships of America's merchant marine appear to have functioned in a similar fashion, furnishing a distinct space and community wherein long-term sailors fashioned and expressed their professional pride and personal values in an altogether unique manner.

While the tattoos of some reveal them to have been alienated wanderers, others self-consciously identified themselves as the husbands, lovers, sons, fathers, and brothers of people ashore. Similarly, although many showed no sign of being anything other than skeptics, some presented themselves as having faith in a combination of religious, spiritual, and superstitious beliefs. These men were strongly nationalistic and vehemently Democratic Republican in politics, although they would feel betrayed by President Thomas Jefferson's embargo. In such ways these seafarers displayed themselves as men who were defined by their seafaring career, yet the tattoos also define them in terms of the people, politics, patriotism, and religion of the shore-bound society whence they came and, in the end, most returned.

It was a culture that could be seen, too, on the streets of the early republic. Seafarers and their families dominated certain parts of the Philadelphia cityscape, and with their belief that "If we've troubles at sea, boys, we've pleasures ashore," sailors enjoyed a vibrant and highly visible culture.[107] Many assembled in taverns and grog shops like one on Shippen Street, close to the Delaware, above which hung a tavern sign picturing a sailor and a woman, bearing the inviting lines "The seaworn sailor here will find, The porter good, the treatment kind."[108] Set apart from other working men by the appearance of their bodies and their unique culture, long-term and indeed all seafarers were instantly recognizable. The tanned, scarred, and pock-marked bodies of professional sailors revealed something of the human cost involved in constructing a commercial Atlantic world. But with their tattoos, these men took some control of their image by writing their own stories in their own fashion on their own skin.

The result is an instructive picture of a man like Richard Dunn. Twenty-two years old when he applied for a protection in 1809, Dunn was a full five inches shorter than the most of the Continental Army soldiers raised from his native Middle Atlantic region three decades earlier. Born in Philadelphia in the year of the Federal Convention, Dunn had a "stout" nose and wrote a well-formed signature that suggested a higher degree of literacy than the majority of his long-term seafaring brethren. The scar on his chin was perhaps less noticeable than the "Crucifix sun and moon" on his right arm and the foul anchor and letters "AD" he wore on his left arm.[109] Short, scarred, and tattooed, Dunn proclaimed his profession with his body, reminding himself and informing other members of the seafaring community of his values, beliefs, experiences and craft.

Dunn was still at sea three years later. By then the United States was at war with Britain and he was serving in the navy on board the *Constitution*. He was wounded in a triumphant battle against the *Guerrière*, as his leg was amputated, he called those who held him down "a hard set of butchers."[110] Although partly incapacitated, he remained a professional seafarer, reenlisting after the war and eventually attaining officer status as a gunner.[111] Dunn refused to abandon the world and work he knew best, even when his injury made it impossible to continue aboard ship. The recipient of a naval pension, he spent his declining years employed in the navy yards, ending his days at the yard in Portsmouth, New Hampshire.[112]

The information recorded on Richard Dunn's body and on the bodies of other professional seafarers complicates our understanding of the early national seafaring community by revealing tensions, complexities, and contradictions that were part of the working lives of long-term sailors. Poor and with limited opportunities on land, they made the sea their career and with pride embraced professional status within the seafaring community. Yet although many spent years and even decades at sea, they inscribed on their bodies images and names that showed the importance of connections to loved ones ashore, and when they applied for protections a good number were accompanied by close relatives. They remained deeply involved in the politics of the new nation, but very much on their own terms, and those who gave expression to religious and spiritual beliefs displayed a quite distinctive outlook. More than anything else, it was the tensions between the worlds of land and sea that defined the bodies of professional seafarers in the early republic.

Chapter 6

Dead Bodies

Illness, disease, and injury were everyday occurrences and experiences for Philadelphia's lower sort, and while some recovered their health many more died in and around their homes and workplaces. Death was a public ritual in which neighbors, friends, and relatives gathered around the dying person. Disease, ill health, accidents, and violence made such scenes common, and impoverished Philadelphians were more than familiar with the demise of the bodies of children, young adults, and old people, for most had gazed upon the dying and dead bodies of siblings, parents, children, or other friends and loved ones. So familiar, so everyday, indeed so domestic was death, that Philadelphia's lower sort were constantly reminded of the mortality of their own bodies.[1]

Death was closest to the children of the poor, weakened as they were by malnutrition and constant exposure to unhealthy conditions and myriad infections. James Saring was little more than two years old when he died, and the diarrhea and vomiting that preceded his death were most likely caused by the white worms, each over half-a-foot in length, that evacuated his body just before death.[2] For those of the lower sort fortunate enough to survive childhood, death remained close. Hannah Burns died as many women knew they might, in childbirth. The wife of Peter Burns, "a poor Labouring man," and the mother of three children, she died in September 1798 "just as her new child was born." Adult men shared the risk of death by infection or disease with women and children, but also faced danger in their work. Ship's carpenter Joseph Wayne, for example, injured his back and suffered internal injuries while working; he spent several weeks lying in damp conditions aboard a storm-tossed ship, and his condition steadily deteriorated until he "died in a deep decay."[3]

The nature and causes of death, the manner of dying, the ways the living experienced the deaths of others, and the rites surrounding death all provide fertile ground for historians interested in everyday existence, culture, and belief.[4] While death was a regular occurrence within the households of early national America, the letters and diaries of the more affluent suggest that they enjoyed better health and greater longevity than did poorer Americans. These men and women had the means to make projects of their bodies, feeding them a nutritious and balanced diet, exercising and molding them to Enlightenment standards of beauty, and when necessary removing them from the fetid atmosphere of city and plantation alike.[5]

Such options were seldom available to the urban poor, who have left us far fewer of their words, making it more difficult for us to recapture the ways they experienced death. We may assume that those with little or no means developed a rather more instrumental relationship with their bodies: the luxury of the body as project was unavailable to those whose bodies were a means to an end.[6] With some confidence we can speculate that insufficient quantities of food, fuel, and clothing, demanding work regimens, and exposure to myriad infections and diseases must surely have made ill health and death far more likely in poor than in wealthy households.[7] The romanticization of both life and death that was beginning to spread through affluent society was as yet far removed from the everyday lives of lower sort Philadelphians, for whom death was too real, too constant, and even too mundane to encourage such fanciful notions.

Death was the ultimate and the most potent inscriber upon the body, and in descriptions of death and of dead bodies—that is, records of how death came to the lower sorts of early national Philadelphia, how it was experienced by those who died, and how it was interpreted by those they left behind—we may learn as much about daily life as death among the lower sorts of early national Philadelphia.[8] More vulnerable than those who were better fed, clothed, and housed, the poor made sense of death by observing, analyzing, and explaining what happened to the bodies of people around them and then, eventually, what happened to their own bodies.[9]

The most complete and detailed descriptions of the dying bodies of lower sort early national Philadelphians are contained in the burial records kept by the Reverend Nicholas Collin between 1786 and 1831.[10] Collin served as the rector of Philadelphia's oldest church, the Swedish Lutheran Gloria Dei church, which stands to this day in Southwark, a ten-minute walk south from Independence Hall. A fast-growing new suburb, Southwark developed among the swamps and marshes south of the city center. The area was flanked by wharves along the bank of the Delaware and was filled with tightly packed houses crammed with working families. Many of the streets were unpaved, and sewage, household waste, and even dead animals decomposed in privies, sink holes, and the river itself. The water was impure, and in summer the air was filled with flies and mosquitoes. Undernourished bodies were ill matched for the illnesses brought by winter and summer, or even the rigors of work and play in Southwark. Collin found himself burying a good many members of the families of Philadelphia's sailors and waterfront workers. The courage and resilience of the meaner folk facing either the death of loved ones or their own demise colored Collin's objective medical records, which are consequently suffused with the tension between bodies as the hapless objects of a social condition that could destroy them and a vigor and passion for life that comprised a demand to be acknowledged and valued in death.[11]

Collin's tenure at Gloria Dei was an unusually long one, stretching from 1786 to 1831. A friend of Dr. Benjamin Rush, Collin was a member of the American Philosophical Society, where he presented papers on a variety of medical and scientific subjects. Medicine fascinated him, and he kept remarkably detailed records of the Philadelphians he buried; no doctor appears to have been present in cases such as those of Elizabeth Ervin, yet Collin felt it necessary to record the length of her illness, her symptoms, and the regularity of her excretions.[12] He saw himself as part of an Enlightenment progress that would eradicate common ailments and diseases, not least the yellow fever that took the life of his beloved wife in 1797.[13] The usurpation of midwives and folk medicine by professional doctors is hinted at by Collin's brief yet moving account of the stillbirth of the young male child of Rebecca Hubbert. Living in great poverty in Mead Alley, with her seafaring husband absent on a voyage, Rebecca was "in great danger" and her life was saved by taking the child "from her by instruments," most likely the forceps that in the hands of qualified yet inexperienced men could cause such great damage to women and children alike.[14]

However, while professional medicine was growing and changing at an ever increasing rate, Collin drew also on the relatively static medical system of interpretations of illness, disease, and dying that had evolved over centuries and was slow to fade away.[15] Relatively few of his records indicate that a doctor had participated in the treatment of the patient. Doctors—and Collin too—had no diagnostic tools available other than their own senses, but the symptoms and treatment of many illnesses, diseases, and conditions were well known among the community. William Buchan's *Domestic Medicine*, first published in 1769 and the best known and most popular general medical treatise in Britain and the United States alike, clearly assumed a general diffusion of medical knowledge among readers. Every community had someone with the skill to bleed or purge a patient, and Buchan did not expect a physician to be called in unless the patient failed to respond to the treatment administered by relatives, friends, and community experts.[16]

Medicine and the care of the sick were part and parcel of everyday life, and they were family and communal endeavors built upon popular folk

wisdom of long standing. Sickness, dying, and death itself remained nego-
tiated public events, with rites of treatment and interaction between the
dying and those around them that had evolved over many centuries. Doctors were often no more than occasional participants in the process. Ten-
month-old John Potts, for example, who was suffering from the common
infant ailment of worms, was unlikely to have been treated by a doctor;
his parents administered powders in an attempt to rid his body of worms,
which they may have obtained from a druggist, the Philadelphia Dispensary, or various other sources. In this case the treatment was unsuccess-
ful and the child died, but centuries of accrued knowledge and practice
meant that folk medicine was just as often successful, and Collin had no
doubt that the worms had "been too long neglected, otherwise he would
probably have overcome the vermine."[17]

Given that the Pennsylvania Hospital had room for no more than a
handful of impoverished patients, it is hardly surprising that so few
Southwark residents Collin buried appear to have died in the hospital.
Moreover, the institution was new and unfamiliar, and many of the area's
lower sort may well have preferred to care or be cared for within the
home and the community. Institutionalization in either the sick wards
of the almshouse or the Pennsylvania Hospital appears very much as a
last resort, to be avoided if at all possible, and even those with sufficient
means resisted the surrender of loved ones to such institutions. Although
often "out of his head" as a result of a childhood head injury, it was only
during the four or five months preceding his death that Samuel Condor's
wife institutionalized him.[18] Collin implies that Condor had not been
working for some time, and as such he must have been a drain on the
meager resources of the household, but his family struggled to keep him
among them. Similarly, Collin describes an orphaned teenage girl and
her widowed older sister who for years had cared for their broken-backed
brother Edward Kirby.[19] Collin was never slow to make note of such acts
of familial love, for he could see the sacrifices that were involved.

Collin framed illness, disease, and death in his burial records, making
sense of what he saw by constructing a scientific and rational explana-
tion of cause, symptoms, and effect. The actual experiences of ill health
and death remain elusive, but what we see is how Collin—an observer
imbued with eighteenth-century education and values—made sense of
the dying and dead bodies of the lower sorts in Southwark. With his
layman's interest in medical science, a firm religious faith, and a con-
descending yet compassionate attitude toward the poor among whom
he lived, Collin organized his observations with precision. Integral to
Collin's burial records were his drive to understand and document how
and why a person died, the ways they were treated, and his own reactions
to both person and process. Collin embodied the medical gaze by which

enlightenment-era men objectified patients, prisoners, lunatics, and others by institutionalizing, studying, and categorizing them and their conditions. Yet his concern for the people he buried and those he consoled allowed him to balance a sense of individual agency and passion against a more strictly rational perspective.[20]

In the case of the unfortunate Daniel Conover, who died during the first summer of Jefferson's presidency at the age of twenty-one, both popular and professional medicine agreed on the course of treatment. Collin recorded that a horse had trodden upon and wounded Conover's foot but that this had healed over with no apparent ill effects, Collin believed that it was Conover's over-exuberance on Independence Day that cost him his life. Having "joined with other young people in the frolics of the days, and being heated by dancing in the evening," he lay down on the ground and consequently contracted "a very great cold." Collin echoed the agreement of professionals and lay people alike that the lockjaw that killed Conover was a result of the cold rather than of infection within the foot wound, since an expensive course of treatment "of mercury taken inwardly, and rubbed externally" did little to help the young man and quite likely speeded his departure.[21]

The interpretation of Collin's records requires us to position ourselves in the middle ground between the early modern world and the scientific enlightenment. Collin, more than many of his contemporaries, had some understanding of contemporary advances in understanding and treating the human body. Yet he retained a sense of the human body as a series of dynamic interactions with its environment, believing that either good health or disease resulted from certain kinds of interactions between environmental circumstance and the body. He believed that one must achieve a balance between one's body and its surrounding circumstances, hence the continued reliance on diet and excretion to rectify imbalances. Almost all medicine was intended to help correct such imbalances, employing such remedies as bloodletting, emetics, and blistering to purge the body of dangerous impurities.[22] Similarly, Collin shared with his contemporaries a belief that what one ingested, and the quantities one took in, were vital to one's health.

Collin's account of the weeklong illness of Mary Norbury, and the treatment administered to her, reflects these beliefs. Because her father was dead and her stepfather had abandoned the family, Mary had been bound out to John Grover, a justice of the peace who resided on Second Street. Sixteen-year-old Mary was sick for just over a week, and her symptoms—"first a chill, moderate headache, pain in the back, bowels & some in the stomach"[23]—suggested an imbalance "between constitutional endowment and environmental circumstance."[24] Good health was believed by contemporaries to be based upon an equilibrium between the constituent parts of the body and the environment in which it functioned, which explains the contemporary emphasis upon what went into and what came out of the body as a key to maintaining or restoring health. In Mary Speer's case this involved regulating the secretions by the application of blisters.

In many similar cases physicians, folk practitioners, and even friends and family members employed tools or drugs in order to supply or diminish the body. Thus the doctor called in to treat five-year-old Elizabeth Loudon "gave medicine to expell the disorder, supposed [to be] the measles," and another physician treated seven-year-old Henry Hoover's worms with "a strong purgative, which did not work well," and no doubt contributed to his death. One-year-old Hester Smith, suffering teething problems, was probably treated by family and friends who dealt with her fever by applying laxatives to drain the fever from her and allow the new teeth to enter, while feverish five-year-old Mellin Hutton was bled four times, again probably not by a doctor.[25] Treatment was designed to attack symptoms, and thus drugs were categorized and administered according to their effects—diuretics, cathartics, narcotics, emetics, and diaphoretics—rather than by disease or ailment.[26]

Collin's burial records contain the names of church members and of local residents who sought a final resting-place in consecrated ground. Most Philadelphians were not church members, and as the congregation of the Swedish Lutheran Church dwindled, the numbers of non-members buried by Collin grew, accounting for 76 percent (764) of the thousand burials between 1791 and 1809 that are examined in this chapter.[27] While members of Collin's congregation could expect burial free of charge, non-members—"Strangers," as Collin labeled them—were required to pay the considerable sum of ten dollars for an adult and five dollars for a child. Few of the impoverished residents of Southwark could afford such fees, but in the majority of cases Collin remitted part of the amount owing. Sometimes he justified this by allowing families to bury young children in the graves of their siblings, as in the case of Mary Ann Hobart, whose father was at sea when she died. Noting that Mary's mother Rebecca was poor, Collin allowed Mary to be interred in the same grave as two of her siblings, thus enabling Collin to offer "a considerable abatement." Similarly Hannah Cassidy, the nineteen-month-old daughter of widowed Matilda Cassidy, was laid to rest in her grandfather's grave, while the stillborn child of Jacob and Elizabeth Riss was buried in the grave of its deceased sibling, thus allowing Collin to reduce the burial costs for the impoverished families.[28]

On occasion, the families of "strangers" were vocal in their pleas for a Christian burial for their children and loved ones, as in the case of Manuel Peterson, an "indigent" fish seller who "pleaded with tears, his desire to enter the babe in consecrated ground." Although Manuel and Abigail Peterson were unable to pay the full cost of the funeral of their five-day-old son, they paid what they could and added a string of perch, recorded by Collin with a mixture of wry amusement, sympathy for the suffering, and respect for the pride of the bereaved couple.[29]

The lower sort of Southwark had good reasons for seeking the burial of loved ones in the cemetery of a church to which they did not belong. Lack of funds made interment in the unconsecrated ground of Potter's Field the most viable option, but the large number of Southwark's poor who knocked on Collin's door indicate that this was to be avoided if at all possible. Southwark's closest Potter's Field was located in one of the four squares planned by William Penn, now known as Washington Square, which lay conveniently close to the three great institutions of the Philadelphia poor, the Walnut Street Jail, the Pennsylvania Hospital, and the almshouse: many who died within their walls were, with a minimum of ceremony, interred in the Potter's Field. During the War for Independence thousands of both British and American soldiers who were housed in these institutions died of disease, malnutrition, and their wounds, and their bodies were added to those in the square. John Adams wrote to his wife Abigail about spending an hour "in the Congregation of the dead." He had taken

a Walk into the Potters Field, a burying ground between the new stone Prison, and the Hospital, and I never in my whole Life was affected with so much Melancholly. The Graves of the soldiers, who have been buried in this Ground, from the Hospital and bettering House . . . dead of the small Pox, and Camp Diseases, are enough to make the Heart of stone melt away.[30]

The great yellow fever epidemic of 1793 brought thousands more bodies to this Potter's Field, but rather than these great tragedies it was the regular burials of impoverished men, women, and children that would have been most familiar to the city's lower sorts. It was a horrible, dreaded place, surrounded by a thick privet hedge. Dark and dank, it resembled a pit, descending from the western side well below street level, with a deep gully and stream coursing through the eastern part: and a pit it was, a depository for the bodies of criminals and paupers who were not entitled to or could not afford proper Christian burials.[31]

Manuel and Abigail Peterson's gift of fish symbolizes the pride of many impoverished families, who sought to avoid the ignominy of a pauper's grave for their loved ones. Moreover, non-membership did not mean, of course, that local residents did not share elements of a basic Christian belief system and did not think it important to bury family members in consecrated ground. Perhaps most important, like the generations of European peasants from whom they were descended, the poor of Southwark were likely to gain comfort from the burial of family members close to one another in a church cemetery that was in the center of their community, a fixed point that their surviving relatives might pass several times each day, allowing as much of a sense of connection with the dead as the living required. Collin recorded hundreds of cases where families begged him to allow burial of parents, siblings, and children beside or even in the graves of dead relatives. Elizabeth Low's mother "was anxious to bury her . . . along with her children," and on April 24, 1801, the single mother was laid to rest alongside four of her children. Elizabeth's mother, her surviving children, and the friends who paid a token amount for the grave and burial were unlikely to be able to afford a permanent marker for the graves of Elizabeth and her children: nonetheless, all would have known the locations of the graves, and they may well have felt a tangible connection to those they had buried.[32]

On occasion, it was the dying themselves who begged Collin for burial at Gloria Dei. Jane Willard "earnestly wished to be buried here," while twenty-nine-year-old Mary Ryan "requested on her deathbed to be buried in our cemetery, where her 2 children had been interred." Jane and George Willard were "poor people," while Mary "had for 5 years been palsical & for the last 5 mos. had a flux," and was thus unable to work. Moreover, her husband Edward was "very indigent, owing to her long sickness & want of imployment as a ship joiner," the result of the collapse of the maritime economy during Jefferson's embargo.[33]

Collin noted full or partial addresses for almost one-quarter (227) of the one thousand decedents, and the large majority—church members and non-members alike—lived within a few blocks of Gloria Dei. Fully 85 percent of the smallpox and yellow fever victims whose addresses were recorded lived no farther away than Third Street to the west and Lombard Street to the north. Similarly, all the women who died from puerperal fever or other factors related to childbirth and almost 93 percent of the children who were stillborn or who succumbed during infancy had lived within the few blocks bounded by Fifth and Pine Streets. The urban poor were Collin's neighbors, and whether or not they were members of his congregation, the minister did what he could for them, fashioning his own informal poor relief by drastically reducing the price of burials. Although striving for a dispassionate and indeed almost scientific objectivity in his records of death and dying, Collin's burial records reveal his respect and compassion for the poor who surrounded him. He wrote often of "affecting" cases, recording details of the condition of families that had little to do with his scientific record of the causes and nature of deaths. He was clearly moved when, for example, he was approached by Mary Moore, who sought burial of her infant son Dougal, describing her as the "wife [of] an absent seaman, struggling hard to support two children and an old sickly mother, [who] pleaded pathetically her poverty." Similarly, Collin concluded his record of Edward Ryan's plea for the burial of his wife Mary by noting it as "a very affecting case & his grief told by a tearful sensibility."[34]

That men and women of limited means sought full Christian burial for stillborn and young children is of no small significance. During excavations of a late eighteenth-century privy pit adjacent to Head House Square in the early 1970s, archaeologists discovered the bones of two infants, one a nine-month-old fetus or newborn and the other a seven-month fetus or premature newborn. The circumstances surrounding the deaths of these infants will never be known, but it is possible that unfortunate mothers did away with the bodies of babies they could not cope with or care for. Yet such sad cases do not appear to have been common, and Collin records many, many more instances of adults seeking burial of infants than there have been discoveries of the illegal burial of babies whose unhappy and brief existence mothers sought to hide.[35]

Perhaps what most affected Collin was the unremitting cycle of child mortality. The majority of those Collin buried in Southwark were children, and this fearsome infant mortality rate reveals a great deal about the straitened circumstances of their families.[36] The pastor recorded the ages of almost 95 percent (948) of the decedents, and both age and a cause of death in almost 94 percent of cases (938). Those interred in Gloria Dei shared a mean age at death of eighteen years, although even this statistic fails to reveal how strikingly commonplace was premature death among the infants and children of poor Philadelphians. Almost one-third (286) were no older than one year when Collin buried them, while almost one-half (458) never reached their fifth birthdays. Once past these hurdles, life became somewhat less hazardous, and only one-tenth (76) died between their fifth and sixteenth years. A further 28 percent (264) died between the ages of sixteen and thirty nine, and within Southwark's cramped and crowded confines less than 16 percent (150) lived beyond the age of forty, with only 5 percent (51) reaching the age of sixty.

The fact that Southwark was a relatively new and rapidly growing community helps explain why so many of those who died were children, and why so few were elderly. Southwark differed from longer established sections of Philadelphia, for it was home to a disproportionately large number of young people who came to live and work in the rapidly expanding maritime community. In their hundreds, young people from Europe, from rural America, and from other urban centers flocked to Southwark and the Northern Liberties in Philadelphia, and to similar areas in and around other American cities, finding what work they could and building lives and families. The Gloria Dei burial records illustrate that many of the urban poor died young as Philadelphia grew into a large city.

Collin furnishes further information about the occupations of those living around his church, inadvertently reinforcing the image of an impoverished community of the lower sort. In 157 cases, Collin recorded the occupation of the deceased, or of the husband or father of the deceased, confirming the lowly socioeconomic status of those who lived and died within his Southwark parish. Fully 46 percent (73) were sailors, perhaps the poorest of all urban white men, and when those in related occupations such as ship's carpenters, boatswains, riggers, and rivermen are included, the figure reaches 69 percent (109). Collin made a point of recording numerous instances of sailors' absence at sea when family members and dependents died: Benjamin Garret was away on a voyage when his year-old daughter Jane died of smallpox, and again when his two-year-old son Benjamin, weakened by worms, died shortly after falling from an upper-story window. Infectious disease, infection, malnutrition, and unsupervised play were constant threats to the "indigent" families of absent sailors.[37]

Other men identified by Collin worked at a variety of urban occupations: 4 percent (6) were bound laborers, 5 percent (8) were apprentices or journeymen, and over 12 percent (20) were artisans producing barrels, clothes, shoes, and so forth. Only 1 percent (2) were shopkeepers, and a further 1 percent (2) were merchants. Thus, while Collin did bury several ship captains, mates, and masters, the very large majority of those he interred were drawn from the ranks of the urban lower sort. It is the lives and deaths of sailors, carters, laborers, and their families that speak to us through these burial records, such as the shoemaker Jacob High and his wife Eliza, who died within two days of one another, or the rope-maker James Ellis, whose infant daughter died while he was stricken with fever, and thus "hindered from his business" and unable to provide for his family.[38]

Collin's interpretative frameworks require surprisingly little deciphering. On occasion his listing of symptoms cannot satisfactorily explain the cause of death, but in many cases his lucid accounts and analyses are persuasive. In such cases as accident, infectious disease, or childbirth, the general cause of death is clear. Similarly, the infant deaths caused by teething or worms refer to the hazards of weaning and the introduction of all manner of germs to young children taking their first solid foods. Less obvious, and yet very revealing, are the children for whom prescribed vomiting and purging heralded an end to their existence.

Almost 58 percent (543) of those whose age and cause of death Collin recorded died before reaching their sixteenth birthdays. A further 17 percent (94) had no childhood, for they were premature, stillborn, or died within a day or so of birth. Only 4 percent (22) died in accidents, the nature of which changed as they grew older. The majority of infants who died accidentally resembled three-year-old James Conden, who died from burns. His mother was a widow, and the greater burden of work that this condition would have placed on her perhaps explains how James met his death, "standing along by the fire his cloathing catch the flames and much burnt him."[39] However, as the children of Southwark grew older and began playing and working away from home, they stood a far greater chance of death by drowning, as in the case of eleven-year-old apprentice Elisha Talman, who drowned in the Delaware by Chestnut Street Wharf, or six-year-old Caleb Pierce, who drowned within a stone's throw of the churchyard in which he was buried.[40]

Disease and infectious illness, broadly defined, were by far the greatest danger faced by children, accounting for the deaths of over 70 percent (383) of those who died before their sixteenth birthdays.[41] Cholera morbus, the intestinal disease commonly recorded as "vomiting and purging," accounted for 23 percent (125) of all childhood deaths, including one-year-old John Bailey in August 1804.[42] John's two-week illness and death must have been hard for his widowed mother Hester, who had buried three children before him. Sometimes the burials of such victims outnumbered all others, as during July and August of 1803, during which time Collin interred eight young victims of "vomiting and purging," none of them more than two years old; during the same period, only three other children died and were buried in the Gloria Dei cemetery.[43] Cholera morbus was far more of a threat to children than to adults, taking the lives of fewer than 2 percent (5) of those older than sixteen.

Although not as pervasive as cholera, smallpox and yellow fever nevertheless took the lives of a further 16 percent of children. While yellow fever struck in less frequent epidemics, smallpox was endemic, and both diseases reappeared with life-threatening regularity in a community visited by hundreds of ships and thousands of sailors every year. Reappearing about twice every decade, when a sizeable population of non-immune youngsters encouraged an epidemic, smallpox struck hardest at the youngest. Thirty children were claimed by smallpox before they reached their second birthdays, a further twenty aged between two and five, and eight between the ages of five and sixteen, while the disease claimed only eight adults. Those who survived established some immunity, displaying their hard-earned resilience with pockmarked faces. Others were inoculated with the disease itself, a procedure that could be fatal and was resisted by many of the poor. It was not until after 1803 that the shift to cowpox inoculation provided the means to eliminate the disease, although it would be decades before smallpox completely disappeared from impoverished communities like Southwark.

In contrast, the yellow fever epidemics struck with greater venom as children grew older, claiming only seven children under the age of five, but taking the lives of twenty-two children between the ages of five and sixteen. In adulthood, yellow fever was an even more potent killer, taking the lives of almost one-third (81) of those who died between the ages of sixteen and forty, and eventually accounting for over one-quarter (102) of the deaths of all who survived beyond their sixteenth birthday. Unsanitary conditions encouraged the disease to spread rapidly within families and the closely knit communities of Southwark, especially during epidemics such as that of 1793, which claimed the lives of twenty-three-year-old Thomas Parram and his mother Esther in the same week.[44] When a second major epidemic struck Philadelphia in 1797 and 1798, Collin's own wife Hannah succumbed to the disease. He recorded her death in the same manner that he recorded all others, but then entered the only prayer to be found in his burial records, asking that "The God of consolation give me support under this dispensation." In the midst of records kept with rational, scientific detachment, the pain caused by the death of a loved one and the difficulty of continuing with normal life echoes through the simple plea. Collin knew the pain and difficulties that were so familiar to the people of Southwark.[45]

There were other dangers and killers that were peculiar to adulthood. Childbirth remained as dangerous as ever, and puerperal fever, loss of blood, and related causes claimed the lives of more than 15 percent (18) of women who—like thirty-three-year-old Mary Evans—died in or shortly after childbirth while they were between the ages of sixteen and forty.[46] Many more women were like Eleanor Grey, the forty-year-old wife of a man regarded by Collin as a "worthless" mariner, who after a period of general illness "was more debilitated by childbirth" and died as a result. Collin's records reveal something of the role of the female community in the birthing process, recording that it was Eleanor's "female friends [who] made charitable exertions for a decent funeral."[47]

Accidents, too, claimed a far higher proportion of adults than children, and the large majority of these were men who died while at work. Fully 20 percent (29) of all of the men buried by Collin who were aged between sixteen and forty died as the result of accidents in their work. When sections of the Delaware froze early in 1791, twenty-six-year old John Hastings was trapped aboard his shallup for three days, and he died of cold and exposure within a day of his return.[48] Indeed, since the river and the sea gave work to so many of those who lived within Collin's parish, it is hardly surprising that it was responsible for the premature deaths of men such as Joseph Taylor of Fuller's Alley, who died two days after falling between his ship and the wharf.[49]

Insufficient diet, infectious illness, and grueling work weakened the bodies of impoverished Philadelphians, and as they grew older more and more succumbed to "decay" and "mortification," general categories that signaled an erosion of good health and the wasting away of bodily strength. Such conditions affected people of all ages, and had a variety of causes, from juvenile tuberculosis or other wasting diseases to severe protein or vitamin deficiencies, low birth-weight, and general malnutrition. Daniel Berger was only thirty-six years old when he died of "Dropsy & mortification," while Simon Atsong "had a decay for 2 years" before finally succumbing.[50] Less than 1 percent (7) of the 938 whose ages and causes of death were recorded by Collin lived long enough to die of old age. Remarkable indeed were people like Heckless Fugerie, whose husband had died in the American army that had invaded Canada during the War for Independence, but who lived to see Madison elected president.[51]

It is the sheer normality of death that is most striking in these burial records, something that on occasion numbed Collin yet never stopped distressing him. He understood how the urban lower sort of the new republic struggled to achieve the necessaries of food, shelter, heat, and clothing, and also to cope with the constancy of illness and death among those who surrounded them. They saw the broken bodies of those who died unexpectedly from falls, burns, shooting accidents, and drowning carried home, where they nursed them as best they could. So too did they see mothers, sisters, and daughters die in childbed, and they knew better than to expect that most of the neighborhood's children would live to adulthood. Illness and disease, both familiar and unknown, surrounded them, and living in a port community they knew better than to expect a lull in its regular cull. From cholera to dropsy, dysentery to measles, yellow fever to whooping cough, potentially fatal illnesses were always present. Moreover, malnutrition and general ill health made the residents of Southwark vulnerable to conditions that would not normally have proved fatal. Thus Collin listed teething as the cause of death for over 4 percent (15) of infants who died in their first two years: the rigors of teething and the shift to solid food rendered young children particularly vulnerable to infection. Worms appeared as one of the causes of death for 12 percent (14) of children who died between their second and fifth birthdays.

Living amid the poor, and burying them week in and week out over a period of almost fifty years, gave Collin a unique insight into the causes and nature of poverty. Attacks on poverty in early national America were grounded in the belief that the poor were themselves to blame for their condition, and the almshouse stood as a monument to the resulting attempt to eliminate the "undeserving" poor.[52] But Collin never adopted such attitudes, for he knew well that the poor he lived among and buried had precious little control over their circumstances. When Isaac Richards, for example, sought to bury his four-year-old son William, Collin described Isaac as "an indigent journey-man taylor, working at very low wages, like many others."[53] Similarly, after burying two-week-old Ann Mary Johnson, Collin lamented the pitiable state of her mother, who was "poor as the generality of seaman's wives."[54]

It was readily apparent to Collin that even those who labored hard and lived respectable lives were never far from poverty and dependence. When Barney Clayton died of consumption in December 1799, Collin discounted the price of burial because Clayton and his family had lost everything "in the fire in Moravian Alley some weeks ago."[55] Economic downturns, harsh winters, and Jefferson's embargo all dragged more people into poverty, and when Collin made such notes as "Indigent, like many others this cruel winter," he attached no blame to those who suffered through no fault of their own. Moreover, the minister recognized that even men like Andrew Dam, "an industrious" man who had enjoyed "employment sufficient for a pretty comfortable living," might slide all too easily into poverty. Dam lived far longer than most, and after he had bestowed much of his property upon his two daughters, "the infirmities of old age obliged him to seek a retreat in the Bettering house for the last." But rather than defining the old man by the dependence and poverty that darkened his final years, Collin preferred to remember a gentle old soul who "had considerable skill in gardening and aided many in that capacity," and who "prepared for death with great devotion."[56]

Collin was, however, a man of his class and time, and he was never slow to condemn the moral failings of the men and women who lived around him, and the "licentious manners" and an "extreme want of order" in early national society that he found distressing.[57] Runaway servants or young people who sought marriage without proper permission, potential bigamists, and all who treated his religious responsibilities with less than proper respect shocked and scandalized Collin. At times the minister's harsh Calvinist moralizing is quite striking, as when he condemned a young couple who sought marriage without proper permission, prompting Collin to rage against "Liberty! Liberty, in a shape often seen by me! Wretched manners!"[58]

Yet when visiting the injured, ill, and diseased poor of Southwark, and recording their journeys to the grave, Collin's judgments of deserving and undeserving poverty, and of morality and immorality, were tempered by an unwillingness to hold the poor responsible for their condition. He had little sympathy for intemperance and the suffering that it caused, and recorded the death of Andrew Armstrong, a fifty-year-old rigger who "had for 3 years occasional twitchings in his nerves, with low spirits and a degree of delerium after imprudent use of strong liquors." But even Armstrong's drunkenness did not lead to outright condemnation, and Collin admitted that apart from "this fault [he] was a person of good character," and he gave a Christian burial to an old drunken sailor the almshouse authorities would have consigned to the Potter's Field.[59]

Collin demonstrated a good understanding of how the desperation of the poor might lead to intemperance and other evils. Although the pastor often made note of intemperance, "disorderly conduct," and "dissolute life," he did not embrace the notion that these moral failings were the primary cause of the poverty suffered by so many of the men, women, and children that he buried, and only rarely did he condemn these unfortunates. He took note, for example, of the conditions surrounding the death of Catherine Smith, whose demise resulted from "the unhappy life that she led with her husband, & the habit of intoxication, probably occasioned by it." Adam Smith had beaten his wife, and their neighbors "often heard her screams." Collin's compassion for her condition was matched by his disgust at the behavior of her husband; his record concludes with the hope "God have mercy on the not few savages in this city."[60]

While the community were unable to save Catherine Smith, in many cases family members and friends stretched meager resources to care for sick and injured loved ones. Catherine Peterson had almost reached her fifth birthday when she died, but she had been so incapacitated by fits during her short life as to need almost constant care and attention, for she was unable to do anything for herself: she died, however, in her parents' home, and not in the almshouse.[61] Such care commanded Collin's respect, as in the case of Aaron and Elizabeth Bryan, who for two years had maintained Aaron's ailing father and were then burdened by the death of their nine-day-old son; the minister concluded that a much reduced fee was "reasonable."[62]

While Collin's records illustrate the pervasive nature of accident, illness, and death, thus emphasizing the fragility of life among the poor in early national Southwark, they also tell a tale of remarkable human resilience. There is both helplessness and agency here, both abject misery and defiant pride. To the civic authorities, many of those Collin buried would have appeared as the undeserving poor, a segment of society to be controlled through the rule of law and such coercive institutions as the almshouse and the prison. At times the poor of Southwark had no choice but to accept such institutional aid and coercive control. But the very tone of Collin's records communicates his respect for a community who refused to accept responsibility for their deprived condition, who lived life as fully as possible, and who demanded respect even in death. While their deaths tell us much of the hardships of life and work among the poor of early national Philadelphia, so too do they tell us of their spirit and resilience, and the courage they found to confront life head on.

Even in Collin's accounts of the deaths of children, for example, we may see something of how impoverished youngsters endeavored to live and play. Eight-year-old Eliza Preston "was killed in playing with other children by a pile of scantling falling on her," while Thomas Turner and his two playmates were "playing on a bateau" that overturned, drowning all three.[63] For the impoverished children of Southwark, there were no sheltered gardens or rural parks, and the crowded streets, building sites, ropewalks, and riverfront provided them with playgrounds. Most moving of all was Collin's record of the strange bruises found on the side of thirteen-year-old orphan Anthony Nealy, an apprentice shoemaker who died of apoplexy. By noting that the marbles in the boy's pocket most likely caused the bruises, Collin acknowledged that, although already working, Anthony Nealy was still a child who played.[64]

There is passion for life in these records, both in the joyous playing of children, and in the raucous activities of adults. How else are we to make sense of the death of John Call, a young militiaman who was accidentally shot during an Independence Day celebration outside a tavern just south of Gloria Dei? And what of the "intemperate" Francis Cooper, who overindulged and "was taken ill on the evening of the 4th of July," or John Smith, who died after falling from a tree while trying to catch a parrot?[65] Even as death approached them, many of the poor commanded Collin's respect, for their hard work, their Christian devotion or their irrepressible joi de vivre. The pastor's admiration for fifty-nine-year-old Sarah Garrigues was obvious in his account of how, despite having been "lame with rheumatism eighteen years," she had employed a chair in order to move around the house and perform her domestic tasks. So, too, did he respect the sixteen-year-old servant Maria Sprole, who had sung hymns on her deathbed, and seventy-one-year-old Samuel Davis, who had kept up his spirits during a year of confinement to his bed by smoking and imbibing "weak mixtures of wine with water."[66]

Collin's records suggest that the lower sort were not slow to seek pleasure, enjoyment, and fulfillment from an often harsh existence that could scar or maim their bodies, yet at any moment might be extinguished. Even their tavern songs reveal a desire to enjoy life, and to do what they could to stop worrying about forces over which they enjoyed little if any control. Thus, one song recorded in a Philadelphia tavern account book asked

Will care cure the toothache or cancel a debt
Will duns or the gout be assuaged by a fret
Repining and whining both double our woe
So I'll laugh and be fat and take things as they go.[67]

Even more interesting is "The Song of the Brown Jug," which acknowledges that for the lower sorts, death was never far away, but which meets this knowledge not with fear and dread but rather with a desire to enjoy life to the fullest and then welcome one's demise as heralding an end to the "grief and vexation" that had filled their lives. "To Death I am Shortly Resigned," went the song, "So we'll Laugh Drink and Smoke and leave Nothing to Care."[68]

At times, then, the lower sorts were able to confront harsh living conditions and imminent mortality with exuberant lives. Evangelical religion, the culture of festive celebration, and a passion for riotous and alcoholic excess all marked adult life and culture among the urban lower sort. They might, for example, have relaxed in such establishments as the widow Martha Smallwood's Man Full of Trouble tavern, an establishment on the northern edge of Southwark that catered to waterfront workers, sailors, and others who lived and worked close by. Warmed by a large iron stove, such people might have relaxed in one of her two comfortable armchairs, or more likely perched on the cheaper rush-bottomed chairs, played cards on her mahogany card table, smoked tobacco in their cheap white clay pipes and drunk rum and ale from cheap leather and pewter mugs; glass was too expensive for the customers of the Man Full of Trouble.[69]

Such release from the cares of everyday life could extend to alcoholic excess, carousing, and even violence, as in the case of ropemaker Robert Jarvis, who was killed "in a tumult between the rope makers, below the church . . . and the crew of a French Privateer." Admitting that the trouble had begun "some days ago in a house of ill-fame," Collin inadvertently revealed more of the culture of the lower sort who inhabited the taverns of the Southwark riverfront, and who were not slow to defend their neighborhood against those they identified as threatening or undesirable.[70] Whether struggling against illness to keep working within or without their households, or finding solace in religion as death approached, or playing children's games on the streets and waterfront, or enjoying riotous celebrations of Independence Day, or fighting against French sailors, the lower sorts of Southwark appear to have fashioned a social life and popular culture that allowed them to live short and fragile lives to the fullest.

Collin's records of the passing of generations of Philadelphia's poor tell us not just about the ways in which death ravaged the bodies of Philadelphia's lower sort. They tell us, too, of these folks' passion and enthusiasm for life. During the early nineteenth century affluent Americans were beginning to embrace what Philippe Ariès has referred to as the era of *la mort de toi*, a romanticization of death expressed in fiction, poetry, art, religious practice, and even the rites and conventions of burial.[71] For the poor of Nicholas Collin's Southwark, however, it was all but impossible to view a consumptive death, for example, as beautiful. There were subtle hints that perceptions of death were changing: it was new for the poor to devote scarce resources to the burial of a stillborn child, for example, and for parents to record in detail the lives of children who had died at a very young age. But for the poor of Gloria Dei parish, life was too hard and too precious for excessive romanticization, and it took all that the laboring poor had to live life to the full and then to accept death with grace and dignity.

Afterword

Perhaps more than any of his contemporaries it was Benjamin Franklin—late eighteenth-century Philadelphia's most famous resident—who popularized and indeed epitomized the rhetoric of opportunity. Franklin famously proposed—both in his autobiography and in the advice of "Poor Richard" that he penned for his popular almanacs—that "if we are industrious we shall never starve," adding that hard work would be rewarded by material success, for "God gives all Things to Industry." In contrast, Franklin condemned those who refused to work hard or who succumbed to "vice," with the admonition that "Laziness travels so slowly, that Poverty soon overtakes him."[1] Success for those who worked hard was assured, while poverty would be the lot of the lazy and dissolute.

Descriptions of the bodies of the poor folk who inhabited Franklin's Philadelphia give the lie to these trite maxims. As described in the runaway advertisements, seamen's protection certificate applications, burial records, and almshouse, prison, and hospital records of early national Philadelphia, these bodies tell stories of lives often filled with hard work yet empty of material well-being and success. What of, for example, Ben, an African American man who chose liberty by running away from slavery in northern Virginia and seeking refuge in Philadelphia? His back had been scarred by the whip, and his body was thus permanently marked in a manner illustrating his servile status. As a slave, Ben had been cautious in his dealings with all white men and women, hiding his thoughts and feelings by lowering his eyes and avoiding eye contact. In the company of friends, however, and after a few drinks, he was more likely to open up, playing the fiddle, singing, and speaking his mind. In these moments of relaxation, and in his bright and colorful clothing and distinctive hairstyle, the young slave had displayed some independence even before running away.[2]

Liberty and the existence of a free black community in Philadelphia did not, however, much improve his lot. Suspecting his destination, Ben's master had advertised for him in the *Pennsylvania Gazette*, describing his body, mannerisms, and dress in pejorative but reasonably accurate fashion. Lacking papers that would prove his freedom, the runaway had limited options, and he could expect only occasional and poorly paid work. At first Ben shared a small room near the waterfront in South-wark with several other impoverished African Americans, playing his fiddle and socializing in a small grog shop favored by black and white sailors, waterfront workers, and the men and women who lived and worked alongside them, for he hoped that those hunting runaways or rounding up the many underemployed masterless men in the city would avoid such a low dive.

But work on the waterfront was irregular and poorly paid, and even-tually Ben joined the crew of a small merchant ship whose captain knew and liked him, and who was short-handed enough to overlook his lack of papers. Hard work earned him more respect from his white co-workers than Ben could have ever hoped for on land, but for this he paid a heavy price. Assuming the dress, demeanour, and even language and song of the seafaring profession, his body was soon scarred by his work, his leg broken by a fall from the rigging, his fingers scarred and raw from hours of frenzied work topside during bitter Atlantic storms, and his face scarred by smallpox contracted in a Caribbean port. It was disease that eventually killed him, for he was back in Philadelphia when a yellow fever epidemic struck. Ben could neither afford nor risk leaving the unhealthy climes of Southwark for the safer air of the countryside, and after eight years of liberty and hard work the runaway died and was buried in a mass grave in the pauper's cemetery that lay adjacent to the prison and the Pennsylvania State House.

And what of Sarah, the Irish woman who had arrived in the city dur-ing Washington's presidency as a young and hopeful immigrant? She began her new life working as the servant of a city merchant, but when toward the end of her term of service she became pregnant her master threw Sarah out. Four years of hard work counted for nothing, and without home, money, or a recommendation Sarah had few options. Sev-eral days later a constable found her hungry and crying in the streets and led her to the almshouse. The almshouse clerk, Joseph Marsh, Jr., cast a disapproving eye on the weeping and heavily pregnant women, and after entering her name in the Daily Occurrence Docket he added the words "Young Irish hussey." Sarah gave birth to a son in the maternity ward of the almshouse, and for months thereafter she received paltry rations in exchange for long hours of sewing.

In the almshouse, however, Sarah made friends with others who, like herself, were trapped by circumstance. Several of these were prostitutes, some no older than herself, whose raucous company and disrespectful attitude toward the almshouse authorities were very appealing to a woman who felt that she deserved better than the derogatory attitudes and harsh rules of the almshouse authorities. With a young child to support, Sarah knew she stood little chance of securing a position as a domestic servant, and she decided to join several of her new friends when they left the almshouse. Soon, she too was working as a prostitute, supporting herself and her child in the only way available to her. The cost was real and immediate, for within a year Sarah had contracted syphilis, and for the rest of her adult life she would suffer from the disease and from the mercury she and other prostitutes took to counter the effects. On several occasions her condition so deteriorated that she was forced back into the almshouse, where the disgusted clerk admitted her to the venereal wards. During one such interlude her young son was taken from her and apprenticed out to a craftsman living in Frankford, a few miles north of Philadelphia. It proved difficult for Sarah to see her son on a regular basis, and the boy grew up hardly knowing his mother. Finding solace in alcohol, she was on one occasion incarcerated in the Walnut Street Jail after being found lying drunk in the market.

And what of John, a young laborer, who was born and raised in revolutionary Philadelphia? His father had been a laborer who had served in the Continental Army, and John had grown up playing in the alleys and streets before following his father into work as a day laborer. At the age of nineteen John married Mary, a woman he had known since childhood. They lived in two rooms in a back alley between Christian and Queen Streets, fifty yards from the waterfront and ten blocks south of the Pennsylvania State House. Mary took in laundry and lodgers while John worked on the streets and waterfront. During the quiet winter months, and when the economy slowed, there was not always enough work or food. Their six children played on the docks and in the alleys and streets, all weakened by malnutrition and intestinal worms, for despite John and Mary's hard work the family seldom enjoyed a full, balanced, and nutritious diet, with the result that the children's ragged, patched clothing, their short stature, and their pale countenances contrasted sharply with the appearance of the children of wealthier Philadelphians who lived within a half-mile of their home.

Yellow fever and "vomiting and purging" (cholera morbus) took the lives of three of the children before their fifth birthdays. Living one block north of the Swedish Lutheran church, the hard-working and respectable family were well known to the Reverend Nicholas Collin, who buried all three children in a single grave for a minimal charge. Their mother regularly visited the grave in the years before she, too, was placed within it, but she knew other women in the neighborhood who had lost even more children than she. John's work made him old before his time, and a poor diet exacerbated the arthritis that made an old and crippled man of him before he reached the age of forty. As a hard-working and respected man, he was admitted into the Pennsylvania Hospital, but since the doctors were unable to cure him John was soon returned home, where he became a dependent of his wife and children, whose combined income was never able to raise the family back above the poverty line.

The lives of such men and women as Ben, Sarah, and John reveal the hollowness of Franklin's pieties, for it was all too easy for members of Philadelphia's lower sort to drop into the poverty that both physically and culturally marked their bodies. Social historians have long relied on such sources as almshouse and prison records or runaway advertisements in order to explore the material conditions of the impoverished lower sort, but few have employed these records in the spirit and manner in which they were compiled, as descriptions of bodies. This book has demonstrated the embodiment of poverty, employing such records to show in graphic and often painful detail the ways in which poverty and the conditions of life and work marked and molded the bodies of the laboring poor.

Philadelphia and the nation as a whole grew rapidly in the wake of independence, and the sudden increase in readily identifiable poor bodies alarmed middling and elite Philadelphians. They responded by categorizing more and more of the poor bodies surrounding them as undeserving of charity, and as warranting incarceration and correction designed to refashion them into less threatening form. When William Birch chose to include the lower sort in his engravings, he featured only relatively well-dressed and respectable working folk, usually portraying them at work; by excluding ragged and poorly dressed bodies he was able to eliminate the poor from the streets of an idealized city in which undesirable bodies were incarcerated, corrected, and then released back into society as well-dressed, hard-working, and deferential members of society (Figure 13). Poverty marked and identified the bodies of the poor, and with runaway advertisements and such institutions as the jail, the almshouse, and the hospital, propertied Philadelphians sought to classify, control, and then condition these impoverished bodies.

But the spirit and resilience of the poor speak through these records, as many resisted such control and sought to express identity and liberty through and even on their very bodies. The streets of Philadelphia were filled with bodies that frightened middling and elite citizens, from the tattooed professional sailor; to the African American runaway with a highly personalized hairstyle and distinctive mannerisms and gestures; to the vigorous and lively Irish woman who used her body in the only way she could but who refused to be cowed by the condemnation of others, to the hard-working laboring family whose weakened and diseased children played and sang in the alleys. In a new republic premised upon liberty and equality, the rapidly increasing ranks of masterless bodies threatened to overwhelm traditional notions of deference, hierarchy, and order (Figure 14).

But try as they might to regulate and control impoverished bodies, middling and elite Philadelphians were unable to completely master them. The independence and vitality of the poor and the lower sort led them to contest such control inside and outside such institutions as the prison, the almshouse, and the hospital. The resulting struggles were played out in and on the very bodies of the poor, for upon these bodies poverty was etched and power and discipline were enacted, and through these bodies agency and liberty were asserted. Almost all of the words of early national Philadelphia's lower sort died with them, but the records documenting their bodies breathe new life into these long dead souls.

Figure 13. William Birch, South East Corner of Third and Market Streets, Philadelphia, 1799. Courtesy of the Library Company of Philadelphia. In a somewhat more densely populated street scene than those usually produced by Birch, the relatively well dressed bodies of the respectable, deserving, and usually hardworking poor are seen alongside respectable men and women. Almshouse, prison, and other records, however, suggest that in areas close to the market such as this one could be found the less wellclad bodies of those categorized as the undeserving poor.

They tell us a great deal about their physical experiences of life and death as conditioned by their economic circumstances, they demonstrate the attempts of middling and elite Philadelphians to control and refashion the bodies of their poorer fellow citizens, and they reveal the attempts of the poor to retain a sense of self and of individual agency through control of their own bodies. Thus, in these dry and dusty records, the bodies of the impoverished lower sort in early national Philadelphia live again.

Figure 14. William Birch, Bank of the United States in Third Street, Philadelphia, 1799. Based on the original at the Library Company of Philadelphia, with additions by Anthony King. Alexander Hamilton's Bank of the United States lay very close to the geographical center of the city, approached along Third Street from north and south and along Dock Street from the east. Each day merchants, bankers, politicians, and men and women of means walked past the neoclassical edifice, but so too did all manner of lower sort Philadelphians, and the bodies of such folk as immigrants from Europe and migrants from the countryside, sailors, runaway servants and slaves, and working-class children mixed freely with those of their betters.

Notes

Introduction

1. Alexander Dick, "Travels in America, 1806–1809: The Journal of Alexander Dick," Special Collections Department, University of Virginia Library, Mss. 4528, 48–49; J. P. Brissot de Warville, *New Travels in the United States of America, Performed in 1788* (New York: T. and J. Swords for Berry and Rogers, 1792), 172.

2. Carole Shammas, "The Space Problem in Early American Cities," *William and Mary Quarterly* 3rd. ser. 60 (2000): 506, 509. Shammas provides a telling critique of the "urban village" portrayed by William Birch.

3. Robert Waln, *The Hermit in America on a Visit to Philadelphia* (Philadelphia: M. Thomas, 1819), 72; Petition to the Select Council, Philadelphia, 1806, quoted in Margaret B. Tinkcom, "The New Market in Second Street," *Pennsylvania Magazine of History and Biography* 82 (1958): 393; *The Cries of Philadelphia: Ornamented with Elegant Wood Cuts* (Philadelphia: Johnson and Warner, 1810), 32; Henry Bradshaw Fearon, *Sketches of America* (London: Longman, Hurst, Rees, Orme, and Brown, 1818), 150; Brissot de Warville, *New Travels*, 115. Historical studies of the poor in late eighteenth- and early nineteenth-century America include Billy G. Smith, *The "Lower Sort": Philadelphia's Laboring People, 1750–1800* (Ithaca, N.Y.: Cornell University Press, 1990); John K. Alexander, *Render Them Submissive: Responses to Poverty in Philadelphia, 1760–1800* (Amherst: University of Massachusetts Press, 1980); Gary B. Nash, *The Urban Crucible: Social Change, Political Consciousness, and the Origins of the American Revolution* (Cambridge, Mass.: Harvard University Press, 1979); Raymond A. Mohl, *Poverty in New York, 1783–1825* (New York: Oxford University Press, 1971); Carla Gardiner Pestana and Sharon Salinger, eds., *Inequality in Early America* (Hanover, N.H.: Dartmouth College Press, 1999).

4. See, for example, Peter Burke, "The Language of Orders in Early Modern Europe," in *Social Orders and Social Classes in Europe Since 1500: Studies in Social Stratification*, ed. M. L. Bush (London: Longman, 1992), 1–12; Keith Wrightson, "'Sorts of People' in Tudor and Stuart England," in *The Middling Sort of People: Culture, Society, and Politics in England, 1550–1800*, ed. Jonathan Barry and Christopher Brooks (London: Macmillan, 1994), 28–51; Penelope J. Corfield, ed., *Language, History, and Class* (Oxford: Blackwell, 1991); and David Cannadine, *Class in Britain* (New Haven, Conn.: Yale University Press, 1998).

5. These terms were employed by William Harrison, a sixteenth-century English

writer, and are quoted in Robert Jütte, *Poverty and Deviance in Early Modern Europe* (Cambridge: Cambridge University Press, 1994), 11.

6. See Wrightson, "Sorts of People," and Smith, *"Lower Sort"*, 4–6.

7. John K. Alexander, "Poverty, Fear, and Continuity: An Analysis of the Poor in Late Eighteenth-Century Philadelphia," in *The Peoples of Philadelphia: A History of Ethnic Groups and Lower-Class Life, 1790–1840*, ed. Allen F. Davis and Mark H. Haller (1973; Philadelphia: University of Pennsylvania Press, 1998), 13.

8. For more on the definition of poverty, see Smith, *"Lower Sort"*, 4–6; Alexander, "Poverty, Fear, and Continuity," 17–19; Jütte, *Poverty and Deviance*, 8–9.

9. Richard L. Bushman, *The Refinement of America: Persons, Houses, Cities* (New York: Knopf, 1992), 63–72.

10. Joanne Finkelstein, *The Fashioned Self* (Oxford: Polity Press, 1991), 51.

11. Chris Schilling, *The Body and Social Theory* (London: Sage, 1993), 131–32.

12. For a discussion of the culturally contingent ways in which people read elements of character on and through the bodies of others, see Finkelstein, *Fashioned Self*, 4–5, and Nicole Sault, "Introduction," in *Many Mirrors: Body Image and Social Relations*, ed. Sault (New Brunswick, N.J.: Rutgers University Press, 1994), 1–7.

13. This process—employed in almshouses, prisons, and hospitals alike—was most powerfully articulated by Michel Foucault in *Discipline and Punish: The Birth of the Prison* (1977), trans. A. M. Sheridan (New York: Pantheon, 1977), and *The Birth of the Clinic: An Archaeology of Medical Perception* (1973), trans. A. M. Sheridan (London: Routledge, 1989). See also Norbert Elias, who first developed the concept of social disciplining in Elias, *The Civilizing Process: The History of Manners* (1939), trans. Edmund Jephcott (Oxford: Blackwell, 1978), and *The Civilizing Process: State Formation and Civilization* (1939), trans. Edmund Jephcott (Oxford: Blackwell, 1982). For American case studies making use of these approaches, see David J. Rothman, *The Discovery of the Asylum: Social Order and Disorder in the New Republic* (Boston: Little, Brown, 1971); Michael Meranze, *Laboratories of Virtue: Punishment, Revolution, and Authority in Philadelphia, 1760–1835* (Chapel Hill: University of North Carolina Press, 1996); and Alexander, *Render Them Submissive.*

14. Brissot de Warville, *New Travels*, 203.

15. Foucault argued that the institutions that controlled and disciplined bodies aggressively stifled individual agency as a significant historical force. Other scholars have argued that individuals resisted the hegemonic authority of knowledge and power in such institutions as the prison. For examples of analysis of some of the ways such agency took shape, see Anne Cranny-Francis, *The Body in the Text* (Melbourne: Melbourne University Press, 1995); David Armstrong, "Bodies of Knowledge/Knowledge of Bodies," in *Reassessing Foucault: Power, Medicine, and the Body*, ed. Colin Jones and Roy Porter (London: Routledge, 1994), 17–27; Judith Butler, "Foucault and the Paradox of Bodily Inscriptions," in *The Body: Classic and Contemporary Readings*, ed. Don Welton (Oxford: Blackwell, 1999), 307–13; Nick Crossley, "Body-Subject/Body-Power: Agency, Inscription, and Control in Foucault and Merleau Ponty," *Body and Society* 2 (1996): 99–116.

16. Examples of the ways scholars have explored how to "read" bodies include Anne Brydon and Sandra Niessen, eds., *Consuming Fashion: Adorning the Transnational Body* (New York: Berg, 1998); Butler, "Foucault and the Paradox of Bodily Inscriptions"; Cranny-Francis, *Body in the Text*; Crossley, "Body-Subject/Body-Power"; Pasi Falk, "Written in the Flesh," *Body and Society* 1 (1995): 95–105; Mike Featherstone and Bryan S. Turner, "Body and Society: An Introduction," *Body and Society* 1 (1995): 1–12; Michel Feher, Ramona Naddaff, and Nadia Tazi, eds., *Fragments for a History of the Human Body*, three volumes published as volumes 3,

4, and 5 of *Zone* (1989); Finkelstein, *Fashioned Self;* Gary Kielhofner and Trudy Mallinson, "Bodies Telling Stories and Stories Telling Bodies," *Human Studies* 20 (1997): 365–69; Sarah Nettleton and Jonathan Watson, eds., *The Body in Everyday Life* (London: Routledge, 1998); Schilling, *Body and Social Theory;* Bryan S. Turner, *The Body and Society: Explorations in Social Theory* (Oxford: Blackwell, 1984); Simon J. Williams and Gillian Bendelow, *The Lived Body: Sociological Themes, Embodied Issues* (London: Routledge, 1998).

17. *Pennsylvania Gazette* (Philadelphia) 21 October 1795 (11132). All of the runaway advertisements employed in this book have been drawn from Folio Four of the Accessible Archives CD-ROM edition of the *Pennsylvania Gazette,* and the number in parentheses is the Accessible Archives Folio Four item number.

18. This information is taken from Augustus Reading's application for a Seamen's Protection Certificate (SPCA), 29 April 1805. The Seamen's Protection Certificate Applications are in the National Archives, Record Group 36, Records of the Board of Customs.

19. The best study of the radicalism of seafarers is Peter Linebaugh and Marcus Rediker, *The Many-Headed Hydra: Sailors, Slaves, Commoners, and the Hidden History of the Revolutionary Atlantic* (Boston: Beacon Press, 2000).

20. Lyndal Roper has explored aspects of this tension, in a history of the relationship between physical, lived bodies and bodies as they are imagined and constructed. See Roper, *Oedipus and the Devil: Witchcraft, Sexuality, and Religion in Early Modern Europe* (London: Routledge, 1994).

21. More than anyone else, Michel Foucault is associated with the interpretation of the body as a site upon which power is exercised and inscribed, especially in *Discipline and Punish* and *Birth of the Clinic.* However, while subsequent scholars have agreed with much of Foucault's interpretation, some have rejected such an instrumental conception of the body, exploring the tension between Foucault's inscribed body and the lived body that exercised agency and resisted elements of this inscription. See, for example, Crossley, "Body-Subject/Body-Power"; Cranny-Francis, *Body in the Text,* 66–79; Diane Crane, "Clothing Behavior as Non-Verbal Resistance: Marginal Women and Alternative Dress in the Nineteenth Century," *Fashion Theory: The Journal of Dress, Body, and Culture* 3 (1999): 241–68; and Anne Brydon and Sandra Niessen, "Introduction: Adorning the Body," in *Consuming Fashion: Adorning the Transnational Body,* ed. Brydon and Niessen (Oxford: Berg, 1998), ix.

22. Gary B. Nash, *Forging Freedom: The Formation of Philadelphia's Black Community, 1720–1840* (Cambridge, Mass: Harvard University Press, 1988).

23. See, for example, Smith, *"Lower Sort";* Susan E. Klepp, *"The Swift Progress of Population": A Documentary and Bibliographic Study of Philadelphia's Population, 1642–1860* (Philadelphia: American Philosophical Society, 1991).

Chapter 1. Almshouse Bodies

1. J. P. Brissot de Warville, *New Travels in the United States of America, Performed in 1788* (New York: T. and J. Swords for Berry and Rogers, 1792), 114. For examples of histories of almshouses in this era, see Michael B. Katz, *In The Shadow of the Poorhouse: A Social History of Welfare in America* (1986; New York: Basic Books, 1996), 3–36; Walter I. Trattner, *From Poor Law to Welfare State: A History of Social Welfare in America,* 4th ed. (New York: Free Press, 1989); Benjamin Joseph Klebaner, "Public Poor Relief in America, 1790–1860," Ph.D. dissertation, Columbia University, 1952.

2. Brissot de Warville, *New Travels*, 115.

3. John Smith, 8 March 1788, Daily Occurrence Dockets (hereafter cited as Dockets), Overseers of the Poor, Philadelphia City Archives. This chapter is based upon 1,000 records drawn from over the course of the decade between 1787 and 1797, comprising runs of entries for 1787–88, 1790, 1792, 1793–94, 1796, and 1797.

4. Isabella Wallington, 1 July 1788, Dockets.

5. Ambrose Robinson, 24 May 1790, Dockets; Thomas White, 5 May 1790, Dockets.

6. Susannah Bond, 27 November 1787, Dockets; Daniel Boyd, 4 December 1787, Dockets; Ann Smith, 17 December 1787, Dockets.

7. Charles E. Rosenberg, *The Care of Strangers: The Rise of America's Hospital System* (New York: Basic Books, 1987), 15–16.

8. Klebaner, "Public Poor Relief," 132–34.

9. Michel Foucault, *The Birth of the Clinic: An Archaeology of Medical Perception* (1973), trans. A. M. Sheridan (London: Routledge, 1989).

10. This point is made rather forcefully by Anne Brydon and Sandra Niessen, eds., *Consuming Fashion: Adorning the Transnational Body* (Oxford: Berg, 1998), ix.

11. For useful discussions of this tension, see Nick Crossley, "Body-Subject/Body-Power: Agency, Inscription, and Control in Foucault and Merleau-Ponty," *Body and Society* 2 (1996): 99–116.

12. Anne Cranny-Francis, *The Body in the Text* (Melbourne: Melbourne University Press, 1995), 79.

13. Hugh Stewart, 1 November 1787, Dockets; Mary Chubb, 29 December 1787, Dockets.

14. Clara McCord, 1 November 1787, Dockets; Elizabeth White, 1 November 1787, Dockets.

15. Ann Newgent, 10 November 1787, Dockets; Elizabeth McClinch, 27 March 1788, Dockets.

16. Sarah Summers, 9 December 1793, Dockets; Sarah Overturf, 1 November 1787, Dockets.

17. Deborah Lupton makes this point about bodies in general, as perceived in public health discourse. See Lupton, *Medicine as Culture: Illness, Disease, and the Body in Western Societies* (London: Sage, 1994), 30.

18. Robert Aitken, 4 December 1787 and 20 November 1790, and see also 1 November 1787, Dockets; Sarah Simpson, 6 December 1791, Dockets; Ann Johnson, 11 December 1787, Dockets.

19. Gary Kielhofner and Trudy Mallinson, "Bodies Telling Stories and Stories Telling Bodies," *Human Studies* 20 (1997): 365–69.

20. William Harrison, as quoted in Robert Jütte, *Poverty and Deviance in Early Modern Europe* (Cambridge: Cambridge University Press, 1994), 11.

21. Among the best accounts of the workings of the Philadelphia almshouse are Billy G. Smith, *The "Lower Sort": Philadelphia's Laboring People, 1750–1800* (Ithaca, N.Y.: Cornell University Press, 1990), 166–75, and John K. Alexander, *Render Them Submissive: Responses to Poverty in Philadelphia, 1760–1800* (Amherst: University of Massachusetts Press, 1980), 110–17.

22. Quoted in Alexander, *Render Them Submissive*, 116–17.

23. Alexander, *Render Them Submissive*, 112; Brissot de Warville, *New Travels*, 112, 113, 115.

24. James Berry, 7 April 1791, Dockets.

25. Daniel McCalley, 16 January 1796, Dockets.

26. Murdock Morris, 26 January 1796, Dockets; James Smith, 22 December 1790, Dockets; William Payne, 1 November 1787, Dockets.

27. Catherine Burley, 18 January 1796, Dockets.

28. Elizabeth Dollason, 1 November 1787, Dockets; Elizabeth White, 1 November 1787, Dockets.

29. Hannah McDonald, 10 February 1788, Dockets; Mary Hensel, 21 February 1788, Dockets.

30. Cudgo Briant, 11 January 1796, Dockets.

31. George Mullen, 14 January 1796, Dockets.

32. Jacob Howtchel, 1 November 1787, Dockets; John Vent, 5 December 1787, Dockets; Daniel Boyd, 4 December 1787, Dockets; Daniel Boyd, 24 March 1788, Dockets.

33. Jane Burns, 6 December 1787, Dockets; Ann Smith, 17 December 1787, Dockets.

34. Judith Boyd, 1 November 1787, Dockets; Mary Lindsey, 1 November 1787, Dockets.

35. Mary Bursly, 1 November 1787, Dockets.

36. In 1800 Philadelphia, the Northern Liberties, and Southwark (the second, sixth, and seventh largest urban areas in the nation) had a combined population of 61,559. See Campbell Gibson, "Population of the 100 Largest Cities and Other Urban Places in the United States: 1790 to 1990" (Washington, D.C.: U.S. Bureau of the Census, on-line Population Working Division Paper 27, 1998).

37. Guardians of the Poor, Almshouse Clothing Issues Ledger (Male), 1805–14, Philadelphia City Archives, 1; Guardians of the Poor, Almshouse Clothing Issues Ledger (Female), 1805–14, Philadelphia City Archives, 5, 13.

38. Randal McDonald (and his wife Ann), 1 July 1792, Dockets; Ann Pettit, 29 July 1792, Dockets.

39. Of the 1,000 people included in the database, places of referral were recorded for 872. Of these, 561 (64.3%) were drawn from Philadelphia, 107 (12.3%) from the Northern Liberties, 186 (21.3%) from Southwark, and 18 from elsewhere in Pennsylvania, New Jersey, New York, and even the Chesapeake or New England. The proportions change slightly when gender is taken into account: 59.8 percent of men entered the almshouse from the city of Philadelphia, as compared to 68.7 percent of women, while Southwark accounted for 15.3 percent of men and 26.9 percent of women, and the Northern Liberties 14 percent of men and 11.3 percent of women.

40. In 1790 the population of Philadelphia stood at 28,522 (64.7%), Northern Liberties 9,913 (22.5%), and Southwark 5,661 (12.8%); by 1800 these figures had grown to 41,220 (67%) for Philadelphia, 10,718 (17.4%) for the Northern Liberties, and 9,621 (15.6%) for Southwark. Gibson, "Population of the 100 Largest Cities."

41. Simon Corney, 6 December 1793, Dockets; James Willis, 11 December 1787, Dockets.

42. In 829 of the 1,000 cases, some kind of description is included as part of the record.

43. William Hill, 1 November 1787, Dockets; Eleanor Fitzgerald, 6 February 1796, Dockets.

44. Charles Proud, 18 October 1790, Dockets.

45. These and the following percentages are taken from the 829 cases including descriptive terms: "old," 126 (15.2%); "distress" or "distressed," 83 (10%); "infirm," 24 (2.9%); "feeble," (18) 2.2%; "helpless," (9) 1.1%; and "ailing," 1 (.1%).

46. "Lame," 39 (4.7%); "invalid," 5 (.6%); "cripple," 4 (.5%); "blind," 34 (4.1%); "deaf," 3 (.4%); frostbite, 4 (.5%); beaten 4 (.4%); injured by fall, 7 (.8%); scalded or burned, 7 (.8%); rupture, 3 (.4%); broken or missing limbs 19 (2.3%).

47. "Sore" legs, 50 (6%); rheumatism, 9 (1.1%); consumption, 14 (1.7%); dropsy, 3 (.4%); fits, 25 (3%); pleurisy, 3 (.4%); fever 6 (.7%), small pox 5 (.6%).

48. Such terms appear in 105 (10.5%) of the records.

49. Sarah Summers, 9 December 1793, Dockets; John Morrison, 17 June 1790, Dockets.

50. Thomas Musgrove, 18 February 1788, 21 December 1790, 22 December 1790, Dockets.

51. John Brown, 6 November 1790, Dockets; Daniel Stevenson, 28 January 1796, Dockets.

52. Isabella Wallington, 24 March 1788, 1 July 1788, Dockets.

53. Mario Perniola, "Between Clothing and Nudity," in *Fragments for a History of the Human Body*, ed. Michel Feher, Ramona Naddaff, and Nadia Tazi, one of three special issues of *Zone* 4 (1989): 237.

54. Mary Peel, 8 July 1794, Dockets.

55. Jane Kean, 23 May 1797, Dockets.

56. William Laird, 9 February 1796, Dockets.

57. John McLean, 3 February 1796, Dockets.

58. John Yard, 27 June 1798, Dockets; Isaac Potter, 25 January 1796, Dockets; John and Ann Shepherd, 21 October 1793, Dockets.

59. Jane Morton, 21 May 1797, Dockets.

60. Elizabeth Philips, 7 August 1792, Dockets.

61. George Yard, 19 December 1790, 16 June 1792, 22 June 1792, Dockets.

62. Alexander Thomas, 29 April 1794, Dockets; John Hutchinson, 21 March 1788, Dockets.

63. October 1790, 25 October 1790, Dockets.

64. July 1792, Dockets.

65. Margaret Summers, 13 December 1787, Dockets; Barbara O'Neal, 3 January 1788, Dockets.

66. Rachel Davis and Sarah Smith, 16 October 1790, Dockets.

67. July 1788, Dockets.

68. Mary Bowgh, 3 December 1787, Dockets.

69. Ann Williams, 3 February 1796, Dockets.

70. John Shepheard, 1 November 1787, Dockets; Catherine Johnston, 1 November 1787, Dockets.

71. W. J. Rorabaugh, *The Alcoholic Republic: An American Tradition* (New York: Oxford University Press, 1979), 9.

72. James Maloy, 1 November 1787, Dockets.

73. Mary Lane, 23 November 1790, Dockets; Ann Johnson, 11 December 1787, Dockets.

74. Alexander Cramsey, 28 July 1792, Dockets; Mary Anne Lawrence, 8 January 1796, Dockets; Benjamin Moffat, 11 January 1796, 12 January 1796, Dockets; James Lynch, 28 November 1793, Dockets.

75. Rorabaugh, *The Alcoholic Republic*, 169–170.

76. Mary Carrol, 1 November 1787, Dockets; Jacob Houtchel, 14 November 1793, Dockets (probably same as Jacob Howtchel, 1 November 1787; see note 32).

77. Thomas Salvester, 1 November 1787, Dockets; James Boyd, 18 December 1787, Dockets; Thomas McCain, 27 December 1790, Dockets; Robert Aitken, 4 December 1787, 20 November 1790, Dockets.

78. Carole Shammas, "The Space Problem in Early American Cities," *William and Mary Quarterly* 3rd ser. 60 (2000): 506.

79. Ann Johnson, 11 December 1787, Dockets: James Lynch, 28 November 1793, Dockets; Patrick Murphy, 7 December 1793, Dockets.

80. Charles William Janson, *The Stranger in America: Containing Observations Made During a Long Residence in That Country, on the Genius, Manners, and Customs of the People of the United States* . . . (London: Albion Press, 1807), 180.

81. Quoted in Margaret B. Tinkcom, "The New Market in Second Street," *Pennsylvania Magazine of History and Biography* 82 (1958), 393, 394.

82. For a detailed discussion of this development see Peter Thompson, *Rum Punch and Revolution: Taverngoing and Public Life in Eighteenth-Century Philadelphia* (Philadelphia: University of Pennsylvania Press, 1999), 145–204.

83. "The Song of the Brown Jug," quoted in Ric Northrup Caric, "'To Drown the Ills That Discompose the Mind': Care, Leisure, and Identity Among Philadelphia Artisans and Workers, 1785–1840," *Pennsylvania History: A Journal of Mid-Atlantic Studies* 64 (1997): 480. In this article Caric demonstrates that in their songs Philadelphia's workers celebrated an abandonment of the cares and worries of their life by means of an exuberant culture of drink and song.

84. Hugh Henry Brackenridge, *Modern Chivalry: Containing the Adventures of Captain John Farrago, and Teague Oregan, His Servant* (Philadelphia: John McCulloch, 1792), 62.

85. For a brief discussion of prostitution in this era, see Timothy J. Gilfoyle, *City of Eros: New York City Prostitution and the Commercialization of Sex, 1790–1920* (New York: W.W. Norton, 1992), 17–26.

86. *Advice to a Magdalen*, broadside (Philadelphia, 1800), Library Company of Philadelphia.

87. Daniel Boyd, 24 March 1788, Dockets; Jane Williams, 28 March 1788, Dockets.

88. Submit Hickman, 14 July 1792, Dockets; Ann Clark, 2 February 1796, Dockets.

89. Cato Cox, 4 November 1790, Dockets.

90. Lynn Hunt, "Introduction," in *Eroticism and the Body Politic*, ed. Hunt (Baltimore: Johns Hopkins University Press, 1991), 2.

91. Catherine Miller, 1 November 1787, Dockets; Ann Wall, 1 November 1787, Dockets; Kitty Jones, 20 December 1787, Dockets.

92. Sarah Wilson, 20 October 1790, Dockets; Susannah Glass, 4 November 1790, Dockets; Grace Boon, 21 December 1790, Dockets.

93. Mary Pothemus, 3 October 1793, Dockets.

94. Mary Killgallant, 10 February 1796, Dockets; Margaret White, 10 January 1791, Dockets; Sarah Simpson, 6 December 1791, Dockets.

95. Sarah Simpson, 3 January 1792, Dockets; Ann Till, 3 January 1792, Dockets.

96. Elizabeth Buckman, 13 August 1792, Dockets.

97. Catherine Delaney, 2 December 1793, 4 December 1793, Dockets.

98. Brackenridge, *Modern Chivalry*, 62, 67.

99. Mary Fitzgerald, 6 November 1790, Dockets; Catherine Hayes, 16 November 1790, Dockets.

100. Eleanor Redman, 9 August 1792, 29 August 1792, Dockets; Hannah Giles, 16 August 1792, Dockets.

101. Elenaor Redman, 9 August 1792, 29 August 1792, Dockets; Grace Boon, 21 December 1790, Dockets.

102. Jane Bickerdite, 22 December 1789, Dockets.

103. Quoted in Rosenberg, *Care of Strangers*, 15–16.

104. Brackenridge, *Modern Chivalry*, 67.

105. Rebecca Tucker, 7 January 1796, Dockets.

106. James Dryor, 1 November 1787, 21 December 1787, Dockets; John Smith, 9 October 1790, Dockets; James Connolly, 13 October 1790, Dockets.

107. Hugh O'Hara, 30 December 1788, 11 March 1789, 21 November 1789, 13 December 1789, Dockets. The problem of almshouse residents selling clothing was hardly new: English historian Steven King points out that he has "never seen a set of workhouse records which fail to record concerns that paupers were pawning poor law clothing for what were substantial sums." See King, "Reclothing the English Poor, 1700–1834," *Textile History* (forthcoming), ms. copy provided by author, 13.

108. Daniel Boyd, 18 November 1793, Dockets.

109. Leah McGee, 1 November 1787, Dockets; Archibald McGowan, 22 October 1790, 4 January 1790, Dockets; Margaret McLean, 3 December 1793, Dockets; Mary Carroll, 13 March 1790, Dockets; John McKinley, 11 December 1793, Dockets.

110. John Cooney, 11 October 1790, Dockets; Archibald McGowan, 22 October 1790, Dockets.

111. (Whitsun) 24 May 1790, Dockets.

112. Cornelius Buckley, 28 December 1787, Dockets; Harry Musgrove, 8 November 1793, Dockets.

113. Elizabeth McClinch, 27 March 1788, Dockets.

114. John Yard, 27 June 1798, Dockets; Thomas McCain, 27 December 1790, Dockets; Mary Ann Lawrence, 8 January 1796, Dockets.

Chapter 2. Villainous Bodies

1. Lady Henrietta Liston, wife of the British minister to the United States during Washington's presidency, as quoted in James C. Nicholls, "Lady Henrietta Liston's Journal of Washington's 'Resignation,' Retirement, and Death," *Pennsylvania Magazine of History and Biography* 95 (1971): 514; George Washington, *Rules of Civility*, ed. Richard Brookhiser (New York: Free Press, 1997). Joanne Finklestein has argued that, ever since the Middle Ages, "Western culture has represented the body, with increasing frequency, as an architectural metaphor of society at large. . . . [T]he individual's display of material competence and bodily control have been used to distinguish class and status." Finklestein, *The Fashioned Self* (Oxford: Polity Press, 1991), 51.

2. Noah Webster, *A Dictionary of the English Language* . . . (1828; London: Black, Young and Young, 1832), vol. 2, entry for "vagrancy"; George Puttenham, *The Arte of English Poesie* . . . (1589; Menston, Yorkshire: Scolar Press, 1968), 3; Webster, *Dictionary*, vol. 1, entry for "idle," and vol. 2, entry for "vicious."

3. William Harrison, quoted in Robert Jütte, *Poverty and Deviance in Early Modern Europe* (Cambridge: Cambridge University Press, 1994), 11.

4. Elias Helm, Michael Duffy, Jane Stewart, 21 July 1796, Vagrancy Dockets, Philadelphia City Archives (hereafter cited as VD); Timothy Wallington, Elizabeth Gifford, Mary Rhee, 22 July 1796, VD; Eleanor Bryan, Jane Brady, 25 July 1796, VD; Alexander McKinsey, Lydia McKinsey, Mary Bennet, Catherine Lynch, Elizabeth McLaughlin, Mary Wilson, Elizabeth Holton, Jacob Spry, Rosanna Spry, Ann Galagher, 25 July 1796, VD.

5. *The Mail; or Claypoole's Daily Advertiser* (Philadelphia), 29 June 1791; "The Dram-Shop," *The Mail,* 20 September 1792. See also John K. Alexander, *Render Them Submissive: Responses to Poverty in Philadelphia, 1760–1800* (Amherst: University of Massachusetts Press, 1980), 26–60; Stephanie Grauman Wolf, *As Various as Their Land: The Everyday Lives of Eighteenth-Century Americans* (New York: Harper Collins, 1993), 15–21; Jütte, *Poverty and Deviance,* 8–11. Deborah Lupton,

in her study of illness and medicine, proposes that the bodies of the poor may well be regarded as out of control and threatening by the elite. See Lupton, *Medicine as Culture: Illness, Disease and the Body in Western Societies* (London: Sage, 1994), 30.

6. Thomas Jefferson, First Annual Message to Congress, 8 December 1801, excerpted in *The Portable Thomas Jefferson*, ed. Merrill D. Peterson (New York: Viking, 1975), 300.

7. Carole Shammas, "The Space Problem in Early United States Cities," *William and Mary Quarterly*, 3rd ser. 60 (2000): 509.

8. Jefferson, First Annual Message to Congress, 300.

9. See, for example, Nicholas Scull, *Plan of the Improved Part of the City of . . . Philadelphia* (Philadelphia: unknown, 1762).

10. "Flower Girl," *Philadelphia Minerva*, 7 May 1796.

11. The best account of the decline of deference among the lower sort is Alfred F. Young's study of the Boston shoemaker George Robert Twelves Hewes. See Young, *The Shoemaker and the Tea Party: Memory and the American Revolution* (Boston: Beacon Press, 1999). For similar developments in Philadelphia, see Steven Rosswurm, *Arms, Country, and Class: The Philadelphia Militia and the "Lower Sort" During the American Revolution, 1775–1783* (New Brunswick, N.J.: Rutgers University Press, 1987), and John K. Alexander, "The Fort Wilson Incident of 1779: A Case Study of the Revolutionary Crowd," *William and Mary Quarterly* 3rd ser. 31 (1974): 589–612. On the rapid increase in the ranks of the poor, see Billy G. Smith, *The "Lower Sort": Philadelphia's Laboring People, 1750–1800* (Ithaca, N.Y.: Cornell University Press, 1990), and Alexander, *Render Them Submissive*.

12. See Alexander, *Render Them Submissive*, 48–60.

13. William Ofrey, 1 November 1787, Daily Occurrence Dockets (hereafter cited as Dockets), Overseers of the Poor, Philadelphia City Archives; Daniel Murphy, 7 November 1787, Dockets. The information employed in this chapter is drawn from a database of 500 vagrants recorded in the Vagrancy Dockets, Philadelphia City Archives, half from May 1790–November 1790, and half from June 1796–October 1796. Further information is drawn from the Daily Occurrence Dockets of the almshouse; from 250 records of Philadelphians convicted and sentenced to jail between March 1795 and December 1797, whose cases were recorded in the Prison Sentence Dockets (hereafter cited as PSD); and from the Prisoner for Trial Dockets (hereafter cited as PTD), which provide more detailed information about those who were convicted. Taken together these sources, all located in the Philadelphia City Archives, reveal much about the bodies and lives of those incarcerated in the almshouse and the prison for vagrancy.

14. Elizabeth Shipheard, 14 November 1787, Dockets.

15. Mary Allen, 24 November 1787, Dockets; James Willis, 11 December 1787, Dockets.

16. Joseph Gale, quoted in Alexander, *Render Them Submissive*, 78–79.

17. John Bryant, PSD, 21 March 1795; Henry Grimm, PSD, 30 September 1795; for examples of scars, see John Davis, PSD, 24 September 1795, David Wills, PSD, 7 January 1796, John Conner, PSD, 23 June 1796, and John Johnson, PSD, 5 December 1797.

18. For an excellent discussion of the tension between the "lived" body and the "inscribed" body, see Nick Crossley, "Body-Subject/Body-Power: Agency, Inscription, and Control in Foucault and Merleau-Ponty," *Body and Society* 2 (1996): 99–116.

19. A total of 268 (54%) of vagrants were male, and 232 (46%) were female; the proportions for those convicted of other offenses were 78 percent male and 22 percent female.

20. Sarah Harrington, VD, 21 June 1790; Violet Rogers, VD, 30 October 1790; Rosey, VD, 30 October 1790; James Walker, VD, 9 August 1790.

21. Sarah Gault, VD, 26 June 1790; Margaret Simons, VD, 19 August 1790.

22. Eleanor Bryan, VD, 25 July 1796; Jane Brady, VD, 25 August 1796.

23. Philip Skamp, VD, 27 June 1796; John Stuart, VD, 25 June 1790.

24. Joseph Kelly, VD, 24 June 1790.

25. Francis McMarron, VD, 18 September 1790.

26. Mary Gorman, VD, 11 October 1790; Lawrence Gorman, VD, 11 October 1790; Patrick Dalton, VD, 11 October 1790; Cornelius Ridle, VD, 11 October 1790; William Tholley, VD, 15 October 1790; John Reiley, VD, 15 October 1790; John Brown, VD, 15 October 1790; Thomas McKean, VD, 15 October 1790; Martin Campbell, VD, 25 October 1790; Jared Newberry, VD, 25 October 1790; George Robinson, VD, 25 October 1790; Philip Shaw, VD, 25 October 1790;Charles Ames, VD, 25 October 1790; Daniel Connolly, VD, 25 October 1790; John Reed, VD, 25 October 1790; James Walker, VD, 25 October 1790; Jesse Cooper, VD, 25 October 1790; Sarah Smith, VD, 25 October 1790; Mary Head, VD, 25 October 1790.

27. Joseph Kelly, VD, 24 June 1790.

28. Toney, Tom, VD, 17 June 1790.

29. Anthony, VD, 22 October 1790, and 31 October 1790.

30. Minga, VD, 2 August 1790; Tom, VD, 2 August 1796.

31. Peter, VD, 1 June 1796; Tilbry, VD, 1 June 1796; James, VD, 1 June 1796.

32. Bob, VD, 9 July 1796.

33. Nelly, VD, 30 June 1796; Phyllis, VD, 5 October 1796.

34. Cuff, VD, 3 November 1790.

35. Jacob Drummer, VD, 21 July 1790, "delivered to his Master" 29 July 1790; Peter Smilie, VD, 12 July 1796, "deld. to his Master" 4 August 1796.

36. Peter Dickson, VD, 19 August 1796; William Carey, VD, 18 June 1790.

37. Michael Van Keek, VD, 13 June 1796; Maria Van Keek, VD, 13 June 1796.

38. Mary Smilie, VD, 30 June 1796; Jane McElroy, VD, 18 June 1796.

39. David Humpskill, VD, 16 June 1790; Lewis Simon, VD, 6 September 1796.

40. Mary Evans, VD, 22 June 1790; Edward Serjeant, VD, 12 August 1796.

41. Joseph Kennedy, VD, 13 June 1796; Mary Ray, VD, 3 September 1796; Elizabeth Griffiths, VD, 3 September 1796.

42. Jane Peck, VD, 21 July 1790; Catherine Courtney, VD, 30 July 1790; Dubain, VD, 28 June 1796.

43. Sarah Thompson, VD, 29 July 1790; Martha Patterson, VD, 31 July 1790.

44. Michael Meranze, *Laboratories of Virtue: Punishment, Revolution, and Authority in Philadelphia, 1760–1835* (Chapel Hill: University of North Carolina Press, 1996), 22–24, 53–54. For more on the history of almshouses during this era, see Michael B. Katz, *In the Shadow of the Poorhouse: A Social History of Welfare in America* (1986; New York: Basic Books, 1996), 3–36.

45. *Rules, Orders, and Regulations for the Goal [sic] of the City and County of Philadelphia* (Philadelphia: broadside, printed by David Humphreys, 1792). For further discussion of these reforms, see Meranze, *Laboratories of Virtue*, 55, 89–91, 131, 167–68, and Negley K. Teeters, *The Cradle of the Penitentiary: The Walnut Street Jail at Philadelphia, 1773–1835* (Philadelphia: Pennsylvania Prison Society, 1955), 39, 44–46.

46. *Rules, Orders, and Regulations for the Goal*; Benjamin Rush, *An Enquiry into the Effects of Public Punishments Upon Criminals, and upon Society. Read in the Society for Promoting Political Enquiries, Convened at the House of his Excellency Benjamin Franklin, Esquire, in Philadelphia, March 9th, 1787* (Philadelphia: Joseph James, 1787), 13.

47. François-Alexandre-Frédéric, duc de La Rochefoucauld Liancourt, *On the Prisons of Philadelphia, by an European* (Philadelphia: Moreau de Saint-Mery, 1796), 12–13.

48. La Rochefoucauld Liancourt, *On the Prisons,* 13.

49. La Rochefoucauld Liancourt, *On the Prisons,* 16–17.

50. Robert J. Turnbull, *A Visit to the Philadelphia Prison; Being an Accurate and Particular Account of the Wise and Humane Administration Adopted in Every Part of That Building . . .* (Philadelphia: unknown, 1796), 26.

51. *Rules, Orders, and Regulations for the Goal.*

52. Michel Foucault, *Discipline and Punish: The Birth of the Prison,* trans. Alan Sheridan (New York: Pantheon, 1977), 195–308.

53. The best study of this process in Philadelphia is Meranze, *Laboratories of Virtue.*

54. La Rochefoucauld Liancourt, *On the Prisons,* 12–13.

55. Turnbull, *Visit to the Philadelphia Prison,* 79.

56. Ann Carson, *The History of the Celebrated Mrs. Ann Carson, Widow of the Late Unfortunate Lietenant Richard Smith . . .* (Philadelphia: author, 1822), 299.

57. Gary Kielhofner and Trudy Mallinson make a similar point in their analysis of how health care providers conceptualize and treat bodies as objects, rather than treating patients as people experiencing a variety of medical conditions in many different ways. See Kielhofner and Mallinson, "Bodies Telling Stories and Stories Telling Bodies, *Human Studies* 20 (1997): 365–66.

58. Peter Grant, PTD, 20 April 1795, and PSD, 16 June 1795.

59. Henry Holmes, PTD, 13 March 1797, and PSD, 5 May 1797.

60. Jack Smith, Cuff, PTD, 1 September 1795, and PSD, 30 September 1795; Jethro, Cuff, VD, 3 November 1790; Minga, VD, 2 August 1790; Phebe Mines, PTD, 20 February 1796, and PSD, 27 May 1796.

61. Flora, VD, 26 July 1796; William Moody, VD, 2 July 1796.

62. Walter Rosalio, VD, 29 June 1790; Elizabeth Johnson, VD, 7 July 1790; John Hazle, VD, 2 June 1796.

63. William Kennedy, VD, 28 June 1796.

64. Peter, VD, 28 July 1790; Phebe Bowers, VD, 11 September 1790; John Kirpatrick, VD, 12 July 1796; Claude, VD, 7 October 1796.

65. John L. Cotter, Daniel G. Roberts, and Michael Parrington, eds., *The Buried Past: An Archaeological History of Philadelphia* (Philadelphia: University of Pennsylvania Press, 1993), 177–80.

66. Carson, *History of the Celebrated Mrs. Ann Carson,* 301.

67. Turnbull, *Visit to the Philadelphia Prison,* 39.

68. Phebe Mines, PTD, 20 February 1796; Catherine Lynch, PTD, 20 February 1796, Phebe Mines, PSD, 18 March 1796.

69. Margaret Jeffreys, VD, 1 November 1790.

Chapter 3. Hospitalized Bodies

1. The materials used in this chapter are drawn from the annual accounts published by the Hospital Managers in 1796, 1797, and 1798, and from three databases created from records in the Pennsylvania Hospital Archives and Historic Library, Philadelphia. These databases are comprised of the 500 men and women admitted to the hospital between 26 June 1780 and 1 August 1793, recorded in the Book of Patients, 1791–96, Series 5, Item 160, Archives of the Pennsylvania Hospital (almost all these records are drawn from the years

1791–93, but they contain some earlier admissions of long-term patients suffering from insanity); the 200 seafarers admitted to the hospital between 18 August 1800 and 5 November 1803, Admissions for U.S. Seamen, 1800–1809, Series 5, Archives of the Pennsylvania Hospital; and the 100 men and women whose cases were recorded between 10 October 1808 and 16 November 1808 in the Admissions and Discharges, 1804–1927, Item 161, Series 5, Archives of the Pennsylvania Hospital. In accordance with the policies of the Pennsylvania Hospital, the names of actual patients have been omitted or changed in accordance with patient confidentiality, although all dates and other information are as found in the sources.

2. Charles E. Rosenberg, *The Care of Strangers: The Rise of America's Hospital System* (New York: Basic Books, 1987), 15.

3. Rosenberg, *Care of Strangers*, 18–19.

4. J. P. Brissot de Warville, *New Travels in the United States of America, Performed in 1788* (New York: T. and J. Swords for Berry and Rogers, 1792), 117. For general histories of the Pennsylvania Hospital, see William Henry Williams, *America's First Hospital: The Pennsylvania Hospital, 1751–1841* (Wayne, Pa.: Haverford House, 1976); Thomas George Morton and Frank Woodbury, *The History of the Pennsylvania Hospital, 1751–1895* (1895; New York: Arno Press, 1973); and Francis R. Packard, *Some Account of the Pennsylvania Hospital* (Philadelphia: Florence M. Greim, 1957).

5. Rosenberg, *Care of Strangers*, 24.

6. Roy Porter, "Introduction," in *Patients and Practitioners: Lay Perceptions of Medicine in Pre-Industrial Society*, ed. Porter (London: Cambridge University Press, 1985), 16–17.

7. Book of Patients, 1791–96, 17 September 1791, discharged 8 October 1791.

8. Yellow fever decimated Philadelphia during the late eighteenth and early nineteenth centuries, killing a disproportionately large number of the poor, whose close living quarters and inability to flee to safer climes rendered them particularly vulnerable. For more on the yellow fever epidemics, see J. M. Powell, *Bring Out Your Dead: The Great Plague of Yellow Fever in Philadelphia in 1793* (1949; Philadelphia: University of Pennsylvania Press, 1993); J. Worth Estes and Billy G. Smith, eds., *A Melancholy Scene of Devastation: The Public Response to the 1793 Philadelphia Yellow Fever Epidemic* (Canton, Mass.: Science History Publications, 1997); Jacquelyn C. Miller, "The Body Politic: Passions, Pestilence, and Political Culture in the Age of the American Revolution," Ph.D. dissertation, Rutgers University, 1996.

9. Nancy Tomes, *The Art of Asylum-Keeping: Thomas Story Kirkbride and the Origins of American Psychiatry* (Philadelphia: University of Pennsylvania Press, 1994), 23–25; Charles S. Rosenberg, "From Almshouse to Hospital," in *Explaining Epidemics and Other Studies in the History of Medicine* (New York: Cambridge University Press, 1992), 178–214.

10. Admission Form, 15 September 1794, Admission Forms, Series 5, Archives of the Pennsylvania Hospital.

11. Williams, *America's First Hospital*, 111–12.

12. Patient quoted in Williams, *America's First Hospital*, 117; for Ezra Stiles Ely's visits, see Rosenberg, *Care of Strangers*, 15–18.

13. The foods purchased by the hospital are recorded in the Matron and Steward's Cash Books, Pennsylvania Hospital Archives and Historic Library, Philadelphia. Billy G. Smith has employed these records in order to reconstruct the diet of the laboring poor in early national Philadelphia: see Smith, *The "Lower Sort":*

Philadelphia's Laboring People, 1750–1800 (Ithaca, N.Y.: Cornell University Press, 1990), 95–99.

14. During the year ending April 25, 1801, for example, the Pennsylvania Hospital "Attended to, and supplied with medicines" 188 "Poor" Philadelphians, while admitting only 153 sick and injured for residential treatment. Moreover, only a minority of those who were hospitalized were categorized as "poor." See *State of the Accounts of the Pennsylvania Hospital, Adjusted by the Managers . . . 1801* (Philadelphia: broadside, 1801). Hereafter cited as *State of the Accounts, 1801* (and similarly for other years).

15. Williams, *America's First Hospital,* 113–14.

16. Williams, *America's First Hospital,* 114.

17. *State of the Accounts, 1801.* These show that during the year ending 25 April 1801, for example, medical students paid a total of $585.75, 2.8 percent of the hospital's income.

18. See Charles E. Rosenberg, "The Therapeutic Revolution: Medicine, Meaning, and Social Change in Nineteenth-Century America," in *The Therapeutic Revolution: Essays in the Social History of Medicine,* ed. Morris J. Vogel and Charles E. Rosenberg (Philadelphia: University of Pennsylvania Press, 1979), 3–25.

19. Rosenberg, "Therapeutic Revolution," 7; J. Worth Estes, "But It Was Worse in 1784," *American Heritage* 35 (1984): 28.

20. Deborah Lupton, *Medicine as Culture: Illness, Disease, and the Body in Western Societies* (London: Sage, 1994), 11.

21. Gary Kielhofner and Trudy Mallinson, "Bodies Telling Stories and Stories Telling Bodies," *Human Studies* 20 (1997): 365–66.

22. "Wound in the Thorax," Collection of Cases, Pennsylvania Hospital, 1803–29, 5–6, Archives of the Pennsylvania Hospital. Hereafter cited as Cases.

23. "Fracture of the Cervical Vertabra," Cases, 32–34.

24. "A Case of Fractured Scull," Cases, 75.

25. "Fractured Ribs and Injured Head," Cases, 183.

26. Charles Rosenberg, "Disease and Social Order," in *Explaining Epidemics,* 258–77.

27. In the 1796 report, 95 (34%) of the cases were lunatics; in 1797 the number increased slightly to 98 (36.5%); in 1801 the number was 92 (37.5%). See *State of the Accounts, 1796; State of the Accounts 1797; State of the Accounts, 1801.*

28. Tomes, *Art of Asylum-Keeping,* 27.

29. Tomes, *Art of Asylum-Keeping,* 25–26.

30. Samuel Coates, "Memorandum Book: Cases of Several Lunaticks in the Pennsylvania Hospital and the Causes thereof in Many Cases," Rare Book Collection, Pennsylvania Hospital Archives and Historic Library, Philadelphia, 1, 3, 11–12, 5.

31. Coates, "Memorandum Book," 8–11, 16.

32. Coates, "Memorandum Book," 26–27.

33. Coates, "Memorandum Book," 39–42. On the taunting of patients within the hospital, see Williams, *America's First Hospital,* 115.

34. "Wound," Cases, 5–6.

35. Tomes, *Art of Asylum-Keeping,* 28.

36. Four (12.5%) black men, 14 (18.1%) white women, and 58 (15.2%) white men in the Book of Patients database suffered from venereal disease.

37. Admissions for U.S. Seamen, 1800–1809, 26 July 1802, 4 December 1802.

38. Book of Patients, 1791–1796, 29 May 1791, died 19 June 1791.

39. Book of Patients, 1791–1796, 29 August 1791, died 20 September 1791.

40. Book of Patients, 1791–1796, 2 October 1791, died 5 October 1791.

41. Book of Patients, 1791–1796, 22 December 1790, died 7 January 1791.

42. Book of Patients, 1791–1796, 17 July 1793, discharged 11 August 1793.

43. Book of Patients, 1791–1796, 7 August 1792, discharged 21 August 1792.

44. Book of Patients, 1791–1796, 4 October 1791, discharged 5 November 1791.

45. Book of Patients, 1791–1796, 15 April 1790, discharged 11 December 1790; 7 July 1792, discharged 1 August 1792; 15 August 1792, discharged 8 May 1793.

46. Book of Patients, 1791–1796, 7 December 1790, discharged 31 January 1791.

47. Book of Patients, 1791–1796, 15 August 1791, discharged 7 September 1791.

48. Book of Patients, 1791–1796, 2 January 1792, died 6 January 1792; Book of Patients, 1791–1796, 28 October 1791, discharged 2 November 1791.

49. Book of Patients, 22 October 1791, eloped 4 November 1791.

50. Book of Patients, 26 November 1791, discharged 12 April 1792; Book of Patients, 14 February 1793, discharged 21 February 1793.

51. Book of Patients, 8 May 1793, discharged 3 July 1793, 18 May 1793 and 31 May 1793 respectively.

52. "Case 1, Accidents from Blood Letting," Cases, 25.

53. "Case 2, Accidents from Blood Letting," Cases, 25–26.

54. "Fracture of the Os Humeric United by a Setory," Cases, 13–14.

55. "Fracture of the Cervical Vertabra," Cases, 32–34; "Neglected compound fracture of the tibia," Cases, 206–7.

56. "Popliteal Anuerism," Cases, 9–10.

57. "Case of Injury of the Pelvis and Abdomen, by a Loaded Waggon," Cases, 196–97.

58. "Diseased Pudenda," Cases, 173. The tumor was drawn in the manuscript record, and once excised was then preserved.

59. Online edition of the *Oxford English Dictionary*, <http://dictionary.oed.com>, entry 3.a under "tumor."

60. "Fracture of the Os Humeric United by a Setory," Cases, 13–23,.

61. "A Wound in the Foot," Cases, 57–60.

62. "Teeth Replaced," Cases,170.

63. Cases, 104.

64. "Hydrophobia," Cases, 162–64.

65. "Puerperal Fever," Cases, 165–66.

66. "A Case of Dropsy," Cases, 53–55.

67. "Mortification of the Foot," Cases, 29–30.

68. "A Case of Amputation," Cases, 61–71.

69. "Fracture of the Pubis and Rupture of the Uretha," Cases, 187–88.

70. "Singular Growth of Tumors Apparently from Perforating the Ears," Cases, 193.

Chapter 4. Runaway Bodies

1. *Pennsylvania Gazette* (Philadelphia), 4 September 1793 (9613). All the runaway advertisements employed in this chapter have been drawn from Folio Four of the Accessible Archives CD-ROM edition of the *Pennsylvania Gazette*; the number in parenthesis is the Accessible Archives Folio Four item number.

2. *Pennsylvania Gazette*, 21 October 1795 (11132).

3. Shane White has discussed the ways this use of print media enabled white masters to define their black slaves. The same was true for the white indentured servants featured in early national runaway advertisements, especially those imported from Ireland. See White, *Somewhat More Independent: The End of Slavery in New York City, 1770–1810* (Athens: University of Georgia Press, 1991), 116–17. David Waldstreicher has built on this observation, noting that runaway slaves were able to manipulate the form and content of such advertisements in their reaction against the power and control exercised by masters. See Waldstreicher, "Reading the Runaways: Self Fashioning, Print Culture, and Confidence in Slavery in the Eighteenth-Century Mid-Atlantic," *William and Mary Quarterly* 56 (1999): 243–72.

4. Jonathan Prude makes this point in "To Look upon the 'Lower Sort': Runaway Ads and the Appearance of Unfree Laborers in America, 1750–1800," *Journal of American History* 78 (1991): 137. One of the best studies of the presentation and perception of slaves as property can be found in Walter Johnson, *Soul by Soul: Life Inside the Antebellum Slave Market* (Cambridge, Mass.: Harvard University Press, 1999).

5. The past quarter-century has witnessed a significant increase in interest in runaway advertisements, although most scholars have tended to focus on runaway slaves more than runaway servants. See, for example, Gerald W. Mullin, *Flight and Rebellion: Slave Resistance in Eighteenth-Century Virginia* (New York: Oxford University Press, 1972); Philip D. Morgan, "Colonial South Carolina Runaways: Their Significance for Slave Culture," *Slavery and Abolition* 6 (1985): 57–78; Sharon Salinger, *"To Serve Well and Faithfully": Labor and Indentured Servants in Pennsylvania, 1682–1800* (New York: Cambridge University Press, 1987); Billy G. Smith and Richard Wojtowicz, eds., *Blacks Who Stole Themselves: Advertisements for Runaways in the* Pennsylvania Gazette, *1728–1790* (Philadelphia: University of Pennsylvania Press, 1989); Prude, "To Look upon the 'Lower Sort'"; White, *Somewhat More Independent;* Daniel E. Meaders, *Dead or Alive: Fugitive Slaves and White Indentured Servants Before 1830* (New York: Garland, 1993); Freddie L. Parker, *Running for Freedom: Slave Runaways in North Carolina, 1775–1840* (New York: Garland, 1993); Graham Russell Hodges and Alan Edward Brown, eds., *Pretends to Be Free: Runaway Slave Advertisements from Colonial and Revolutionary New York and New Jersey* (New York: Garland, 1994); Billy G. Smith, "Runaway Slaves in the Mid-Atlantic Region During the Revolutionary Era," in *The Transforming Hand of Revolution: Reconsidering the American Revolution as a Social Movement,* ed. Ronald Hoffman and Peter J. Albert (Charlottesville: University Press of Virginia, 1995), 199–230; John Hope Franklin and Loren Schweninger, *Runaway Slaves: Rebels on the Plantation* (New York: Oxford University Press, 1999); Waldstreicher, "Reading the Runaways"; Billy G. Smith, "Black Women Who Stole Themselves in Eighteenth-Century America," in *Inequality in Early America,* ed. Carla Gardina Pestana and Sharon V. Salinger (Hanover, N.H.: University Press of New England, 1999), 134–59.

6. *Pennsylvania Gazette,* 19 March 1794 (9948); *Pennsylvania Gazette,* 2 September 1795 (11018).

7. For more information on runaways and Philadelphia in this era, see Salinger, *To Serve Well and Faithfully;* Gary B. Nash, *Forging Freedom: The Formation of Philadelphia's Black Community, 1720–1840* (Cambridge, Mass.: Harvard University Press, 1988); Billy G. Smith, *The "Lower Sort": Philadelphia's Laboring People, 1750–1800* (Ithaca, N.Y.: Cornell University Press, 1990); and Smith and Wojtowicz, *Blacks Who Stole Themselves.*

8. While all the runaway advertisements appearing between 1784 and 1800

were examined, one hundred of the most complete and detailed advertisements for runaway blacks and another one hundred similarly full advertisements for runaway whites provided the base group for the examples used. This chapter features a qualitative rather than a quantitative analysis, and the advertisements employed in the samples were the lengthiest and most detailed that appeared during these years.

9. Nick Crossley is one of a number of commentators who have sought to demonstrate that Foucault's functionalist theory of the body as controlled and acted upon, and Merleau-Ponty's belief in the agency displayed by and inherent within individual bodies, can be reconciled in this fashion. See Crossley, "Body-Subject/Body Power: Agency, Inscription and Control in Foucault and Merleau-Ponty," *Body and Society* 2 (1996): 99–116.

10. White, *Somewhat More Independent*, 116–17; Waldstreicher, "Reading the Runaways," 244–47.

11. Jean-Claude Schmitt, "The Ethics of Gesture," in *Fragments for a History of the Human Body*, ed. Michel Feher, Ramona Naddaff, and Nadia Tazi, special issue of *Zone* 2 (1989): 129–130.

12. *Pennsylvania Gazette*, 4 August 1790 (7310).

13. *Pennsylvania Gazette*, 14 December 1791 (8414).

14. *Pennsylvania Gazette*, 25 June 1794 (10152).

15. *Pennsylvania Gazette*, 30 December 1795 (11282).

16. *Pennsylvania Gazette*, 20 August 1794 (10281).

17. For a detailed discussion of the context for sexual relationships between black men and white women, see Martha Hodes, *White Women, Black Men: Illicit Sex in the Nineteenth-Century South* (New Haven, Conn.: Yale University Press, 1997), and Hodes, "The Sexualization of Reconstruction Politics: White Women and Black Men in the South After the Civil War," *Journal of the History of Sexuality* 3 (1993): 402–17.

18. *Pennsylvania Gazette*, 27 September 1786 (3670); *Pennsylvania Gazette*, 10 June 1795 (10892); *Pennsylvania Gazette*, 15 September 1790 (7428); *Pennsylvania Gazette*, 25 May 1796 (11577).

19. *Pennsylvania Gazette*, 6 June 1798 (12805); *Pennsylvania Gazette*, 1 May 1790 (8854).

20. *Pennsylvania Gazette*, 10 June 1793 (9510); *Pennsylvania Gazette*, 29 November 1787; *Pennsylvania Gazette*, 15 October 1794 (10405).

21. On slaves' employment of surnames, and their increasing use over the course of the eighteenth and early nineteenth centuries, see White, *Somewhat More Independent*, 192–94; Herbert G. Gutman, *The Black Family in Slavery and Freedom, 1750–1925* (New York: Pantheon, 1976), 230–56.

22. *Pennsylvania Gazette*, 31 March 1787 (4344).

23. Nash, *Forging Freedom*, 81–86; White, *Somewhat More Independent*, 192.

24. *Pennsylvania Gazette*, 7 January 1789 (5885); *Pennsylvania Gazette*, 16 March 1796 (11440); *Pennsylvania Gazette*, 26 September 1792 (8925).

25. *Pennsylvania Gazette*, 9 June 1790 (7166).

26. *Pennsylvania Gazette*, 4 August 1790 (7310) ; *Pennsylvania Gazette*, 28 May 1788 (5301); *Pennsylvania Gazette*, 10 June 1793 (9510).

27. Mullin, *Flight and Rebellion*, 89.

28. Mullin, *Flight and Rebellion*, 98–99.

29. *Pennsylvania Gazette*, 9 April 1791 (7950); *Pennsylvania Gazette*, 21 October 1795 (11132).

30. *Pennsylvania Gazette*, 21 October 1795 (11132).

31. *Pennsylvania Gazette*, 13 October 1790 (7490).

32. bell hooks describes "back talk" in terms of "daring to disagree," or even just having an opinion, "an act of risking and daring." See hooks, "Talking Back," in *Out There: Marginalization and Contemporary Cultures*, ed. Russell Ferguson, Martha Gever, Trinh T. Minh-ha, and Cornel West (New York: New Museum of Contemporary Art, 1990), 337.

33. *Pennsylvania Gazette*, 13 April 1796 (11481); *Pennsylvania Gazette*, 4 December 1793 (9685).

34. Mullin, *Flight and Rebellion*, 98–100.

35. *Pennsylvania Gazette*, 1 September 1790 (7392); *Pennsylvania Gazette*, 7 December 1791 (8405); *Pennsylvania Gazette*, 25 April 1792 (8646); *Pennsylvania Gazette*, 9 November 1785 (2634); *Pennsylvania Gazette*, 4 September 1793 (9613).

36. *Pennsylvania Gazette*, 25 February 1795 (10687); *Pennsylvania Gazette*, 11 March 1795 (10713).

37. *Pennsylvania Gazette*, 5 May 1790 (7098); *Pennsylvania Gazette*, 10 November 1790 (7568).

38. Lindon Barrett, "African-American Narratives: Literacy, the Body, Authority," *American Literary History* 7 (1995): 415–19.

39. *Pennsylvania Gazette*, 20 August 1788 (5496); *Pennsylvania Gazette*, 8 August 1792 (8839); *Pennsylvania Gazette*, 25 April 1792 (8646).

40. *Pennsylvania Gazette*, 12 September 1787 (4619); *Pennsylvania Gazette*, 29 March 1797; *Pennsylvania Gazette*, 27 March 1794 (10001).

41. Mullin, *Flight and Rebellion*, 94–98.

42. Richard L. Bushman, *The Refinement of America: Persons, Houses, Cities* (New York: Alfred A. Knopf, 1992), 66.

43. Kenneth R. Johnson, "Black Kinesics: Some Non-Verbal Communication Patterns in Black Culture," in *Perspectives on Black English*, ed. John Dillard (The Hague: Mouton, 1975), 296–306.

44. According to Johnson, reluctance to look an authority figure in the eye was common to many West African cultures, and this strategy may well have assumed renewed significance in the context of New World racial slavery. See Johnson, "Black Kinesics," 299–300.

45. *Pennsylvania Gazette*, 3 April 1790 (7098); *Pennsylvania Gazette*, 19 March 1794 (9948); *Pennsylvania Gazette*, 15 October 1794 (10405).

46. *Pennsylvania Gazette*, 10 January 1785; *Pennsylvania Gazette*, 16 July 1788 (5404); *Pennsylvania Gazette*, 20 June 1792 (8751); *Pennsylvania Gazette*, 7 August 1793 (9566).

47. *Pennsylvania Gazette*, 10 November 1790 (7567).

48. Shane White has compared the "down look" of runaway blacks with the rather more aggressive posture of runway white convicts, and has suggested that the down look was thus more race than class specific. While the *Pennsylvania Gazette* runaway advertisements employed in this sample described more black men than white men as adopting this stance, it was common enough among whites to challenge White's assertion. See White, *Somewhat More Independent*, 202.

49. *Pennsylvania Gazette*, 10 June 1795 (10892); *Pennsylvania Gazette*, 1 February 1792 (8491).

50. *Pennsylvania Gazette*, 16 April 1788 (5192).

51. Primus was recorded as having run away with Bob, a fellow New Jersey slave: see *Pennsylvania Gazette*, 16 April 1788 (5192).

52. *Pennsylvania Gazette*, 3 September 1794 (10314); *Pennsylvania Gazette*, 4 August 1790 (7324).

53. *Pennsylvania Gazette*, 4 December 1793; *Pennsylvania Gazette*, 29 August 1787 (4581).

54. Pasi Falk, "Written in the Flesh," *Body and Society* 1 (1995): 95.

55. Mullin, *Flight and Rebellion*, 40–41.

56. *Pennsylvania Gazette*, 2 December 1789 (6702).

57. Smith, "Runaway Slaves in the Mid-Atlantic Region," 211; Shane White and Graham White, *Stylin': African American Expressive Culture from Its Beginnings to the Zoot Suit* (Ithaca, N.Y.: Cornell University Press, 1998), 40.

58. *Pennsylvania Gazette*, 8 January 1794 (9794); *Pennsylvania Gazette*, 4 September 1793 (9613).

59. *Pennsylvania Gazette*, 6 June 1787 (4378); *Pennsylvania Gazette*, 9 May 1792 (8679); *Pennsylvania Gazette*, 5 August 1789 (6415).

60. *Pennsylvania Gazette*, 29 March 1797 (12144).

61. White and White, *Stylin'*, 40; Smith, "Runaway Slaves in the Mid-Atlantic Region," 211–12.

62. *Pennsylvania Gazette*, 29 May 1793 (9414); *Pennsylvania Gazette*, 3 October 1795 (11132).

63. *Pennsylvania Gazette*, 30 March 1791 (7872).

64. Prude, "To Look Upon the 'Lower Sort,'" 143–44.

65. *Pennsylvania Gazette*, 7 November 1792 (9016).

66. See Prude, "To Look Upon the 'Lower Sort,'" 145–46, and Joanne Early, "Runaway Advertisements: A Source for the Study of Working-Class Costume," *Pennsylvania Folklife* 27 (1978): 46–49.

67. *Pennsylvania Gazette*, 9 July 1794 (10176).

68. White and White, *Stylin'*, 23–35.

69. *Pennsylvania Gazette*, 29 May 1793 (9414).

70. *Pennsylvania Gazette*, 3 October 1792 (8938).

71. *Pennsylvania Gazette*, 5 February 1794 (9847).

72. *Pennsylvania Gazette*, 11 October 1788 (6091); *Pennsylvania Gazette*, 27 September 1786 (3670); *Pennsylvania Gazette*, 7 August 1793 (9565).

73. John Hope Franklin and Loren Schweninger have argued of runaways that "principally they took along changes of clothing to use for disguise." See Franklin and Schweninger, *Runaway Slaves*, 222.

74. *Pennsylvania Gazette*, 9 April 1788 (5162); *Pennsylvania Gazette*, 31 October 1792 (8999).

75. See Beverly Lemire, "The Theft of Clothes and Popular Consumerism in Early Modern England," *Journal of Social History* 24 (1990): 255–76, and Patricia Allerston, "Clothing and Early Modern Venetian Society," *Continuity and Change* 15 (2000): 367–90, and "The Market in Second Hand Clothes and Furnishings in Venice, c. 1500–c. 1600," Ph.D. dissertation, European History Institute, 1996. See also Daniel Roche, *The Culture of Clothing: Dress and Fashion in the "Ancien Régime*," trans. Jean Birrell (New York: Cambridge University Press, 1994). One of the few historians to probe the significance of this market for American runaways is Shane White in *Somewhat More Independent*, 195–97.

76. John Styler, "Servants," *Textile History*, forthcoming: manuscript provided by author.

77. Paricia Calefato, "Fashion and Worldliness: Language and Imagery of the Clothed Body," trans. Lisa Adams, *Fashion Theory: The Journal of Dress, Body and Culture* 1 (1997): 69–70; Joanne Finkelstein, *The Fashioned Self* (Oxford: Polity Press, 1991), 5; Dick Hebdige, "Style as Intentional Communication," in *Subculture: The Meaning of Style* (London: Methuen, 1979), 100–102.

78. Prude, "To Look Upon the 'Lower Sort,'" 155.

79. *Pennsylvania Gazette*, 6 April 1796 (11475); *Pennsylvania Gazette*, 5 February 1794 (9847); *Pennsylvania Gazette*, 18 November 1789 (6670).

80. *Pennsylvania Gazette*, 3 September 1794 (10314); *Pennsylvania Gazette*, 11 May 1785 (1987).

81. White, *Somewhat More Independent*, 195.

82. *Pennsylvania Gazette*, 7 August 1793 (9320).

83. Diane Crane has argued that clothing may function as a nonverbal "form of symbolic communication." See Crane, "Clothing Behavior as Non-Verbal Resistance: Marginal Women and Alternative Dress in the Nineteenth Century," *Fashion Theory: The Journal of Dress, Body, and Culture* 3 (1999): 242.

84. White, *Somewhat More Independent*, 197.

85. Kobena Mercer, "Black Hair/Style Politics," in *Out There*, ed. Ferguson et al., 247–64; White and White, *Stylin'*, 40–51.

86. *Pennsylvania Gazette*, 5 February 1794 (9847).

87. See, for example, the advertisements for Dinah and for Armstrong, *Pennsylvania Gazette*, 6 June 1798 (12805), and *Pennsylvania Gazette*, 16 November 1791 (8351).

88. *Pennsylvania Gazette*, 21 October 1795 (11132). For a complete description of black hair styles, see White and White, *Stylin'*, 41.

89. *Pennsylvania Gazette*, 14 May 1788 (5265).

90. *Pennsylvania Gazette*, 4 May 1791 (7950); *Pennsylvania Gazette*, 19 February 1794 (9883).

91. Mercer, "Black Hair/Style Politics," 249–59.

Chapter 5. Seafaring Bodies

1. This information is taken from George Ribble's application for a Seamen's Protection Certificate (SPCA), 18 December 1805. The SPCAs are in the National Archives, Record Group 36, Records of the Bureau of Customs. Ribble stood 65.5 inches tall; military records from the American War for Independence reveal that native-born white males had a mean height of 68.1 inches. See Kenneth L. Solokoff, *The Heights of Americans in Three Centuries: Some Economic and Demographic Implications*, NBER (Cambridge, Mass.: National Bureau of Economic Research, 1984), Working Paper 1384, 6, and Kenneth L. Sokoloff and Georgia C. Villaflor, "The Early Achievement of Modern Stature in America," *Social Science History* 6 (1982): 453–81.

2. Daniel Vickers, "Beyond Jack Tar," *William and Mary Quarterly* 3rd ser. 50 (1993): 422. Some two decades ago, David Alexander eloquently suggested that seafarers "were simply working men who got wet." See Alexander, "Literacy Among Canadian and Foreign Seamen, 1863–1899," in *Working Men Who Got Wet*, ed. Rosemary Ommer and Gerald Panting (St. John's: Memorial University of Newfoundland, 1980), 32. His point has been echoed and enlarged by such scholars as Eric W. Sager and Daniel Vickers: see Sager, *Seafaring Labour: The Merchant Marine of Atlantic Canada, 1820–1914* (Montreal: McGill-Queen's University Press, 1989), and Vickers, "Beyond Jack Tar" and *Farmers and Fishermen: Two Centuries of Work in Essex County, Massachusetts, 1630–1850* (Chapel Hill: University of North Carolina Press, 1994), 182–83.

3. Herman Melville, "Daniel Orme," in *Billy Budd, Sailor, and Other Stories*, ed. Harold Beaver, (New York: Penguin, 1970), 417.

4. Dick Hebdige, *Subculture: The Meaning of Style* (London: Methuen, 1979), 18, 80, 100–102.

5. Michel Foucault used "political anatomy" to describe the process whereby institutions with power—in this case merchant and naval ships—manifested

discipline and control by inscribing the bodies of those who lived and labored within them. But the body was both acted upon and active, a contested terrain, and seafarers projected a measure of independence through the presentation of their bodies. For further discussion of this contest over and upon the body, see David Armstrong, "Bodies of Knowledge/Knowledge of Bodies," in *Reassessing Foucault: Power, Medicine, and the Body*, ed. Colin Jones and Roy Porter (London: Routledge, 1994), 20–22; Judith Butler, "Foucault and the Paradox of Bodily Inscriptions," in *The Body: Classic and Contemporary Readings*, ed. Donn Welton (Oxford: Blackwell, 1999), 307–13; Simon J. Williams and Gillian Bendelow, *The Lived Body: Sociological Themes, Embodied Issues* (London: Routledge, 1998), 28–29; Nick Crossley, "Body-Subject/Body-Power: Agency, Inscription, and Control in Foucault and Merleau-Ponty," *Body and Society* 2 (1996): 99–116.

6. Under the principle of indefeasible nationality, British authorities argued that any man born a British subject remained one until the day he died, which to their minds justified the impressment of Americans whenever the Royal Navy was short-handed; see Christopher Lloyd, *The British Seaman, 1200–1860: A Social Survey* (1968; Rutherford, N.J.: Fairleigh Dickinson University Press, 1970), 215, 265–66, 115, 117–18. By the turn of the nineteenth century, at least 3,000 native-born citizens of the republic were fighting and dying for a foreign monarch, to say nothing of thousands of British-born impressed mariners who had become legal residents and citizens of the United States.

7. Richard Peters, ed., *The Public Statutes at Large of the United States of America, from the Organization of the Government in 1789, to March 3, 1845 . . .* (Boston: Little and Brown, 1845), 1: 477. See also *The Debates and Proceedings in the Congress of the United States . . . Fourth Congress—First Session* (Washington, D.C.: Gales and Seaton, 1849), 5: 802.

8. Ira Dye, "The Philadelphia Seamen's Protection Certificate Applications," *Prologue: Sources at the National Archives for Genealogical and Local History Research* 18 (1986): 51. See also Ruth Priest Dixon and Katherine George Eberly, *Index to Seamen's Protection Certificate Applications, Port of Philadelphia, 1796–1861*, 2 vols. (Baltimore: Clearfield, 1994–95); Dye, "Early American Merchant Seafarers," *Proceedings of the American Philosophical Society* 120 (1976): 340–44, and "Physical and Social Profiles of Early American Seafarers, 1812–1815," in *Jack Tar in History: Essays in the History of Maritime Life and Labour*, ed. Colin Howell and Richard J. Twomey (Fredericton: Acadiensis, 1991), 220–35.

9. Native Americans were the only other contemporary North Americans who wore tattoos: see, for example, the portrait of a Mahican named Etow Oh Koam painted by John Van Verelst with several simple designs on his face (1710) and John Faber's paintings of Sa Ga Yeath Qua Pieth, a Mohawk with more elaborate designs on his face, chest, and left arm (1710). See *Handbook of North American Indians*, vol. 15, *Northeast*, ed. Bruce G. Trigger (Washington, D.C.: Smithsonian Institution Press, 1978), 201–2, 310.

On the tattoos of seafarers see Ira Dye, "The Tattoos of Early American Seafarers, 1796–1818," *Proceedings of the American Philosophical Society* 133 (1989): 520–54; Simon P. Newman, "Wearing Their Hearts on Their Sleeves," in *American Bodies: Cultural Histories of the Physique*, ed. Tim Armstrong (Sheffield: Sheffield Academic Press, 1996), 18–31; B. R. Burg, "Tattoo Designs and Locations in the Old U.S. Navy," *Journal of American Culture* 18 (1995): 69–75, and "Sailors and Tattoos in the Early American Steam Navy: Evidence from the Diary of Philip C. Van Buskirk, 1884–1889," *International Journal of Maritime History* 6 (1994): 161–74.

10. For further discussion of the British records of the incidence of tattooing

among American soldiers and sailors imprisoned during the War of 1812, see Dye, "The Tattoos of Early American Seafarers," 548–49, 526–27.

11. The relative popularity of tattooing among late eighteenth-century mariners confirms that exposure to the ornate tattooing of the South Sea Islanders, in the wake of Captain Cook's voyages of the 1770s, simply increased interest and proficiency in a custom already well established among seamen. For centuries, European visitors had acquired tattoos in the Holy Land, and the techniques and designs of Coptic Christian tattooists had been appropriated by early modern seafarers. For a detailed description of one pilgrim's account of his acquisition of such a tattoo, see Jean de Thévenot, quoted in C. P. Jones, "Stigma: Tattooing and Branding in Graeco-Roman Antiquity," *Journal of Roman Studies* 77 (1987): 141.

Others who have argued that the custom of seafaring tattooing originated with these religious tattoos in the Mediterranean world include Alan Governar, "Christian Tattoos," *Tattootime* 2 (1983), 7–8; R.W.B. Scutt and Christopher Gotch, *Art and Symbol: The Mystery of Tattooing* (Cranbury, N.J.: A.S. Barnes, 1974), 65; Clinton R. Sanders, *Customizing the Body: The Art and Culture of Tattooing* (Philadelphia: Temple University Press, 1989), 13–14; and Jane Caplan, "Introduction," in *Written on the Body: The Tattoo in European and American History*, ed. Caplan (Princeton, N.J.: Princeton University Press, 2000), xvii–xvii.

For more on the history and culture of tattooing see Robert Brain, *The Decorated Body* (New York: Hutchinson, 1979); W. D. Hambly, *The History of Tattooing and Its Significance* (London: H. F. and G. Witherby, 1925); Samuel M. Steward, *Bad Boys and Tough Tattoos: A Social History of the Tattoo with Gangs, Sailors, and Street-Corner Punks* (New York: Harrington Park, 1990); Victoria Ebin, *The Body Decorated* (London: Thames and Hudson, 1979); Bernard Rudofsky, *The Unfashionable Human Body* (New York: Van Nostrand Reinhold, 1984); Frances E. Mascia-Lees and Patricia Sharpe, eds., *Tattoo, Torture, Mutilation, and Adornment: The Denaturalization of the Body in Culture and Text* (Albany: State University of New York Press, 1992); and André Virel, *Decorated Man: The Human Body as Art*, trans. I. Mark Paris (New York: Abrams, 1980).

12. Dye, " Tattoos of Early American Seafarers," 529–31.

13. Arkady G. Bronnikov, "Body Language," *New York Times*, 6 November 1993, 17, and "Telltale Tattoos in Russian Prisons," *Natural History* 102 (November 1993): 50.

14. William Story, SPCA, 10 July 1815; Jacob McKinsey, SPCA, 2 November 1803.

15. Greg Dening, *Mr. Bligh's Bad Language: Passion, Power, and Theatre on the Bounty* (New York: Cambridge University Press, 1992), 36.

16. Jane Caplan has suggested that tattoos can function extremely effectively as "a marker of difference, an index of inclusion and exclusion." See Caplan, *Written on the Body*, xiv.

17. British officers often justified impressment on the grounds that a large number of British sailors and deserters from the Royal Navy were working in the American merchant marine, and a few of these Britons may well have applied for protection certificates, lying to officials about their place of birth. Well aware of this, Royal Navy officers frequently impressed seamen who they suspected were British "without respect to their protections, which were often taken from them and destroyed." Samuel Leech, *A Voice from the Main Deck: Being the Experiences of Samuel Leech, Who Was for Six Years in the British and American Navies* (Boston: Tappan and Dennet, 1843), 80. Thus some of the 500 applicants for protection certificates who are the subjects of this chapter in all probability lied about their

place of birth. However, these men had become members of the American sea-faring community, a heterogeneous mix of ethnicities and races: whether or not they lied about their birthplace, they were sailors on American ships and members of American seaport communities. For a discussion of the numbers of foreign seamen serving on U.S. navy ships see Christopher McKee, "Foreign Seamen in the United States Navy: A Census of 1808," *William and Mary Quarterly* 3rd ser. 42 (1985): 383–93.

18. For the purposes of this chapter, towns and cities that in 1790 had populations exceeding 5,000 are considered urban. Only Salem, Boston, Newport, Providence, New York, Philadelphia, Baltimore, Charleston, and New Orleans meet this criterion. Riley Moffat, *Population History of the Eastern U.S. Cities and Towns, 1790–1870* (Metuchen, N.J.: Scarecrow Press, 1992). Most historians have accepted that New England provided the early republic with more sailors than any other region. The fact that my data base is formed from applications filed in Philadelphia accounts for the high proportion of Middle Atlantic-born men.

19. Dye, "Early American Merchant Seafarers," 349, 350.

20. W. Jeffrey Bolster, "'To Feel like a Man': Black Seamen in the Northern States, 1800–1860," *Journal of American History* 76 (1990): 1174; Billy G. Smith, *The "Lower Sort": Philadelphia's Laboring People, 1750–1800* (Ithaca, N.Y.: Cornell University Press, 1990), 156–58; Gary B. Nash, *Forging Freedom: The Formation of Philadelphia's Black Community, 1720–1840* (Cambridge, Mass.: Harvard University Press, 1988), 74, 135–37, 146, 149; Dye, "Physical and Social Profiles of Early American Seafarers," unpublished paper, 10–11 (I am grateful to Ira Dye for sharing his research and work with me). According to the Census of 1790, free and enslaved black people constituted just under 5 percent of the population of Philadelphia and its immediate suburbs, but when compared to the white community a far higher proportion of black adult males—both locally based and transitory—were sailors. *Return of the Whole Number of Persons Within the Several Districts of the United States . . .* (Philadelphia: Childs and Swaine, 1791), 45.

21. W. Jeffrey Bolster, *Black Jacks: African American Seamen in the Age of Sail* (Cambridge, Mass.: Harvard University Press, 1997), 93.

22. In most other respects, these black seamen were strikingly similar to the white applicants in this sample: seven were born in rural locations, three in Southern states, and only two in New England. Gary B. Nash has employed both protection certificate applications and crew lists to establish that no more than about one-twelfth of black long- and short-term sailors operating in Philadelphia had actually been born there. The proportion of white sailors was probably significantly higher, suggesting that the city served as a refuge for black Americans from all over the United States and beyond in the decades after the American Revolution, and that for black men seafaring was one of the most accessible careers. See Nash, *Forging Freedom*, 136–37.

23. Because there could be significant differences in adult heights according to race, I measured the heights of white and black seafarers separately. From the total of 485 white sailors I discounted the 14 who were foreign-born or whose birthplace is unrecorded and a further three whose heights are not recorded. Five more were discounted because their applications reveal that they were measured while wearing shoes, leaving a total of 463 native-born white seamen.

24. Roderick Floud, Kenneth Wachter, and Annabel Gregory, *Height, Health, and History: Nutritional Status in the United Kingdom, 1750–1980* (New York: Cambridge University Press, 1990), 17; Sokoloff, *Heights of Americans in Three Centuries*, 1–3.

25. Full adult height is not usually achieved until age twenty-four, and diminution of stature occurs after age forty-nine (see, for example, Floud et al., *Height,*

Health, and History, 24–25). Using these benchmarks, this sample was reduced to the 217 seamen who were born between 1760 and 1789 and had achieved full adult height at the time of their application.

26. While military records from the Revolutionary era furnish a mean height of 68.1 inches for native-born white males, similar records for World War II indicate a mean height of 68.2 inches; see Sokoloff, *Heights of Americans in Three Centuries*, 6. The male population of Europe averaged as much as four inches shorter, which suggests that the white American population were considerably better nourished and lived in much healthier conditions. For the heights of the British military see Sokoloff and Villaflor, "Early Achievement of Modern Stature," 467, 460.

27. Sokoloff and Villaflor, "Early Achievement of Modern Stature," 467–78, 474.

28. On poverty in late eighteenth- and early nineteenth-century middle Atlantic cities, see Smith, *"Lower Sort"*; Gary B. Nash, *The Urban Crucible: Social Change, Political Consciousness, and the Origins of the American Revolution* (Cambridge, Mass.: Harvard University Press, 1979); Raymond A. Mohl, *Poverty in New York, 1783–1825* (New York: Oxford University Press, 1971); John K. Alexander, *Render Them Submissive: Responses to Poverty in Philadelphia, 1760–1800* (Amherst: University of Massachusetts Press, 1980); Robert E. Cray, Jr., *Paupers and Poor Relief in New York City and Its Rural Environs, 1700–1830* (Philadelphia: Temple University Press, 1988).

29. Thirteen witnesses were fathers of the seafarers, and their records suggest that illiteracy was declining over time, albeit slowly. Five seamen (38.46%) enjoyed a higher level of literacy than their fathers, three (23.07%) had the same level of literacy, while only two (15.38%) were less literate. In only three cases (23.07%) were both father and son illiterate.

Of the witnesses to these 500 applications, 56 were women, and they were even less literate than the male seafarers: 62.5 percent were completely illiterate, and a further 26.8 percent could not write a well-formed signature. Well-born functionaries like Benjamin Nones struck out the words "a Citizen" when women like Catherine Adams and Mary Shepperd appeared as witnesses for William Adams and George Ribble. William Adams, SPCA, 22 October 1804; George Ribble, SPCA, 18 December 1805.

30. Lee Soltow and Edward Stevens, *The Rise of Literacy and the Common School in the United States: A Socioeconomic Analysis to 1870* (Chicago: University of Chicago Press, 1981), 52.

31. This pattern was common to all the regions these sailors came from. The illiteracy rate for urban-born New Englanders stood at 44 percent, 35 percent for those from the middle Atlantic, and 58 percent for Southerners. In comparison, illiteracy among the rural-born stood at 20 percent in New England, 27 percent in the middle Atlantic, and 49 percent in the South. Overall, illiteracy was highest in the South; 54 percent of the mariners born there were unable to sign their names. The rate was considerably lower among middle Atlantic applicants, 31 percent, and not surprisingly illiteracy was lowest in New England, 24 percent.

32. Leech, *Voice from the Main Deck*, 105.

33. Over 90 percent of the Royal Navy ships lost during the Napoleonic Wars were destroyed by the elements; well over 80 percent of all sailors' deaths were caused by scurvy and disease. Michael Lewis, *A Social History of the Navy, 1793–1815* (London: Allen and Unwin, 1960), 390; Lloyd, *British Seaman*, 263.

34. William Bentley, *The Diary of William Bentley, D.D., Pastor of the East Church Salem, Massachusetts* (1905; Gloucester, Mass.: Peter Smith, 1962), 1: 19, 270, 271.

35. For a detailed discussion of the work patterns of eighteenth-century seamen and the dangers of this work, see Marcus Rediker, *Between the Devil and*

the Deep Blue Sea: Merchant Seamen, Pirates, and the Anglo-American Maritime World, 1700–1750 (New York: Cambridge University Press, 1987), 85–93.

36. Peter Hanse, SPCA, 5 July 1806; Lawrence Hanson, SPCA, 4 June 1806.

37. William Travis, SPCA, 6 March 1807; Robert Andrews, SPCA, 29 May 1809.

38. John Baker, SPCA, 5 July 1808; John Fullerton, SPCA, 24 November 1815. Many of the scars and injuries recorded on protection certificate applications fit the hazardous work regimen of the seafarers, although others may have occurred during childhood, at work in rural or urban locations, or even in tavern brawls.

39. Smith, *"Lower Sort"*, 53; Reverend Nicholas Collin's record for John Seaburn, 25 Feb. 1798, Burial Records, Old Swedes Church, Gloria Dei Burial Records, 115–16. These records are held by the Pennsylvania Genealogical Society, Historical Society of Pennsylvania, and are hereafter cited as Burial Records. Surprisingly, none of the 500 mariners were recorded as having hernias or, to use their own term for the painful affliction, "bursted bellies." The heavy lifting and pulling required of seamen resulted in close to 15 percent of the sailors in the contemporary Royal Navy wearing trusses, and it is reasonable to suspect that some of these American mariners suffered similar injuries. Perhaps the applications were interpreted in such a way as to render references to hernias unnecessary: perhaps, too, this injury was so common as not to warrant mention. Rediker, *Between the Devil and the Deep Blue Sea*, 93; Lloyd, *British Seaman*, 262.

40. Smith, *The "Lower Sort"*, 54.

41. Throughout the seventeenth and eighteenth centuries, smallpox killed tens of thousands of Americans, but by the turn of the nineteenth century inoculation had become increasingly common. However, Edward Jenner's discovery that a cowpox inoculation conferred immunity did not reach America until the very end of the eighteenth century: for many decades before, and for some years after, a severe form of inoculation had been practiced using long and deep incisions in one or both upper arms and the insertion of material from a human smallpox pustule. The results were deep and malignant scars, a less severe case of smallpox, contagion, and, on occasion, death. Eighteen-year-old John Dixon of Nantucket was one of the seven mariners in this group with "a large Scar occasioned by inoculation." John Dixon, SPCA, 7 June 1804. See Peter Razzell, *The Conquest of Smallpox: The Impact of Inoculation on Smallpox Mortality in Eighteenth Century Britain* (Firle, Sussex: Caliban, 1977), 6, 10, 12–19, 93–94, 142–43. See also Donald R. Hopkins, *Princes and Peasants: Smallpox in History* (Chicago: University of Chicago Press, 1983), 3–4, 261–64.

42. For a discussion of the history of popular resistance to inoculation, see John B. Blake, "The Inoculation Controversy in Boston, 1721–1722," in *Sickness and Health in America: Readings in the History of Medicine and Public Health*, ed. Judith Walzer Leavitt and Ronald L. Numbers (Madison: University of Wisconsin Press, 1985), 347–55.

43. Thomas Dawson, 15 April 1803, Burial Records, 208; John Stubbe, 8 November 1808, Burial Records, 252–53. Collin was unable to determine the nature of the malady that killed Dawson.

44. Collin recorded the ages of 23 of the 25 mariners: the average was 33.6, and 14 (60.9%) were under thirty. During these years Collin buried at least 13 wives or widows of seafarers and at least 18 seamen's children.

45. J. H. admitted to the Pennsylvania Hospital for the Deserving Poor 29 April 1801; S. B., admitted 21 August 1802; I. H., admitted 7 July 1802. See Admissions for U.S. Seamen, 1800–1809, Series 5, Archives of the Pennsylvania Hospital. These data are drawn from the cases of 200 seafarers admitted to the hospital between 18 August 1800 and 5 November 1803.

46. "Spanking Jack," in *Spanking Jack and Other Songs* (songbook, Library Company of Philadelphia, 1805), cited in Ric Nortrup Caric, "'To Drown the Ills That Discompose the Mind': Care, Leisure, and Identity Among Philadelphia Artisans and Workers, 1785–1840," *Pennsylvania History: A Journal of MidAtlantic Studies* 64 (1997): 470–71.

47. A foul or fouled anchor was an anchor with a chain wound around it.

48. William Gaines, SPCA, 19 April 1805; William Adams, SPCA, 22 October 1804; Thomas Milburn, SPCA, 24 March 1807.

49. George Robinson, SPCA, 29 August 1804; John Williams, SPCA, 23 December 1805.

50. Maritime tattoos may thus have functioned as badges of the shared class consciousness, culture, and *mentalité* of seafaring wage laborers described by Marcus Rediker. See Rediker, *Between the Devil and the Deep Blue Sea*.

51. James Henry, SPCA, 26 December 1805; William Watson, SPCA, 17 May 1809.

52. John Berry, SPCA, 14 June 1809; James Henry, SPCA, 26 December 1805.

53. Christopher McKee has established that a sizable minority of the applicants for protection certificates had worked their way up from the bottom of the profession and that future naval officers often sought practical experience before the mast in the merchant marine. See McKee, *A Gentlemanly and Honorable Profession: The Creation of the U.S. Naval Officer Corps, 1794–1815* (Annapolis, Md.: Naval Institute Press, 1991), 99, 160.

54. Steven C. Bullock, "The Revolutionary Transformation of American Freemasonry, 1752–1792," *William and Mary Quarterly* 3rd ser. 47 (1990): 359, 363, 367.

55. Wayne A. Huss, *The Master Builders: A History of the Grand Lodge of Free and Accepted Masons of Pennsylvania*, vol. 1, *1731–1873* (Philadelphia: Grand Lodge F. & A.M., 1986), 53, 82, 297–98.

56. John Fenton, SPCA, 31 December 1803; Francis Montfort, SPCA, 28 June 1809.

57. Jeremy Bentham, *The Theory of Legislation*, trans. Richard Hildreth, ed. C. K. Ogden (New York: Harcourt, Brace, 1931), 416.

58. Joseph Shourds, SPCA, 14 February 1807.

59. Christopher Fenner, SPCA, 18 December 1805; John Peters, SPCA, 22 July 1806.

60. John Hancurne, SPCA, 10 October 1805.

61. William Lane, SPCA, 6 November 1807; Charles Davis, SPCA, 4 November 1808.

62. John Slater, SPCA, 25 October 1803.

63. Margaret S. Creighton, "American Mariners and the Rites of Manhood, 1830–1870," in *Jack Tar in History*, ed. Howell and Twomey, 155, 148.

64. Joseph Golden, SPCA, 30 May 1809. On virtue see Ruth H. Bloch, "The Gendered Meanings of Virtue in Revolutionary America," *Signs: Journal of Women and Culture and Society* 13 (1987): 37–58. For discussion of the ways emotions were sentimentalized and feminized in nineteenth-century America, see Ann Douglas, *The Feminization of American Culture* (New York: Knopf, 1977), and Jane Tompkins, *Sentimental Designs: The Cultural Work of American Fiction, 1790–1860* (New York: Oxford University Press, 1985).

65. Seventeen of the witnesses were identified as parents of the applicants, 5 as siblings, and 2 as relations-by-marriage; 43 had the same last name.

66. Francis White, SPCA, 22 May 1815.

67. James Walker, SPCA, 21 December 1805; John Fenton, SPCA, 31 December 1803; George Hyneman, SPCA, 21 October 1803.

68. Peter Sally, SPCA, 28 December 1807; Lawrence Oliver, SPCA, 28 December 1807.

69. For discussion of gender and masculinity within the seafaring community see Margaret S. Creighton, "Fraternity in the American Forecastle, 1830–1870," *New England Quarterly* 63 (1990): 531–57, "American Mariners and the Rites of Manhood," 143–63, and *Rites and Passages: The Experience of American Whaling, 1830–1870* (New York: Cambridge University Press, 1995).

70. Melville, *Moby-Dick, Or The Whale*, ed. Harrison Hayford (Evanston, Ill.: Northwestern University Press, 1988), 25.

71. Melville, "Billy Budd," in *Billy Budd, Sailor*, 325.

72. For further discussion of same-sex emotional ties see, for example, Carroll Smith-Rosenberg, "The Female World of Love and Ritual: Relations Between Women in Nineteenth-Century America," *Signs: Journal of Women in Culture and Society* 1 (1975): 1–29, and George Chauncey, *Gay New York: Gender, Urban Culture, and the Making of the Gay Male World, 1890–1940* (New York: Basic Books, 1994), 76–86.

73. William Newark, SPCA, 28 August 1809. It is possible that a few of these mariners were in fact Britons who lied about their identity in order to stave off impressment. Yet one can well imagine that Britons who sought to avoid detection would, when they applied for a "protection," have employed a pseudonym with initials matching those tattooed upon their bodies.

74. We know little about same-sex relationships within the seafaring community as a whole. Most of our evidence comes from the tyrannical Georgian Royal Navy, whose commanders sought to root out and punish homosexuality less from a moral or ethical condemnation of such behavior than from fear that it might undermine the hierarchy and order of shipboard life. There is little evidence to suggest that the Royal Navy's brutal campaign against homosexuality was replicated in the American navy or in the far more informal and forgiving environs of merchant ships. See Arthur N. Gilbert, "Buggery and the British Navy, 1700–1861," *Journal of Social History* 10 (1976): 81–82, 87, and B. R. Burg, *Sodomy and the Perception of Evil: English Sea Rovers in the Seventeenth-Century Caribbean* (New York: New York University Press, 1983).

In mid-twentieth-century America it was not unusual for gay men to affirm their relationships by having the initials of their companions, rather than their full names, tattooed on their bodies. Steward, *Bad Boys and Tough Tattoos*, 52–56.

75. Rediker, *Between the Devil and the Deep Blue Sea*, 173, 175.

76. George Gillespie, SPCA, 8 August 1809; Bartlett Wrangham, SPCA, 2 October 1807; James Head, SPCA, 13 May 1804.

77. See J. C. Cooper, *An Illustrated Encyclopedia of Traditional Symbols* (London: Thames and Hudson, 1978), 12.

78. John Hancurne, SPCA, 12 October 1805; James Dixon, SPCA, 30 September 1805; John Frazer, SPCA, 4 October 1805; John Brown, SPCA, 12 December 1805. This figure includes the dozen mariners from New Orleans who wore tattooed crucifixes on their bodies.

79. Melville, "Daniel Orme," 415; Herman Melville, *White-Jacket: Or The World in a Man-of-War*, ed. Harrison Hayford (Evanston, Ill.: Northwestern University Press, 1970), 171.

80. Melville, *White-Jacket*, 170. This would be in keeping with the likely origin of tattooed crucifixes. During the medieval and early modern era, European Crusaders and pilgrims visiting the Holy Land had crucifixes tattooed on their bodies in order to display their commitment to God, to prove that they had reached Jerusalem, and to mark them for a Christian burial should they die far from home.

81. This sailor was Olaf Melin, who, according to Collin, had "sailed from this Port for several years." Olaf Mellin, 20 April 1809, Burial Records, 258.

82. Bronnikov, "Telltale Tattoos," 53.

83. Nicholas Welsh and John Smith, both of Philadelphia, wore tattoos of a cross accompanied by the letters IHS. These had two possible meanings: they were probably an abbreviation of "In Hoc Signo Vinces," meaning "By this sign [of the Cross] thou shalt conquer," although they may have simultaneously represented a latinized contraction of the Greek word for Jesus. See Nicholas Welsh, SPCA, 25 October 1803; F. L. Cross and E. A. Livingstone, eds., *The Oxford Dictionary of the Christian Church*, 2nd ed. (New York: Oxford University Press, 1974), 696.

84. See, for example, William Cox, SPCA, 24 August 1804.

85. For an excellent survey of this constellation of beliefs and practices see Jon Butler, *Awash in a Sea of Faith: Christianizing the American People* (Cambridge, Mass.: Harvard University Press, 1990), 7–97.

86. Two recent surveys of the political history of the early republic completely ignore seafarers. See James Roger Sharp, *American Politics in the Early Republic: The New Nation in Crisis* (New Haven, Conn.: Yale University Press, 1993), and Stanley M. Elkins and Eric L. McKitrick, *The Age of Federalism: The Early American Republic, 1788–1800* (New York: Oxford University Press, 1993). For an examination of the role of ordinary Americans in the early national political process, see Simon P. Newman, *Parades and the Politics of the Street: Festive Culture in the Early American Republic* (Philadelphia: University of Pennsylvania Press, 1997).

87. Susanna Rowson, *Slaves in Algiers* (Philadelphia: Wrigley and Berrima, 1794); *Debates and Proceedings in the Congress*, 5: 802; Rowson, "Independent and Free," from her play *The American Tar*, quoted in Susan Branson, "Politics and Gender: The Political Consciousness of Philadelphia Women in the 1790s," Ph.D. dissertation, Northern Illinois University, 1992, 82. For further discussion of the American sailors imprisoned in Algiers and Rowson's play, see Gary E. Wilson, "American Hostages in Moslem Nations, 1784–1796: The Public Response," *Journal of the Early Republic* 2 (1982): 123–41, and Branson, "Politics and Gender," 61–66.

88. Nathaniel Oliver, SPCA, 8 December 8; Andrew Dodge, SPCA, 10 May 1809; Charles Spinel, SPCA, 20 June 1807.

89. William Sweeney, SPCA, 13 June 1804.

90. For more on the history of American seafarers' resistance to impressment, see Jesse Lemisch, "Jack Tar in the Streets: Merchant Seamen in the Politics of Revolutionary America," *William and Mary Quarterly* 3rd ser. 25 (1968): 396–97.

91. Lemisch, "Jack Tar in the Streets," 401, 403, and Jesse Lemisch, "Listening to the 'Inarticulate': William Widger's Dream and the Loyalties of American Revolutionary Seamen in British Prisons," *Journal of Social History* 3 (1969): 3–4, 25–26. See also Marcus Rediker, "A Motley Crew of Rebels: Sailors, Slaves, and the Coming of the American Revolution," in *The Transforming Hand of Revolution: Reconsidering the American Revolution as a Social Movement*, ed. Ronald Hoffman and Peter J. Albert (Charlottesville: University Press of Virginia, 1996), 155–98, and Alfred F. Young, "George Robert Twelve Hewes (1742–1840): A Boston Shoemaker and the Memory of the American Revolution," *William and Mary Quarterly* 3rd ser. 38 (1981): 561–623.

92. Dye, " Tattoos of Early American Seafarers," 528.

93. William Carson, SPCA, 6 January 1806; Samuel Anderson, SPCA, 4 September 1804.

94. *Aurora. General Advertiser* (Philadelphia), 15 April, 9 March 1801; "Oliver

Oldschool's *Portfolio*," 12 April 1801, quoted in Edward G. Everett, "Some Aspects of Pro-French Sentiment in Pennsylvania, 1790–1800," *Western Pennsylvania Historical Magazine* 43 (1960): 26.

95. William Carson, SPCA, 6 January 1806; John Whyman, SPCA, 11 October 1805; John Thompson, SPCA, 16 November 1805.

96. John Alexander, SPCA, 21 December 1804.

97. See Simon P. Newman, "Principles or Men? George Washington and the Political Culture of National Leadership, 1776–1801," *Journal of the Early Republic* 12 (1992): 490–93; Arthur M. Schlesinger, "The Liberty Tree: A Genealogy," *New England Quarterly* 25 (1952): 435–58; and Jennifer Harris, "The Red Cap of Liberty: A Study of Dress Worn by French Revolutionary Partisans, 1789–1794," *Eighteenth-Century Studies* 14 (1980–81): 283–312.

98. See, for example, *Aurora*, 20 September 1794; "The Tree of Liberty," *Porcupine's Gazette*, 25 March 1797; "Sedition Poles," *Porcupine's Gazette*, 2 February 1799.

99. Newman, *Parades and the Politics of the Street*, 165–76.

100. The "Rules and Regulations" of the Massachusetts Constitutional Society in Boston, for example, made explicit provision for members who were seafarers; see "The Massachusetts Constitutional Society, Rules and Regulations," 13 January 1794, in *The Democratic-Republican Societies, 1790–1800*, ed. Philip S. Foner (Westport, Conn.: Greenwood, 1976), 257.

101. "New-York, July 30," *Porcupine's Gazette*, 31 July 1798.

102. Norman E. Saul, "Ships and Seamen as Agents of Revolution," in *The Consortium on Revolutionary Europe, 1750–1850: Proceedings 1986*, ed. Warren Spencer (Athens: University of Georgia Press, 1987), 248–58; Peter Linebaugh and Marcus Rediker, *The Many-Headed Hydra: Sailors, Slaves, Commoners, and the Hidden History of the Revolutionary Atlantic* (Boston: Beacon, 2000).

103. *New-York Journal*, 6 February 1793. For a more detailed discussion of this festival see Newman, *Parades and the Politics of the Street*, 122–30.

104. Samuel Coates to William Moyer, Jr., 4 November 1796, Samuel Coates Letter Book, September 1795–May 1802, Coates Family Papers, Historical Society of Pennsylvania, 142–43.

105. On the protests in Philadelphia see *American Citizen* (Philadelphia), 16 January 1808, and *Columbian Centinel* (Boston), 27 January 1808; for Boston see *Columbian Centinel*, 9 Jan. 1808; for New York City see *Oracle and Daily Advertiser* (New York), 8 January 1808; and for Baltimore see *Columbian Centinel*, 13 February 1808. See also Frank Folsom, "Jobless Jack Tars, 1808," *Labor's Heritage: Quarterly of the George Meany Memorial Archives* 2 (1990): 6–14.

106. This became less true in the final years of the twentieth century, as tattoos were appropriated by relatively privileged and educated young people.

107. "Spanking Jack," 471.

108. J. Thomas Scharf and Thompson Westcott, *History of Philadelphia, 1609–1884* (Philadelphia: L.H. Everts, 1884), 2: 987.

109. Richard Dunn, SPCA, 8 August 1809.

110. Dunn, quoted in Moses Smith, *Naval Scenes in the Last War; or, Three Years on Board the Constitution, and the Adams; Including the Capture of the Guerriere . . .* (Boston: Gleason's, 1846), 35.

111. Linda M. Maloney, *The Captain from Connecticut: The Life and Naval Times of Isaac Hull* (Boston: Northeastern University Press, 1986), 523, n.112; *List of Officers of the Navy of the United States and of the Marine Corps, from 1775 to 1900*, ed. Edward W. Callahan (New York: Haskell House, 1969), 174.

112. Maloney, *Captain from Connecticut*, 202, 238–40, 285; George Henry Preble, *History of the United States Navy-Yard, Portsmouth, N.H.* (Washington, D.C.:

Government Printing Office, 1892), 73. Comparison of the signature of Richard Dunn on his application for a protection with his signature on a later application for a naval pension confirms that these were one and the same man. Collateral evidence supporting this includes the place of birth recorded on each document. See Richard Dunn, SPCA, 8 August 1809, and Richard Dunn, Pension File, National Archives, Record Group 15, War of 1812 Pension Application Files, Navy Invalid Number 485. I am grateful to Christopher McKee for pointing out this connection and sharing these sources.

Chapter 6. Dead Bodies

1. Philippe Ariès, *Western Attitudes Toward Death: From the Middle Ages to the Present,* trans. Patricia M. Ranum (Baltimore: Johns Hopkins University Press, 1974), 8–12; John McManners, *Death and the Enlightenment: Changing Attitudes to Death Among Christians and Unbelievers in Eighteenth-Century France* (Oxford: Clarendon Press, 1981), 59. Susan E. Klepp has produced some of the most significant work on death in early national Philadelphia. See Klepp, ed., *"The Swift Progress of Population": A Documentary and Bibliographic Study of Philadelphia's Growth, 1642–1859* (Philadelphia: American Philosophical Society, 1991); Klepp, "Zachariah Poulson's Bills of Mortality, 1788–1801," in *Life in Early Philadelphia: Documents from the Revolutionary and Early National periods,* ed. Billy G. Smith (University Park: Pennsylvania State University Press, 1995), 219–42; Klepp, "Demography in Early Philadelphia, 1690–1860," *Proceedings of the American Philosophical Society* 133 (1989): 85–111. See also Billy G. Smith, "Death and Life in a Colonial Immigrant City: A Demographic Analysis of Philadelphia," *Journal of Economic History* 37 (1977): 863–89, and *The "Lower Sort": Philadelphia's Laboring People, 1750–1800* (Ithaca, N.Y.: Cornell University Press, 1990), 7–8, 15, 40–62, 205–10; Roger Lane, *Violent Death in the City: Suicide, Accident, and Murder in Nineteenth-Century Philadelphia* (Cambridge, Mass.: Harvard University Press, 1979).

2. Nicholas Collin's record for James Saring, September 1800, Burial Records, Old Swedes Church, 163. These records are held by the Pennsylvania Genealogical Society, Historical Society of Pennsylvania, and are hereafter cited as Burial Records.

3. Hannah Burns, September 1798, Burial Records, 124–25; Joseph Wayne, 23 May 1801, Burial Records, 174.

4. This point has been made to superb effect in an exhibit at the Museum of London, and the accompanying text: Alex Werner, *London Bodies: The Changing Shape of Londoners from Prehistoric Times to the Present Day* (London: Museum of London, 1988), with an introduction by Roy Porter. See also Ariès, *Western Attitudes Toward Death,* and McManners, *Death and the Enlightenment.*

5. For further discussion of the disparities in health and longevity between wealthy and poor, see Susan E. Klepp, "Philadelphia in Transition: A Demographic History of the City and Its Occupational Groups," Ph.D. dissertation, University of Pennsylvania, 1980, 190, 292.

6. Chris Schilling, *The Body and Social Theory* (London: Sage, 1993), 131–32. For further discussion of the body see Bryan S. Turner, *The Body and Society: Explorations in Social Theory* (Oxford: Blackwell, 1984); Anthony Synnott, *The Body Social: Symbolism, Self, and Society* (London: Routledge, 1993); Gary Kielhofner and Trudy Mallinson, "Bodies Telling Stories and Stories Telling Bodies," *Human Studies* 20 (1997): 365–69; Nicole Sault, ed., *Many Mirrors: Body Image and Social Relations* (New Brunswick, N.J.: Rutgers University Press, 1994).

7. Smith, *"Lower Sort"*, 92–125.

8. Marcel Mauss has written about the ways everyday life is inscribed on the body, and I am arguing that death functions in a similar manner. See Mauss, *Sociology and Psychology: Essays*, trans. Ben Brewster (London: Routledge and Kegan Paul, 1979), 95–123. See also Anne Cranny-Francis, *The Body in the Text* (Melbourne: Melbourne University Press, 1995), 78–79.

9. Deborah Lupton adopts this constructionist approach toward disease and illness, and it may easily be extended to death itself. See Lupton, *Medicine as Culture: Illness, Disease and the Body in Western Societies* (London: Sage, 1994), 11–22.

10. For further information about Collin, see Amandus Johnson, *The Journal and Biography of Nicholas Collin* (Philadelphia: New Jersey Society of Pennsylvania, 1936). Susan E. Klepp and Billy G. Smith have excerpted and commented upon some of Collin's records; see "The Records of Gloria Dei Church: Burials, 1800–1804," *Pennsylvania History* 53 (1986): 56–79, and "Marriage and Death: The Records of Gloria Dei Church" in *Life in Early Philadelphia*, 177–218.

11. This description of conditions in Southwark and Philadelphia is based upon John K. Alexander, *Render Them Submissive: Responses to Poverty in Philadelphia, 1760–1800* (Amherst: University of Massachusetts Press, 1980), 20–21, and J. M. Powell, *Bring Out Your Dead: The Great Plague of Yellow Fever in Philadelphia in 1793* (1949; Philadelphia: University of Pennsylvania Press, 1993), xvii–xviii.

12. Elizabeth Ervin, 6 September 1798, Burial Records, 124–25.

13. Hannah Collin, 29 September 1797, Burial Records, 104–5. On the revolutionary transformations in medical practice, see Roy Porter, ed., *Medicine in the Enlightenment* (Amsterdam: Rodopi, 1995), and Morris J. Vogel and Charles E. Rosenberg, eds., *The Therapeutic Revolution: Essays in the Social History of Medicine* (Philadelphia: University of Pennsylvania Press, 1979).

14. Stillborn child of William and Rebecca Hubbert, 18 December 1805, Burial Records, 392. For the damage forceps could cause, see Irvine Loudon, *Death in Childbirth: An International Study of Maternal Care and Maternal Mortality, 1800–1950* (Oxford: Clarendon Press, 1992), 133, 137, 142, 171, 407.

15. See, for example, Roy Porter, ed., *Patients and Practitioners: Lay Perceptions of Medicine in Pre-Industrial Society* (Cambridge: Cambridge University Press, 1985); Dorothy Porter and Roy Porter, *Patient's Progress: Doctors and Doctoring in Eighteenth-Century England* (Oxford: Polity, 1989); and Guy Williams, *The Age of Agony: The Art of Healing, c. 1700–1800* (London: Constable, 1975).

16. Charles S. Rosenberg, *Explaining Epidemics: Epidemics and Other Studies in the History of Medicine* (New York: Cambridge University Press, 1992). 14, 32–39.

17. John Potts, 23 July 1805, Burial Records, 374.

18. Samuel Condor, 22 October 1795, 83.

19. Edward Kirby, 21 November 1801, 180.

20. Michel Foucault, *The Birth of the Clinic: An Archaeology of Medical Perception*, trans. A. M. Sheridan (London: Tavistock, 1973).

21. Daniel Conover, 10 July 1801, Burial Records, 176–77.

22. Throughout this period people held to their belief that one might best counteract illness by correcting imbalances in the body, either in the four liquid "humors" (blood, phlegm, yellow bile, and black bile) or in the solid organs. Treatment was designed to top up weakened humors or flush them of impurities. See Charles E. Rosenberg, "The Therapeutic Revolution: Medicine, Meaning, and Social Change in Nineteenth-Century America," in *Therapeutic Revolution*, ed. Vogel and Rosenberg, 5–6.

23. Mary Speer, 17 September 1805, Burial Records, 372.

24. Rosenberg, "Therapeutic Revolution," 5.

25. Elizabeth Loudon, October 1801, Burial Records, 169; Henry Hoover, 31 August 1804, Burial Records, 220; Hester Smith, 20 July 1804, Burial Records, 218–19; Mellin Hutton, 3 March 1806, Burial Records, 236–37.

26. Rosenberg, "Therapeutic Revolution," 7.

27. A few of Collin's records contain little more than a brief listing of name, age, cause of death, and burial date. The large majority are far more precise, often featuring precise descriptions of the symptoms and medical treatment, the apparent cause and nature of death, the age, address, and family of the deceased, their social and economic circumstances, and even accounts of their character. All members of the Swedish Lutheran Church were entitled to burial within its cemetery, including anyone who had moved away from Southwark, but this was a small and ever-dwindling group.

28. Mary Ann Hobart, 7 April 1807, Burial Records, 408; Hannah Cassidy, 3 September 1805, Burial Records, 377; stillborn child of Jacob and Elizabeth Riss, 23 April 1803, Burial Records, 207.

29. Male child of Abigail and Manuel Peterson, 22 December 1801, Burial Records, 185.

30. John Adams to Abigail Adams, Philadelphia, 13 April 1777, *Adams Family Correspondence*, ed. L. H. Butterfield (Cambridge, Mass.: Belknap Press, 1963), 2: 209.

31. John F. Watson, *Annals of Philadelphia, and Pennsylvania, in the Olden Time . . .* (Philadelphia: Leary, Stuart, 1909), 1: 405–6; Gary Laderman, *The Sacred Remains* (New Haven, Conn.: Yale University Press, 1997), 41–42; John L. Cotter, Daniel G. Roberts, and Michael Parrington, eds., *The Buried Past: An Archaeological History of Philadelphia* (Philadelphia: University of Pennsylvania Press, 1993), 206.

32. Elizabeth Low, 24 April 1801, Burial Records, 172–73.

33. Jane Willard, November 1794, Burial Records, 73–74; Mary Ryan, 2 March 1809, Burial Records, 447.

34. Dougal More, 29 July 1802, Burial Records, 197–98; Mary Ryan, 2 March 1809, Burial Records, 447.

35. Sharon Ann Burnston, "Babies in the Well: An Underground Insight into Deviant Behavior in Eighteenth-Century Philadelphia," *Pennsylvania Magazine of History and Biography* 106 (1982): 151–86.

36. Susan Klepp, "Malthusiasn Miseries and the Working Poor in Philadelphia, 1780–1830: A Study of Infant Mortality," paper delivered at the annual conference of the Omohundro Institute of Early American History and Culture, Austin, Texas, 1999, 1.

37. Jane Garret, 18 October 1804, Burial Records, 356; Benjamin Garret, 9 September 1805, Burial Records, 377–78.

38. Eliza High, 23 September 1805, Burial Records, 379; Jacob High, 25 September 1805, Burial Records, 382; Louisa Ellis, 20 August 1807, Burial Records, 420–21.

39. James Conden, 1 December 1796, Burial Records, 98.

40. Elisha Talman, 15 June 1806, Burial Records, 400; Caleb Pierce, 25 May 1804, Burial Records, 217–18.

41. On the nature of disease in early America, see Charles E. Rosenberg, *Explaining Epidemics and Other Studies in the History of Medicine* (New York: Cambridge University Press, 1992), and Rosenberg and Janet Golden, eds., *Framing Disease: Studies in Cultural History* (New Brunswick, N.J.: Rutgers University Press, 1992).

42. John Bailey, 21 August 1804, Burial Records, 354.

43. These victims of cholera morbus were Anne Paul, 14 July 1803, Burial

Records, 341; Joseph King, 16 July 1803, Burial Records, 341; Benjamin Martin, 19 July 1803, Burial Records, 341; Eliza Clement, 1 August 1803, Burial Records, 341; William Chittendon, 1 August 1803, Burial Records, 342; Mary Ann Bennet, 4 August 1803, Burial Records, 342; John Grant, 18 August 1803, Burial Records, 342; Robert Watkins, 21 August 1803, Burial Records, 343–44.

44. Thomas Parram, 7 October 1793, Burial Records, 65; Esther Parram, 13 October 1793, Burial Records, 68. For more on the yellow fever epidemic, see J. Worth Estes and Billy G. Smith, eds., *A Melancholy Scene of Devastation: The Public Response to the 1793 Philadelphia Yellow Fever Epidemic* (Canton, Mass.: Science History Publications, 1997).

45. Hannah Collin, 29 September 1797, Burial Records, 104–5.

46. Mary Evans, 5 May 1803, Burial Records, 332.

47. Eleanor Grey, 18 February 1803, Burial Records, 205.

48. John Hastings, 22 February 1791, Burial Records, 54.

49. Joseph Taylor, 21 December 1804, Burial Records, 353.

50. Daniel Berger, 24 March 1808, Burial Records, 430–31; Simon Atsong, 12 May 1801, Burial Records, 173–74.

51. Heckless Fugerie, 7 January 1808, Burial Records, 425–26.

52. Gary B. Nash, "Poverty and Politics in Early American History," paper delivered at the annual conference of the Omohundro Institute of Early American History and Culture, Austin, Texas, 1999, 26–30.

53. William Richards, 24 December 1801, Burial Records, 185–86.

54. Ann Mary Johnson, 2 November 1807, Burial Records, 422.

55. Barney Clayton, 8 December 1799, Burial Records, 140.

56. Andrew Dam, October 1806, Burial Records, 241–43.

57. Nicholas Collin, December 1794, 11 May 1801, quoted in Klepp and Smith, "Marriage and Death," 188, 198.

58. Nicholas Collin, 29 May 1797, Burial Records, 194.

59. Andrew Armstrong, August 1799, Burial Records, 141.

60. Catherine Smith, 11 November 1803, Burial Records, 339.

61. Catherine Peterson, 16 December 1800, Burial Records, 231.

62. William Bryan, 13 January 1805, Burial Records, 360.

63. Eliza Preston, 29 June 1805, Burial Records, 227; Thomas Turner, 23 September 1805, Burial Records, 232. "Scantling" refers to small timber beams.

64. Anthony Nealy, 19 May 1807, Burial Records, 413.

65. John Call, 5 July 1804, Burial Records, 349–50; Francis Cooper, 8 July 1805, Burial Records, 362; Anthony Nealy, 19 May 1807, Burial Records, 413.

66. Sarah Garrigues, January 1795, Burial Records, 75; Maria Sprole, 2 February 1808, Burial Records, 249–50; Samuel Davis, June 1800, Burial Records, 151–52.

67. This song is recorded in Robert and Lydia Moulder's tavern account book. It is quoted, and its intent explored, in Ric Northrup Caric, "'To Drown the Ills That Discompose the Mind': Care, Leisure, and Identity Among Philadelphia Artisans and Workers, 1785–1840," *Pennsylvania History: A Journal of MidAtlantic Studies* 64 (1997): 467.

68. Caric, "'To Drown the Ills," 480–81.

69. The contents of the tavern have been reconstructed from the inventory of Martha Smallwood's goods made when she died in 1826, and from an archaeological dig. See Cotter, et al., *Buried Past*, 164–70.

70. Robert Jarvis, May 1795, Burial Records, 77–78.

71. Ariès, *Western Attitudes Toward Death*, 55–82.

Afterword

1. Richard Saunders [Benjamin Franklin], "The Way to Wealth" (1758), in *Benjamin Franklin: The Autobiography and Other Writings*, ed. Jesse Lemisch (New York: Signet, 1961), 190.

2. The following life courses are composites of a number of individuals. Employing information in the records on which this book is based, I have developed stories linking the different records together in such a way as to show how the lives of members of the early national lower sort might unfold. Thus, these are not real individuals, but all that is described here was experienced by various individuals, and is recorded in runaway advertisements, burial records, vagrancy dockets, and so forth. This approach is based on Billy G. Smith's "Walking the Streets," in *The "Lower Sort": Philadelphia's Laboring People, 1750–1800* (Ithaca, N.Y.: Cornell University Press, 1990), 7–39.

Bibliography

Manuscript Sources

Admissions and Discharges, 1804–8. Series 5, Item 161. Pennsylvania Hospital Archives and Historic Library, Philadelphia.

Admissions for U.S. Seamen, 1800–1809. Series 5. Pennsylvania Hospital Archives and Historic Library, Philadelphia.

Almshouse Clothing Issues Ledger (Female), 1805–14. Guardians of the Poor. Record Group 35.81. City of Philadelphia, Department of Records, City Archives.

Almshouse Clothing Issues Ledger (Male), 1805–14. Guardians of the Poor. Record Group 35.81. City of Philadelphia, Department of Records, City Archives.

Alsmhouse Daily Issues, 1805–32. Guardians of the Poor. Record Group 35.76. City of Philadelphia, Department of Records, City Archives.

Book of Patients, 1791–96. Series 5, Item 160. Pennsylvania Hospital Archives and Historic Library, Philadelphia.

Coates, Samuel. Letter Book, September 1795–May 1802. Coates Family Papers, Historical Society of Pennsylvania, Philadelphia.

———. "Memorandum Book: Cases of Several Lunaticks in the Pennsylvania Hospital and the Causes Thereof in Many Cases." Pennsylvania Hospital Archives and Historic Library, Philadelphia.

Collection of Cases, 1803–29. Rare Book Collection, Pennsylvania Hospital Archives and Historic Library, Philadelphia.

Collin, Nicholas. Burial Records, 1786–1831. Old Swedes Church, Philadelphia. Pennsylvania Genealogical Society, Historical Society of Pennsylvania, Philadelphia.

Daily Occurrence Dockets of the Almshouse (Dockets). Overseers of the Poor. Record Group GP64.1. November 1787–March 1788; October 1790–November 1790; July 1792; September 1793–December 1793; January 1796–February 1796; May 1797. City of Philadelphia, Department of Records, City Archives.

Dick, Alexander. "Travels in America, 1806–1809: The Journal of Alexander Dick." Mss. 4528. Special Collections Department, University of Virginia Library.

Prison Sentence Dockets (PSD). March 1795—December 1797. City of Philadelphia, Department of Records, City Archives.

Prisoner for Trial Dockets (PTD). City of Philadelphia, Department of Records, City Archives.

Seamen's Protection Certificate Applications. 1798–1816. Record Group 36. Records of the Board of Customs, National Archives, Washington, D.C.

Vagrancy Dockets (VD). Overseers of the Poor. 31 May 1790–9 November 1790; 1 June 1796–26 October 1796. City of Philadelphia, Department of Records, City Archives.

Published Primary Sources

An Account of the Philadelphia Dispensary, Instituted for the Medical Relief of the Poor, April 12, 1786. Philadelphia: Budd and Bartram, 1802.

The Accounts of the Guardians of the Poor, Managers of the Alms House and House of Employment of Philadelphia, from 25th of March, 1801, to the 25th of March, 1802. Philadelphia: broadside, 1802.

Adams Family Correspondence. Ed. L. H. Butterfield. 2 vols. Cambridge, Mass.: Belknap Press, 1963.

Advice to a Magdalen. Philadelphia: broadside, 1800. Library Company of Philadelphia.

Bentley, William. *The Diary of William Bentley, D.D., Pastor of the East Church Salem, Massachusetts.* 2 vols. 1905. Gloucester, Mass.: Peter Smith, 1962.

Brackenridge, Hugh Henry. *Modern Chivalry: Containing the Adventures of Captain John Farrago, and Teague Oregan, His Servant.* Philadelphia: John McCulloch, 1792.

Brissot de Warville, J. P. *New Travels in the United States of America, Performed in 1788.* New York: T. and J. Swords for Berry and Rogers, 1792.

Carson, Ann. *The History of the Celebrated Mrs. Ann Carson, Widow of the Late Unfortunate Lieutenant Richard Smith.* Philadelphia: pub. by author, 1822.

Cope, Thomas P. *Philadelphia Merchant: The Diary of Thomas P. Cope, 1800–1851.* Ed. Eliza Cope Harrison. South Bend, Ind.: Gateway Editions, 1978.

The Cries of Philadelphia: Ornamented with Elegant Wood Cuts. Philadelphia: Johnson and Warner, 1810.

Davies, Benjamin. *Some Account of the City of Philadelphia, the Capital of Pennsylvania, And Seat of the Federal Congress.* Philadelphia: Richard Folwell, 1794.

Fearon, Henry Bradshaw. *Sketches of America: A Narrative of a Journey of Five Thousand Miles Through the Eastern and Western States of America . . .* London: Longman, Hurst, Rees, Orme, and Brown, 1818.

Foner, Philip S., ed. *The Democratic-Republican Societies, 1790–1800.* Westport, Conn.: Greenwood Press, 1976.

Franklin, Benjamin. *Benjamin Franklin: The Autobiography and Other Writings.* Ed. Jesse Lemisch. New York: Signet, 1961.

Janson, Charles William. *The Stranger in America: Containing Observations Made During a Long Residence in That Country, on the Genius, Manners, and Customs of the People of the United States. . . .* London: Albion Press, 1807.

Jefferson, Thomas. *The Portable Thomas Jefferson.* Ed. Merrill D. Peterson. New York: Viking, 1975.

J[ones], A[bsalom] and R[ichard] A[llen]. *A Narrative of the Proceedings of the Black People, During the Late Awful Calamity in Philadelphia, In the Year 1793.* Philadelphia: William H. Woodward, 1794.

A Just and True Account, of the Prison of the City and County of Philadelphia; Accompanied with the Rules, Regulations, Manners, Customs, and Treatment of the Untried Prisoners. Philadelphia: D. McKenzie, 1820.

La Rochefoucauld-Liancourt, François Alexandre Frédéric, duc de. *On the Prisons of Philadelphia. By an European.* Philadelphia: Moreau de Saint-Mery, 1796.

————. *Travels Through the United States . . . , 1795–97.* 2 vols. London: R. Phillips, 1800.

Leech, Samuel. *A Voice from the Main Deck: Being the Experiences of Samuel Leech, Who Was for Six Years in the British and American Navies.* Boston: Tappan and Dennet, 1843.

List of Officers of the Navy of the United States and of the Marine Corps, from 1775 to 1900. Ed. Edward W. Callahan. New York: Haskell House, 1969.

Liston, Lady Henrietta. "Lady Henrietta Liston's Journal of Washington's 'Resignation,' Retirement, and Death," ed. James C. Nicholls. *Pennsylvania Magazine of History and Biography* 95 (1971): 511–20.

Lownes, Caleb. *An Account of the Alteration and Present State of the Penal Laws of Penna Containing Also an Account of the Gaol.* Boston: Young and Minns, 1799.

Lyon, Patrick. *The Narrative of Patrick Lyon, Who Suffered Three Months Severe Imprisonment in the Philadelphia Gaol.* Philadelphia: Francis and Robert Bailey, 1799.

The Mail; or Claypoole's Daily Advertiser (Philadelphia).

Melville, Herman. "Daniel Orme." In *Billy Budd, Sailor, and Other Stories.* Ed. Harold Beaver. New York: Penguin, 1970.

————. *Moby-Dick, Or The Whale.* Ed. Harrison Hayford. Evanston, Ill.: Northwestern University Press, 1988.

————. *White-Jacket: Or The World in a Man-of-War.* Ed. Harrison Hayford. Evanston, Ill.: Northwestern University Press, 1970.

Pennsylvania Gazette (Philadelphia). Folio Four, CD-ROM. Accessible Archives, Malvern, Pa., 1999.

Philadelphia Minerva (Philadelphia).

Plan of the Philadelphia Dispensary for the Medical Relief of the Poor. Philadelphia: broadside, 1787.

Puttenham, George. *The Arte of English Poesie. . . .* 1589. Menston, Yorkshire: Scolar Press, 1968.

Rowson, Susanna. *Slaves in Algiers.* Philadelphia: Wrigley and Berrima, 1794.

Rules, Orders, and Regulations for the Goal of the City and County of Philadelphia. Philadelphia: broadside printed by David Humphreys, 1792.

Rush, Benjamin. *An Enquiry into the Effects of Public Punishments upon Criminals, and upon Society. . . .* Philadelphia: Joseph James, 1787.

Sargent, Lucius M. *Dealings with the Dead: By a Sexton of the Old School.* 2 vols. Boston: Dutton and Wentworth, 1856.

Scharf, J. Thomas and Thompson Westcott. *History of Philadelphia, 1609–1884.* 3 vols. Philadelphia: L.H. Everts, 1884.

Scull, Nicholas Scull. *Plan of the Improved Part of the City of . . . Philadelphia.* Philadelphia: unknown, 1762.

Smith, Billy G. and Richard Wojtowicz, eds. *Blacks Who Stole Themselves: Advertisements for Runaways in the* Pennsylvania Gazette, *1728–1790.* Philadelphia: University of Pennsylvania Press, 1989.

Smith, Moses. *Naval Scenes in the Last War; or, Three Years on Board the Constitution, and the Adams; Including the Capture of the Gurriere.* Boston: Gleason's, 1846.

State of the Accounts of the Pennsylvania Hospital, Adjusted by the Managers, Being a Summary of the Receipts and Payments for the Year Ending the 23d of the 4ᵗʰ Month, 1796. . . . Philadelphia: broadside, 1796.

State of the Accounts of the Pennsylvania Hospital, Adjusted by the Managers, Being a Summary of the Receipts and Payments for the Year Ending the 22d of the 4ᵗʰ Month, 1797. . . . Philadelphia: broadside, 1797.

State of the Accounts of the Pennsylvania Hospital, Adjusted by the Managers, Being a Summary of the Receipts and Payments for the Year Ending the Twenty-Fifth day of the Fourth Month, 1801. . . . Philadelphia: broadside, 1801.

Turnbull, Robert J. *A Visit to the Philadelphia Prison.* . . . Philadelphia: unknown, 1796.

Waln, Robert. *The Hermit in America on a Visit to Philadelphia* . . . Philadelphia: M. Thomas, 1819.

Washington, George. *Rules of Civility.* Ed. Richard Brookhiser. New York: Free Press, 1997.

Watson, John Fanning. *Annals of Philadelphia, and Pennsylvania, in the Olden Time.* . . . 1830. 3 vols. Philadelphia: Leary, Stuart, 1909.

Webster, Noah. *A Dictionary of the English Language* . . . 1828. 2 vols. London: Black, Young, and Young, 1832.

Secondary Sources

Alexander, David. "Literacy Among Canadian and Foreign Seamen, 1863–1899." In *Working Men Who Got Wet,* ed. Rosemary Ommer and Gerald Panting. St. John's: Memorial University of Newfoundland, 1980. 3–33.

Alexander, John K. "The Fort Wilson Incident of 1779: A Case Study of the Revolutionary Crowd." *William and Mary Quarterly* 3rd ser. 31 (1974): 589–612.

———. "Poverty, Fear, and Continuity: An Analysis of the Poor in Late Eighteenth-Century Philadelphia." In *The Peoples of Philadelphia: A History of Ethnic Groups and Lower-Class Life, 1790–1840,* ed. Allen F. Davis and Mark H. Haller. 1973. Philadelphia: University of Pennsylvania Press, 1998. 3–35.

———. *Render Them Submissive: Responses to Poverty in Philadelphia, 1760–1800.* Amherst: University of Massachusetts Press, 1980.

Allerston, Patricia. "Clothing and Early Modern Venetian Society." *Continuity and Change* 15 (2000): 367–90.

———. "The Market in Second Hand Clothes and Furnishings in Venice, c. 1500–c. 1600." Ph.D. dissertation, European History Institute, 1996.

Ariès, Philippe. *The Hour of Our Death.* Trans. Helen Weaver. Harmondsworth: Penguin, 1983.

———. *Images of Man and Death* . Trans. Janet Lloyd. Cambridge, Mass.: Harvard University Press, 1985.

———. *Western Attitudes Toward Death: From the Middle Ages to the Present.* Trans. Patricia M. Ranum. Baltimore: Johns Hopkins University Press, 1974.

Armstrong, David. "Bodies of Knowledge/Knowledge of Bodies." In *Reassessing Foucault: Power, Medicine and the Body,* ed. Colin Jones and Roy Porter. London: Routledge, 1994. 17–27.

Barrett, Lindon. "African-American Slave Narratives: Literacy, the Body, Authority." *American Literary History* 7 (1995): 415–42.

Bhattacharya, Nandini. *Reading the Splendid Body: Gender and Consumerism in Eighteenth-Century British Writing on India.* Newark: University of Delaware Press, 1998.

Bender, John. *Imagining the Penitentiary: Fiction and the Architecture of Mind in Eighteenth-Century England.* Chicago: University of Chicago Press, 1987.

Blake, John B. "The Inoculation Controversy in Boston, 1721–1722." In *Sickness and Health in America: Readings in the History of Medicine and Public Health,* ed. Judith Walzer Leavitt and Ronald L. Numbers. Madison: University of Wisconsin Press, 1985. 347–55.

Bloch, Ruth H. "The Gendered Meanings of Virtue in Revolutionary America." *Signs: Journal of Women and Culture and Society* 13 (1987): 37–58.

Bolster, W. Jeffrey. *Black Jacks: African American Seamen in the Age of Sail.* Cambridge, Mass.: Harvard University Press, 1997.

———. "'To Feel like a Man': Black Seamen in the Northern States, 1800–1860." *Journal of American History* 76 (1990): 1173–99.

Brain, Robert. *The Decorated Body.* New York: Hutchinson, 1979.

Branson, Susan. *These Fiery Frenchified Dames: Women and Political Culture In Early National Philadelphia.* Philadelphia: University of Pennsylvania Press, 2001.

———. "Politics and Gender: The Political Consciousness of Philadelphia Women in the 1790s." Ph.D. dissertation, Northern Illinois University, 1992.

Brieger, Gert H. *Medical America in the Nineteenth Century: Readings from the Literature.* Baltimore: Johns Hopkins University Press, 1972.

Bronnikov, Arkady G. "Body Language." *New York Times,* 6 November 1993, 17.

———. "Telltale Tattoos in Russian Prisons." *Natural History* 102 (1993): 50–59.

Brook, Barbara. *Feminist Perspectives on the Body.* London: Longman, 1999.

Brydon, Anne and Sandra Niessen. "Introduction: Adorning the Body." In *Consuming Fashion: Adorning the Transnational Body,* ed. Brydon and Niessen. Oxford: Berg, 1998.

Bullock, Steven C. "The Revolutionary Transformation of American Freemasonry, 1752–1792." *William and Mary Quarterly* 3rd ser. 47 (1990): 347–69.

Burg, B. R. "Sailors and Tattoos in the Early American Steam Navy: Evidence from the Diary of Philip C. Van Buskirk, 1884–1889." *International Journal of Maritime History* 6 (1994): 161–74.

———. *Sodomy and the Perception of Evil: English Sea Rovers in the Seventeenth-Century Caribbean.* New York: New York University Press, 1983.

———. "Tattoo Designs and Locations in the Old U.S. Navy." *Journal of American Culture* 18 (1995): 69–75.

Burke, Peter. "The Language of Orders in Early Modern Europe." In *Social Orders and Social Classes in Europe Since 1500: Studies in Social Stratification,* ed. M. L. Bush. London: Longman, 1992. 1–12.

Burnston, Sharon Ann. "Babies in the Well: An Underground Insight into Deviant Behavior in Eighteenth-Century Philadelphia." *Pennsylvania Magazine of History and Biography* 106 (1982): 151–86.

Bushman, Richard L. *The Refinement of America: Persons, Houses, Cities.* New York: Knopf, 1992.

Butchart, Alexander. *The Anatomy of Power: European Constructions of the African Body.* London: Zed Books, 1998.

Butler, Judith. "Foucault and the Paradox of Bodily Inscriptions." In *The Body: Classic and Contemporary Readings,* ed. Donn Welton. Oxford: Blackwell, 1999. 307–13.

Butler, Jon. *Awash in a Sea of Faith: Christianizing the American People.* Cambridge, Mass.: Harvard University Press, 1990.

Calefato, Patrizia. "Fashion and Worldliness: Language and Imager of the Clothed Body," trans. Lisa Adams. *Fashion Theory: The Journal of Dress, Body, and Culture* 1 (1997): 69–90.

Cannadine, David. *Class in Britain.* New Haven, Conn.: Yale University Press, 1998.

Caplan, Jane, ed. *Written on the Body: The Tattoo in European and American History.* Princeton, N.J.: Princeton University Press, 2000.

Caric, Ric Northrup. "'To Drown the Ills That Discompose the Mind': Care, Leisure, and Identity Among Philadelphia Artisans and Workers, 1785–1840." *Pennsylvania History: A Journal of MidAtlantic Studies* 64 (1997): 465–89.

Cavallaro, Dani. *Fashioning the Frame: Boundaries, Dress and Body.* Oxford: Berg, 1998.

Chaplin, Joyce E. *Subject Matter: Technology, the Body, and Science on the Anglo-American Frontier, 1500–1676.* Cambridge, Mass.: Harvard University Press, 2001.

Chauncey, George. *Gay New York: Gender, Urban Culture, and the Making of the Gay Male World, 1890–1940.* New York: Basic Books, 1994.

Coffin, Margaret. *Death in Early America: The History and Folklore of Customs and Superstitions of Early Medicine, Funerals, Burials, and Mourning.* Nashville, Tenn.: Nelson, 1976.

Copeland, Peter F. *Working Dress in Colonial and Revolutionary America* . Westport, Conn.: Greenwood Press, 1977.

Corfield, Penelope J., ed. *Language, History, and Class.* Oxford: Blackwell, 1991.

Cotter, John L., Daniel G. Roberts, and Michael Parrington, eds. *The Buried Past: An Archaeological History of Philadelphia.* Philadelphia: University of Pennsylvania Press, 1993.

Crane, Diane. "Clothing Behavior as Non-Verbal Resistance: Marginal Women and Alternative Dress in the Nineteenth Century." *Fashion Theory: The Journal of Dress, Body, and Culture* 3 (1999): 241–68.

Cranny-Francis, Anne. *The Body in the Text.* Melbourne: Melbourne University Press, 1995.

Cray, Robert E., Jr. *Paupers and Poor Relief in New York City and Its Rural Environs, 1700–1830.* Philadelphia: Temple University Press, 1988.

Creighton, Margaret S. "American Mariners and the Rites of Manhood, 1830–1870." In *Jack Tar In History: Essays In the History of Maritime Life and Labour,* ed. Colin Howell and Richard Twomey. Fredericton: Acadiensis, 1991. 143–63.

———. "Fraternity in the American Forecastle, 1830–1870." *New England Quarterly* 63 (1990): 531–57.

———. *Rites and Passages: The Experience of American Whaling, 1830–1870.* New York: Cambridge University Press, 1995.

Crossley, Nick. "Body-Subject/Body-Power: Agency, Inscription, and Control in Foucault and Merleau Ponty." *Body and Society* 2 (1996): 99–116.

Cunnington, C. Willet and Phyllis Cunnington. *Handbook of English Costume in the Eighteenth Century.* Boston: Plays, 1972.

Davis, Kathy, ed. *Embodied Practices: Feminist Perspectives on the Body.* London: Sage, 1997.

Dixon, Ruth Priest and Katherine George Eberly. *Index to Seamen's Protection Certificate Applications, Port of Philadelphia, 1796–1861.* 2 vols. Baltimore: Clearfield, 1994–95.

Douglas, Ann. *The Feminization of American Culture.* New York: Knopf, 1977.

Duden, Barbara. *The Woman Beneath the Skin: A Doctor's Patients in Eighteenth-Century Germany.* Trans. Thomas Dunlap. Cambridge, Mass.: Harvard University Press, 1991.

Dye, Ira. "Early American Merchant Seafarers." *Proceedings of the American Philosophical Society* 120 (1976): 331–60.

———. "The Philadelphia Seamen's Protection Certificate Applications." *Prologue: Sources at the National Archives for Genealogical and Local History Research* 18 (1986): 46–55.

———. "Physical and Social Profiles of Early American Seafarers." Manuscript, provided by the author.

———. "Physical and Social Profiles of Early American Seafarers, 1812–1815."

In *Jack Tar in History: Essays in the History of Maritime Life and Labour*, ed. Colin Howell and Richard J. Twomey. Fredericton: Acadiensis, 1991. 220–35.

———. "The Tattoos of Early American Seafarers, 1796–1818." *Proceedings of the American Philosophical Society* 133 (1989): 520–54.

Early, Joanne. "Runaway Advertisements: A Source for the Study of Working-Class Costume." *Pennsylvania Folklife* 27 (1978): 46–49.

Ebin, Victoria Ebin. *The Body Decorated.* London: Thames and Hudson, 1979.

Elias, Norbert. *The Civilizing Process.* Vol. 1, *The History of Manners.* 1939. Trans. Edmund Jephcott. Oxford: Blackwell, 1978.

———. *The Civilizing Process.* Vol. 2, *State Formation and Civilization.* 1939. Trans. Edmund Jephcott. Oxford: Blackwell, 1982.

Elkins, Stanley M. and Eric L. McKitrick. *The Age of Federalism: The Early American Republic, 1788–1800.* New York: Oxford University Press, 1993.

Estes, J. Worth. "But It Was Worse in 1784." *American Heritage* 35 (1984): 28.

Estes, J. Worth and Billy G. Smith, eds. *A Melancholy Scene of Devastation: The Public Response to the 1793 Philadelphia Yellow Fever Epidemic.* Canton, Mass.: Science History Publications, 1997.

Falk, Pasi. "Written in the Flesh." *Body and Society* 1 (1995): 95–105.

Featherstone, Mike, Mike Hepworth, and Bryan S. Turner. *The Body: Social Process and Cultural Theory.* London: Sage, 1991.

Featherstone, Mike and Bryan S. Turner. "Body and Society: An Introduction." *Body and Society* 1 (1995): 1–12.

Finkelstein, Joanne. *The Fashioned Self.* Oxford: Polity, 1991.

Fishurn, Katherine. *The Problem of Embodiment in Early African American Narrative.* Westport, Conn.: Greenwood Press, 1997.

Floud, Roderick, Kenneth Wachter, and Annabel Gregory. *Height, Health, and History: Nutritional Status in the United Kingdom, 1750–1980.* New York: Cambridge University Press, 1990.

Fogel, Robert W., Stanley L. Engerman, and James Trussell. "Exploring the Uses of Data on Height: The Analysis of Long-Term Trends in Nutrition, Labor Welfare, and Labor Productivity." *Social Science History* 6 (1982): 401–21.

Folsom, Frank. "Jobless Jack Tars, 1808." *Labor's Heritage: Quarterly of the George Meany Memorial Archives* 2 (1990): 4–17.

Foucault, Michel. *The Birth of the Clinic: An Archaeology of Medical Perception.* 1973. Trans. A. M. Sheridan. London: Routledge, 1989.

———. *Discipline and Punish: The Birth of the Prison.* 1972. Trans. Alan Sheridan. Harmondsworth: Penguin Books, 1979.

———. *The History of Sexuality.* Vol. 1, *The Will to Knowledge.* 1976. Trans. Robert Hurley. London: Penguin, 1990.

———. *The History of Sexuality.* Vol. 2, *The Use of Pleasure.* 1976. Trans. Robert Hurley. London: Penguin, 1985.

———. *The History of Sexuality.* Vol. 3, *Care of the Self.* 1976. Trans. Robert Hurley. London: Penguin, 1990.

Franklin, John Hope and Loren Schweninger. *Runaway Slaves: Rebels on the Plantation.* New York: Oxford University Press, 1999.

Gadlin, Howard. "Scars and Emblems: Paradoxes of American Life." *Journal of Social History* 11 (1978): 305–27.

Galenson, David W. *White Servitude in Colonial America: An Economic Analaysis.* New York: Cambridge University Press, 1981.

Gibson, Campbell. "Population of the 100 Largest Cities and Other Urban Places in the United States: 1790 to 1990." Washington, D.C.: U.S. Bureau of the Census, on-line Population Working Division Paper 27, 1998.

Gilbert, Arthur N. "Buggery and the British Navy, 1700–1861." *Journal of Social History* 10 (1976): 72–98.

Gilfoyle, Timothy J. *City of Eros: New York City, Prostitution, and the Commercialization of Sex, 1790–1920.* New York: W.W. Norton, 1992.

Gould, Philip. "Race, Commerce, and the Literature of Yellow Fever in Early National Philadelphia." *Early American Literature* 35 (2000): 157–86.

Governar, Alan. "Christian Tattoos." *Tattootime* 2 (1983): 4–11.

Greene, Lorenzo J. "The New England Negro as Seen in Advertisements for Runaway Slaves." *Journal of Negro History* 29 (1944): 125–46.

Gutman, Herbert. *The Black Family in Slavery and Freedom, 1750–1925.* New York: Pantheon, 1976.

Hall, Stuart and Tony Jefferson, eds. *Resistance Through Ritual: Youth Subcultures in Post-War Britain.* London: Hutchinson, 1976.

Hambly, W. D. *The History of Tattooing and Its Significance.* London: H. F. and G. Witherby, 1925.

Harris, Jennifer. "The Red Cap of Liberty: A Study of Dress Worn by French Revolutionary Partisans, 1789–1794." *Eighteenth-Century Studies* 14 (1980–81): 283–312.

Harris, Jonathan Gil. *Foreign Bodies and the Body Politic: Discourses of Social Pathology in Early Modern England.* Cambridge: Cambridge University Press, 1998.

Harris, Ruth. *Lourdes: Body and Spirit in a Secular Age.* London: Allen Lane, 1999.

Hebdige, Dick. *Subculture: The Meaning of Style.* London: Methuen, 1979.

Hicks, Marjorie. *Clothing for Ladies and Gentlemen of Higher and Lower Standing.* Washington, D.C.: U.S. Government Printing Office, 1976.

Hillman, David and Carla Mazzio, eds., *The Body in Parts: Fantasies of Corporeality in Early Modern Europe.* New York, London: Routledge, 1997.

Hodes, Martha. "The Sexualization of Reconstruction Politics: White Women and Black Men in the South After the Civil War." *Journal of the History of Sexuality* 3 (1993): 402–17.

———. *White Women, Black Men: Illicit Sex in the Nineteenth-Century South.* New Haven, Conn.: Yale University Press, 1997.

Hodges, Graham Russell and Alan Edward Brown, eds. *Pretends to Be Free: Runaway Slave Advertisements from Colonial and Revolutionary New York and New Jersey.* New York: Garland, 1994.

Hoffman, Ronald, Mechal Sobel, and Fredrike Teute, eds. *Through a Glass Darkly: Reflections on Personal Identity in Early America.* Chapel Hill: University of North Carolina Press, 1997.

Hopkins, Donald R. *Princes and Peasants: Smallpox in History.* Chicago: University of Chicago Press, 1983.

hooks, bell. "Talking Back." In *Out There: Marginalization and Contemporary Cultures,* ed. Russell Ferguson, Martha Gever, Trinh T. Minh-ha, and Cornel West. New York: New Museum of Contemporary Art, 1990. 337–43.

Howell, Colin and Richard Twomey, eds. *Jack Tar In History: Essays In the History of Maritime Life and Labour.* Fredericton: Acadiensis, 1991

Hunt, Lynn, ed. *Eroticism and the Body Politic.* Baltimore: Johns Hopkins University Press, 1991.

Huss, Wayne A. *The Master Builders: A History of the Grand Lodge of Free and Accepted Masons of Pennsylvania.* Vol. 1, *1731–1873.* Philadelphia: Grand Lodge F. & A.M., 1986.

Isaac, Rhys. *The Transformation of Virginia, 1740–1790.* Chapel Hill: University of North Carolina Press, 1982.

Johnson, Amandus. *The Journal and Biography of Nicholas Collin.* Philadelphia: New Jersey Society of Pennsylvania, 1936.

Johnson, Kenneth R. "Black Kinesics: Some Non-Verbal Communication Patterns in Black Culture." In *Perspectives on Black English,* ed. J. L. Dillard. The Hague: Mouton, 1975. 296–306.

Johnson, Michael P. "Runaway Slaves and the Slave Communities in South Carolina, 1799 to 1830." *William and Mary Quarterly* 38 (1981): 418–41.

Johnson, Walter. *Soul by Soul: Life Inside the Antebellum Slave Market.* Cambridge, Mass.: Harvard University Press, 1999.

Jones, C. P. "Stigma: Tattooing and Branding in Graeco-Roman Antiquity." *Journal of Roman Studies* 77 (1987): 139–155.

Jones, Colin and Roy Porter, eds. *Reassessing Foucault: Power, Medicine and the Body.* London: Routledge, 1994.

Jütte, Robert. *Poverty and Deviance in Early Modern Europe.* Cambridge: Cambridge University Press, 1994.

Kaartinen, Marjo and Anu Korhonen. *Bodies in Evidence: Perspectives on the History of the Body in Early Modern Europe.* Turku: University of Turku, 1997.

Katz, Michael B. *In the Shadow of the Poorhouse: A Social History of Welfare in America.* New York: Basic Books, 1986.

Kerber, Linda K. *Women of the Republic: Intellect and Ideology on Revolutionary America.* Chapel Hill: University of North Carolina Press, 1980.

Kidwell, Claudia B. "Riches, Rags, and In-Between." *Historic Preservation* 28 (1976): 28–33.

Kielhofner, Gary and Trudy Mallinson. "Bodies Telling Stories and Stories Telling Bodies." *Human Studies* 20 (1997): 365–69.

King, Steven. "Reclothing the English Poor, 1700–1834." Manuscript, provided by author.

Klebaner, Benjamin Joseph. *Public Poor Relief in America, 1790–1860.* New York: Arno Press, 1976.

Klepp, Susan E. "Demography in Early Philadelphia, 1690–1860." *Proceedings of the American Philosophical Society* 133 (1989): 85–111.

———. "Malthusian Miseries and the Working Poor in Philadelphia, 1780–1830: A Study of Infant Mortality." Paper delivered at the annual conference of the Omohundro Institute of Early American History and Culture, Austin, Texas, 1999.

———. "Philadelphia in Transition: A Demographic History of the City and Its Occupational Groups." Ph.D. dissertation, University of Pennsylvania, 1980.

———. *"The Swift Progress of Population": A Documentary and Bibliographic Study of Philadelphia's Growth, 1642–1859.* Philadelphia: American Philosophical Society, 1991.

———. "Zachariah Poulson's Bills of Mortality, 1788–1801." In *Life in Early Philadelphia: Documents from the Revolutionary and Early National periods,* ed. Billy G. Smith. University Park: Pennsylvania State University Press, 1995. 219–42.

Klepp, Susan E. and Billy G. Smith. "Marriage and Death: The Records of Gloria Dei Church." In *Life in Early Philadelphia: Documents from the Revolutionary and Early National Periods,* ed. Billy G. Smith. University Park: Pennsylvania State University Press, 1995. 177–218.

———. "The Records of Gloria Dei Church: Burials, 1800–1804." *Pennsylvania History* 53 (1986): 56–79.

Kornfeld, Eve. "Crisis in the Capital: The Cultural Significance of Philadelphia's Great Yellow Fever Epidemic." *Pennsylvania History* 51 (1984): 189–205.

Laderman, Gary. *The Sacred Remains.* New Haven, Conn.: Yale University Press, 1997.

Lane, Roger. *Violent Death in the City: Suicide, Accident, and Murder in Nineteenth-Century Philadelphia*. Cambridge, Mass.: Harvard University Press, 1979.

Langley, Harold D. *A History of Medicine in the Early U.S. Navy*. Baltimore: Johns Hopkins University Press, 1995.

Lemire, Beverly. "The Theft of Clothes and Popular Consumerism in Early Modern England." *Journal of Social History* 24 (1990): 255–76.

Lemisch, Jesse. "Jack Tar in the Streets: Merchant Seamen in the Politics of Revolutionary America." *William and Mary Quarterly* 3rd. ser. 25 (1968): 371–407.

———. *Jack Tar vs. John Bull: The Role of New York's Seamen in Precipitating the Revolution*. New York: Garland, 1997.

———. "Listening to the 'Inarticulate': William Widger's Dream and the Loyalties of American Revolutionary Seamen in British Prisons." *Journal of Social History* 3 (1969): 1–29.

Lewis, Michael. *A Social History of the Navy, 1793–1815*. London: Allen and Unwin, 1960.

Linebaugh, Peter and Marcus Rediker. *The Many-Headed Hydra: Sailors, Slaves, Commoners, and the Hidden History of the Revolutionary Atlantic*. Boston: Beacon Press, 2000.

Lloyd, Christopher. *The British Seaman, 1200–1860: A Social Survey* 1968. Rutherford, N.J.: Fairleigh Dickinson University Press, 1970.

Loudon, Irvine. *Death in Childbirth: An International Study of Maternal Care and Maternal Mortality, 1800–1950*. Oxford: Clarendon Press, 1992.

Lupton, Deborah. *Medicine as Culture: Illness, Disease, and the Body in Western Societies*. London: Sage, 1994.

Lurie, Alison. *The Language of Clothes*. New York: Random House, 1981.

Marly, Diana de. *Dress in North America: The New World, 1492–1800*. New York: Holmes and Meier, 1990.

Mascia-Lees, Frances E. and Patricia Sharpe, eds. *Tattoo, Torture, Mutilation, and Adornment: The Denaturalization of the Body in Culture and Text*. Albany: State University of New York Press, 1992.

Masur, Louis P. *Rites of Execution: Capital Punishment and the Transformation of American Culture, 1776–1865*. New York: Oxford University Press, 1989.

Mauss, Marcel. *Sociology and Psychology: Essays*. 1950. Trans. Ben Brewster. London: Routledge and Kegan Paul, 1979.

Maw, Joan and John Picton, eds. *Concepts of the Body/Self in Africa*. Wien: Afro-Pub, 1992.

McClellan, Elisabeth. *History of American Costume, 1607–1870*. New York: Tudor, 1942.

McGowen, Randall. "The Body and Punishment in Eighteenth Century England." *Journal of Modern History* 59 (1987): 651–79.

McKee, Christopher. "Foreign Seamen in the United States Navy: A Census of 1808." *William and Mary Quarterly* 3rd ser. 42 (1985): 383–93.

McManners, John. *Death and the Enlightenment: Changing Attitudes to Death Among Christians and Unbelievers in Eighteenth-Century France*. Oxford: Clarendon Press, 1981.

Meaders, Daniel E. *Dead or Alive: Fugitive Slaves and White Indentured Servants Before 1830*. New York: Garland, 1993.

———. "South Carolina Fugitives as Viewed Through Local Colonial Newspapers with Emphasis on Runaway Notices, 1732–1801." *Journal of Negro History* 60 (1975): 288–319.

Meranze, Michael. *Laboratories of Virtue: Punishment, Revolution, and Authority in Philadelphia, 1760–1835*. Chapel Hill: University of North Carolina Press, 1996.

Mercer, Kobena. "Black Hair/Style Politics." In *Out There: Marginalization and Contemporary Cultures*, ed. Russell Ferguson, Martha Gever, Trinh T. Minh-ha, and Cornel West. New York: New Museum of Contemporary Art, 1990. 247–64.

Miller, Jacquelyn C. "The Body Politic: Passions, Pestilence, and Political Culture in the Age of the American Revolution." Ph.D. dissertation, Rutgers University, 1996.

Moffat, Riley. *Population History of the Eastern U.S. Cities and Towns, 1790–1870.* Metuchen, N.J.: Scarecrow Press, 1992.

Mohl, Raymond A. *Poverty in New York, 1783–1825.* New York: Oxford University Press, 1971.

Mohl, Ruth. *The Three Estates in Medieval and Renaissance Literature.* New York: Columbia University Press, 1933.

Morgan, Philip D. "Colonial South Carolina Runaways: Their Significance for Slave Culture." *Slavery and Abolition* 6 (1985): 57–78.

Morton, Thomas George and Frank Woodbury, *The History of the Pennsylvania Hospital, 1751–1895* (1895). New York: Arno, 1973.

Mullin, Gerald W. *Flight and Rebellion: Slave Resistance in Eighteenth-Century Virginia.* New York: Oxford University Press, 1972.

Nash, Gary B. *Forging Freedom: The Formation of Philadelphia's Black Community, 1720–1840.* Cambridge, Mass.: Harvard University Press, 1988.

———. "Poverty and Politics in Early American History." Paper delivered at the annual conference of the Omohundro Institute of Early American History and Culture, Austin, Texas, 1999.

———. *The Urban Crucible: Social Change, Political Consciousness, and the Origins of the American Revolution.* Cambridge, Mass.: Harvard University Press, 1979.

Nettleton, Sarah and Jonathan Watson, eds. *The Body in Everyday Life.* London: Routledge, 1998.

Newman, Simon P. *Parades and the Politics of the Street: Festive Culture in the Early American Republic.* Philadelphia: University of Pennsylvania Press, 1997.

———. "Principles or Men? George Washington and the Political Culture of National Leadership, 1776–1801." *Journal of the Early Republic* 12 (1992): 477–507.

———. "Reading the Bodies of Early American Seafarers." *William and Mary Quarterly* 3rd. ser. 55 (1998): 59–82.

———. "Wearing Their Hearts on Their Sleeves." In *American Bodies: Cultural Histories of the Physique*, ed. Tim Armstrong. Sheffield: Sheffield Academic Press, 1996, 18–31.

O'Connor, Erin. "'Fractions of Men': Engendering Amputation in Victorian Culture." *Comparative Studies in Society and History* 39 (1997): 742–77.

Outram, Dorinda. *The Body and the French Revolution: Sex, Class, and Political Culture.* New Haven, Conn.: Yale University Press, 1989.

Packard, Francis R. *Some Account of the Pennsylvania Hospital.* Philadelphia: Florence M. Greim, 1957.

Parker, Freddie L. *Running for Freedom: Slave Runaways in North Carolina, 1775–1840.* New York: Garland, 1993.

Patterson, Orlando. *Slavery and Social Death: A Comparative Study.* Cambridge, Mass.: Harvard University Press, 1982.

Perniola, Mario. "Between Clothing and Nudity." In *Fragments for a History of the Human Body*, ed. Michel Feher, Ramona Naddaff, and Nadia Tazi. *Zone* 2 (1989): 237–65.

Pestana, Carla Gardiner and Sharon Salinger, eds. *Inequality in Early America.* Hanover, N.H.: Dartmouth College Press, 1999.

Porter, Dorothy and Roy Porter. *In Sickness and in Health: The British Experience, 1650–1850*. London: Fourth Estate, 1988.

———. *Patient's Progress: Doctors and Doctoring in Eighteenth-Century England.* Oxford: Polity Press, 1989.

Porter, Roy. "Gout: Framing and Fantasizing Disease." *Bulletin of the History of Medicine* 68 (1994): 1–28.

———. "History of the Body." In *New Perspectives on Historical Writing*, ed. Peter Burke. University Park: Pennsylvania State University Press, 1992. 206–32.

———, ed. *Medicine in the Enlightenment.* Amsterdam: Rodopi, 1995.

———, ed. *Patients and Practitioners: Lay Perceptions of Medicine in Pre-Industrial Society.* Cambridge: Cambridge University Press, 1985.

Powell, J. M. *Bring Out Your Dead: The Great Plague of Yellow Fever in Philadelphia in 1793.* 1949. Philadelphia: University of Pennsylvania Press, 1993.

Preble, George Henry. *History of the United States Navy-Yard, Portsmouth, N.H.* Washington, D.C.: Government Printing Office, 1892.

Price, Janet and Margrit Shildrick, eds. *Feminist Theory and the Body: A Reader.* Edinburgh: Edinburgh University Press, 1999.

Prude, Jonathan. "To Look upon the 'Lower Sort': Runaway Ads and the Appearance of Unfree Laborers in America, 1750–1800." *Journal of American History* 78 (1991): 124–59.

Razzell, Peter. *The Conquest of Smallpox: The Impact of Inoculation on Smallpox Mortality in Eighteenth Century Britain.* Firle, Sussex: Caliban, 1977.

Rediker, Marcus. *Between the Devil and the Deep Blue Sea: Merchant Seamen, Pirates, and the Anglo-American Maritime World, 1700–1750.* New York: Cambridge University Press, 1987.

———. "A Motley Crew of Rebels: Sailors, Slaves, and the Coming of the American Revolution." In *The Transforming Hand of Revolution: Reconsidering the American Revolution as a Social Movement*, ed. Ronald Hoffman and Peter J. Albert. Charlottesville: University Press of Virginia, 1996. 155–98.

Roche, Daniel. *The Culture of Clothing: Dress and Fashion in the "Ancien Régime".* Trans. Jean Birrell. New York: Cambridge University Press, 1994.

Roper, Lyndal. *Oedipus and the Devil: Witchcraft, Sexuality and Religion in Early Modern Europe.* London: Routledge, 1994.

Rorabaugh, W. J. *The Alcoholic Republic: An American Tradition.* New York: Oxford University Press, 1979.

———. *The Craft Apprentice: From Franklin to the Machine Age in America.* New York: Oxford University Press, 1986.

Rosenberg, Charles E. *The Care of Strangers: The Rise of America's Hospital System.* New York: Basic, 1987.

———. "Deconstructing Disease." *Reviews in American History* 14 (1986): 110–15.

———. "Disease and Social Order." In *Explaining Epidemics and Other Studies in the History of Medicine*, ed. Charles Rosenberg. New York: Cambridge University Press, 1992.

———. "The Therapeutic Revolution: Medicine, Meaning, and Social Change in Nineteenth-Century America." In *The Therapeutic Revolution: Essays in the Social History of Medicine*, ed. Morris J. Vogel and Charles E. Rosenberg. Philadelphia: University of Pennsylvania Press, 1979. 3–25.

Rosenberg, Charles E. and Janet Golden. *Framing Disease: Studies in Cultural History.* New Brunswick, N.J.: Rutgers University Press, 1992.

Rosswurm, Steven. *Arms, Country, and Class: The Philadelphia Militia and the 'Lower Sort' During the American Revolution, 1775–1783.* New Brunswick, N.J.: Rutgers University Press, 1987.

Rothman, David J. *The Discovery of the Asylum: Social Order and Disorder in the New Republic.* Boston: Little, Brown, 1971.

Rudofsky, Bernard. *The Unfashionable Human Body.* New York: Van Nostrand Reinhold, 1984.

Sager, Eric W. *Seafaring Labour: The Merchant Marine of Atlantic Canada, 1820–1914.* Montreal: McGill-Queen's University Press, 1989.

Salinger, Sharon. *"To Serve Well and Faithfully": Labor and Indentured Servants in Pennsylvania, 1682–1800.* New York: Cambridge University Press, 1987.

Sanders, Clinton R. *Customizing the Body: The Art and Culture of Tattooing.* Philadelphia: Temple University Press, 1989.

Sankar, Pamela. "State Power and Record-Keeping: The History of Individualized Surveillance in the United States, 1790–1935." Ph.D. dissertation, University of Pennsylvania, 1992.

Saul, Norman E. "Ships and Seamen as Agents of Revolution." In *The Consortium on Revolutionary Europe, 1750–1850: Proceedings 1986,* ed. Warren Spencer. Athens: University of Georgia Press, 1987: 248–58.

Sault, Nicole, ed. *Many Mirrors: Body Image and Social Relations.* New Brunswick, N.J.: Rutgers University Press, 1994.

Saum, Lewis O. *The Popular Mood of Pre-Civil War America.* Westport, Conn.: Greenwood Press, 1980.

Sawday, Jonathan. *The Body Emblazoned: Dissection and the Human Body in Renaissance Culture.* London: Routledge, 1995.

Sawicki, Jana. *Disciplining Foucault: Feminism, Power, and the Body.* New York, London: Routledge, 1991.

Schilling, Chris. *The Body and Social Theory.* London: Sage, 1993.

Schlesinger, Arthur M. "The Liberty Tree: A Genealogy." *New England Quarterly* 25 (1952): 435–58.

Schmitt, Jean-Claude. "The Ethics of Gesture." In *Fragments for a History of the Human Body,* ed. Michel Feher, Ramona Naddaff, and Nadia Tazi. *Zone* 2 (1989): 129–47.

Scutt, R. W. B. and Christopher Gotch. *Art and Symbol: The Mystery of Tattooing.* Cranbury, N.J.: A.S. Barnes, 1974.

Seed, John. "From 'Middling Sort' to Middle Class in Late Eighteenth-Century and Early Nineteenth-Century England." In *Social Orders and Social Classes in Europe Since 1500: Studies in Social Stratification,* ed. M. L. Bush. London: Longman, 1992. 114–35.

Sennett, Richard. *Flesh and Stone: The Body and the City in Western Civilization.* London: Faber and Faber, 1994.

Shammas, Carole. "The Space Problem in Early American Cities." *William and Mary Quarterly* 3rd ser. 60 (2000): 505–42.

Sharp, James Roger. *American Politics in the Early Republic: The New Nation in Crisis.* New Haven, Conn.: Yale University Press, 1993.

Shryock, Richard H. *Medicine and Society in America, 1660–1860.* New York: New York University Press, 1960.

———. *Medicine in America: Historical Essays.* Baltimore: Johns Hopkins University Press, 1966.

Shuemaker, Helen. "'This Lock You See': Nineteenth-Century Hair Work as the Commodified Self." *Fashion Theory: The Journal of Dress, Body, and Culture* 1 (1997): 421–46.

Simon, Diane. *Hair: Public, Political, and Extremely Personal.* New York: St. Martin's Press, 2000.

Smith, Billy G. "Black Women Who Stole Themselves in Eighteenth-Century

America." In *Inequality in Early America*, ed. Carla Gardina Pestana and Sharon V. Salinger. Hanover, N.H.: University Press of New England, 1999. 134–59.

———. "Death and Life in a Colonial Immigrant City: A Demographic Analysis of Philadelphia." *Journal of Economic History* 37 (1977): 863–89.

———, ed. *Life in Early Philadelphia: Documents from the Revolutionary and Early National Periods*. University Park: Pennsylvania State University Press, 1995.

———. *The "Lower Sort": Philadelphia's Laboring People, 1750–1800*. Ithaca, N.Y.: Cornell University Press, 1990.

———. "Runaway Slaves in the Mid-Atlantic Region During the Revolutionary Era." In *The Transforming Hand of Revolution: Reconsidering the American Revolution as a Social Movement*, ed. Ronald Hoffman and Peter J. Albert. Charlottesville: University Press of Virginia, 1995. 199–230.

Smith-Rosenberg, Carroll. "The Female World of Love and Ritual: Relations Between Women in Nineteenth-Century America." *Signs: Journal of Women in Culture and Society* 1 (1975): 1–29.

Sokoloff, Kenneth Lee. *The Heights of Americans in Three Centuries: Some Economic and Demographic Implications*. NBER Working Paper 1384. Cambridge, Mass.: National Bureau of Economic Research, 1984.

Sokoloff, Kenneth Lee and Georgia C. Villaflor. "The Early Achievement of Modern Stature in America." *Social Science History* 6 (1982): 453–81.

Soltow, Lee and Edward Stevens. *The Rise of Literacy and the Common School in the United States: A Socioeconomic Analysis to 1870*. Chicago: University of Chicago Press, 1981.

Steward, Samuel M. *Bad Boys and Tough Tattoos: A Social History of the Tattoo with Gangs, Sailors, and Street-Corner Punks*. New York: Harrington Park, 1990.

Styler, John. "Servants." *Textile History*, forthcoming.

Synnott, Anthony. *The Body Social: Symbolism, Self, and Society*. London: Routledge, 1993.

Teeters, Negley K. *The Cradle of the Penitentiary: The Walnut Street Jail at Philadelphia, 1773–1835*. Philadelphia: Pennsylvania Prison Society, 1955.

Thompson, E. P. *Customs in Common*. New York: New Press, 1991.

Thompson, Peter. *Rum Punch and Revolution: Taverngoing and Public Life in Eighteenth-Century Philadelphia*. Philadelphia: University of Pennsylvania Press, 1999.

Thornton, John. *Africa and Africans in the Making of the Atlantic World, 1400–1680*. Cambridge: Cambridge University Press, 1992.

Tinkcom, Margaret B. "The New Market in Second Street." *Pennsylvania Magazine of History and Biography* 82 (1958): 379–96.

Todd, January *Physical Culture and the Body Beautiful: Purposive Exercise in the Lives of American Women, 1800–1870*. Macon, Ga.: Mercer University Press, 1998.

Tomes, Nancy. *The Art of Asylum-Keeping: Thomas Story Kirkbride and the Origins of American Psychiatry*. Philadelphia: University of Pennsylvania Press, 1994.

Tompkins, Jane. *Sentimental Designs: The Cultural Work of American Fiction, 1790–1860*. New York: Oxford University Press, 1985.

Toner, Lawrence W. "A Fondness for Freedom: Servant Protest in Puritan Society." *William and Mary Quarterly* 19 (1962): 201–19.

Trattner, Walter I. *From Poor Law to Welfare State: A History of Social Welfare in America*. New York: Free Press, 1974.

Turner, Bryan S. *The Body and Society: Explorations in Social Theory*. Oxford: Blackwell, 1984.

Turner, Terence S. "The Social Skin." In *Not Work Alone: A Cross-Cultural View of Activities Superfluous to Survival*, ed. Jeremy Cherfas and Roger Lewin. London: Temple Smith, 1980. 112–40.

Vickers, Daniel. "Beyond Jack Tar." *William and Mary Quarterly* 3rd ser. 50 (1993): 418–24.

———. *Farmers and Fishermen: Two Centuries of Work in Essex County, Massachusetts, 1630–1850.* Chapel Hill: University of North Carolina Press, 1994.

Virel, André. *Decorated Man: The Human Body as Art.* Trans. I. Mark Paris. New York: Abrams, 1980.

Vogel, Morris J. and Charles E. Rosenberg, eds. *The Therapeutic Revolution: Essays in the Social History of Medicine.* Philadelphia: University of Pennsylvania Press, 1979.

Waldstreicher, David. "Reading the Runaways: Self Fashioning, Print Culture, and Confidence in Slavery in the Eighteenth-Century Mid-Atlantic." *William and Mary Quarterly* 56 (1999): 243–72.

Watson, Alan D. "Impulse Toward Independence: Resistance and Rebellion Among North Carolina Slaves, 1750–1775." *Journal of Negro History* 63 (1978): 317–28.

Weiss, Gary. *Body Images: Embodiment as Intercorporeality.* New York, London: Routledge, 1999.

Welton, Donn, ed. *The Body: Classic and Contemporary Readings.* Oxford: Blackwell, 1999.

Werner, Alex. *London Bodies: The Changing Shape of Londoners from prehistoric Times to the Present Day.* London: Museum of London, 1988.

White, Shane. *Somewhat More Independent: The End of Slavery in New York City, 1770–1810.* Athens: University of Georgia Press, 1991.

White, Shane and Graham White. *Stylin': African American Expressive Culture From Its Beginnings to the Zoot Suit.* Ithaca, N.Y.: Cornell University Press, 1998.

Whitman, T. Stephen. *The Price of Freedom: Slavery and Manumission in Baltimore and Early National Maryland.* Lexington: University Press of Kentucky, 1997.

Williams, Guy. *The Age of Agony: The Art of Healing, c. 1700–1800.* London: Constable, 1975.

Williams, Simon J. and Gillian Bendelow. *The Lived Body: Sociological Themes, Embodied Issues.* London: Routledge, 1998.

Williams, William Henry. *America's First Hospital: The Pennsylvania Hospital, 1751–1841.* Wayne, Pa.: Haverford House, 1976.

———. "The Pennsylvania Hospital, 1751–1801: An Internal Examination of Anglo-America's First Hospital." Ph.D. dissertation, University of Delaware, 1971.

Winterson, Jeanette. *Written on the Body.* London: Jonathan Cape, 1992.

Wolf, Stephanie Grauman. *As Various as Their Land: The Everyday Lives of Eighteenth-Century Americans.* New York: Harper Collins, 1993.

Wood, Betty. *Slavery in Colonial Georgia, 1730–1775.* Athens: University of Georgia Press, 1984.

Wood, Peter H. *Black Majority: Negroes in Colonial South Carolina from 1670 through the Stono Rebellion.* New York: Knopf, 1974.

Workman, Mark. "Medical Practice in Philadelphia at the Time of the Yellow Fever Epidemic, 1793." *Pennsylvania Folklife* 27 (1978): 33–39.

Wrightson, Keith. "Estates, Degrees, and Sorts: Changing Perceptions of Society in Tudor and Stuart England." In *Language, History, and Class,* ed. Penelope J. Corfield. Oxford: Blackwell, 1991. 30–52.

———. "'Sorts of People' in Tudor and Stuart England." In *The Middling Sort of People: Culture, Society, and Politics in England, 1550–1800,* ed. Jonathan Barry and Christopher Brooks. London: Macmillan, 1994. 28–51.

Young, Alfred F. "George Robert Twelve Hewes (1742–1840): A Boston Shoemaker and the Memory of the American Revolution." *William and Mary Quarterly* 3rd ser. 38 (1981): 561–623.

———. *The Shoemaker and the Tea Party: Memory and the American Revolution.* Boston: Beacon Press, 1999.

Young, Katherine Galloway. *Presence in the Flesh: The Body in Medicine.* Cambridge, Mass.: Harvard University Press, 1997.

Index

Page numbers in italics indicate tables and illustrations.

Acknowledgments

This book has been made possible by the generous support of institutions on both sides of the Atlantic. In Britain, my work has been supported by a Research Grant from the Urban Studies Research Fund of the University of Glasgow, a travel grant from the Wellcome Trust, a Social Science Research Grant from the Nuffield Foundation, and a British Academy Research Grant. In the United States I received a Research Grant from the American Philosophical Society, an Andrew W. Mellon Foundation Fellowship at the Library Company of Philadelphia, and a Coca Cola Residential Fellowship at the International Center for Jefferson Studies in Monticello, Virginia. A sabbatical from the University of Glasgow allowed me to undertake a lengthy period of research and writing, which was extended by a Research Leave Grant from the Arts and Humanities Research Board, affording me the extra term of leave during which I completed the first draft of this book.

A number of colleagues and the staff of various libraries and archives have helped me with my research. At the University of Glasgow, Dr. Helen Marlborough has maintained and improved the library's American history collections, keeping me connected and well supplied. In Philadelphia, Jim Green and the able staff of the Library Company continue to make it one of the best and the friendliest of research libraries, and the Historical Society of Pennsylvania has become a joy to work in. Many of the records on which this book is based are housed in the City Archives of Philadelphia, and surrounded by genealogists I spent many happy months wading through prison and almshouse records. In the Pennsylvania Hospital, archivist Margo Szabunia was of enormous help, as were Roy Goodman and the rest of the late Ted Carter's team in the library of the American Philosophical Society. The International Center for Jefferson Studies provided a very collegial setting, and I treasure the time I spent writing or chatting with Jim Horn and Peter Onuf on "the Mountain." I am also grateful to scholars who have shared primary source materials and their own research, including Tricia Allerston, Ira Dye, Steven King, Susan Klepp, Leslie Patrick, Billy Smith, and Alfred Young.

Bob Lockhart, my editor at the University of Pennsylvania Press, has become a friend and colleague whose opinions and advice I value greatly. He never doubted this book, and he and series editors Kathy Brown and Dan Richter have combined rigorous criticism with generous encouragement. Marguerite DuPree, Michael Meranze, and Billy Smith also helped me with suggestions based on their full and careful readings of the manuscript, and Alison Anderson helped enormously with the final editing.

An earlier version of Chapter 5 appeared as "Reading the Bodies of Early American Seafarers," *William and Mary Quarterly*, 3rd ser. 55 (1998): 59–82, while Chapter 6 is based on the essay "Dead Bodies: Poverty and Death in Early National Philadelphia," which will appear in *Down and Out in Early America*, edited by Billy G. Smith (University Park: Pennsylvania State University Press, 2003); both are reprinted with permission.

I have spent years wading through seemingly endless accounts of debility, disease, and death among the poor of early national Philadelphia. I found relief, however, in the stories of community and friendship among the people I was reading about, from children playing together in the streets, to runaway slaves and servants forming close-knit communities filled with as much joy as fear, to the close bonds forged between professional seafarers. Writing this book made me realize the importance of friends in my own life, and that is why *Embodied History* is for them.

First, thanks to the friends who were colleagues at Northern Illinois University when I first started working on this project, especially Eric Duskin, Bruce Field, and Jim Schmidt. During my last semester at NIU we taught a class together: this was my best teaching experience yet, not least because of the concluding two-day party. In Glasgow I am very fortunate in that I work in an extremely collegial department and university, where the tone is set by Margo Hunter and Alison Peden, my cappuccino companions. My colleagues and students in the Department of History, and in the Andrew Hook Centre for American Studies, constantly remind me how much I enjoy what I do. Special thanks to friends in the English Department, especially Andrew Hook, Nick and Maggie Selby, and Susan Castillo, the latter a fellow early Americanist and a co-conspirator at the Rock. Life and work in Glasgow has been made so much more enjoyable by the many happy hours spent exploring the restaurants and pubs of Glasgow in the company of the Modern History Musketeers, the unlikely trio of Simon Ball, Phil O'Brien, and most especially Marina Moskowitz: they will know how best to celebrate this book with me. Beyond Glasgow I have found new communities of friends among the staff and graduate students in the British Association for American Studies, and in the Scottish Association for the Study of America. Janet Beer, Phil Davies, Jenel Virden, and company form the best of scholarly communities, and they dance well too.

My early Americanist friends form a true Atlantic World community. There are many people in this category, but I want to make special note of Michael Bellesiles, Frank Cogliano, Kon Dierks, Richard Dunn, Laura Edwards, Paul Gilje, Colin Kidd, Susan Klepp, Sarah Knott, Allan Kulikoff, Brendan McConville, Roderick McDonald, John Murrin, Colin Nicolson, Leslie Patrick, Bill Pencak, Darryl Peterkin, Liam Riordan, Betty Wood, and Alfred Young. In particular, I relish the time that I spend with Susan Branson, Alison Games, Tom Humphrey, Mike McDonnell, Billy Smith, and Peter Thompson.

Thanks also to my old friends in the Felixstowe Boys, namely Anthony King (the artist who has contributed the wonderfully evocative additions to the Birch engravings), the irrepressible Dominic Christian, and the crazy Matt Lane. For enthusiastic discussions of history and soccer, usually over many pints of Guinness and games of darts, I thank my old friend Joe Henry. Family was a constant theme in the records I studied for this book, and this work is also for my oldest and my newest friends: my parents Maureen and Peter, my sister Clare, my brothers Giles, Jem, and Tim, my sister-in-law Alison, my nephews Christopher and Joseph, and my niece Lucy.

Most of all, this book is for Sophie, Packy, Sally, and Dan Gordon, and for Moira Peters, who all made me so very welcome during the time I was researching and writing in Philadelphia. The Gordons' house is the madcap headquarters of the Wissahickon Wanderers, who took me in and wrecked my body while cheering my spirit. Whether we were relay-running around Cape Breton or through Hell, Michigan, the camaraderie was wonderful and the running kept me sane.